THE ELEMENTS OF LOGIC

THE ELEMENTS OF

LOGIC

VINCENT EDWARD SMITH

THE BRUCE PUBLISHING COMPANY
MILWAUKEE

NIHIL OBSTAT:

JOANNES A. SCHULIEN
Censor librorum

IMPRIMATUR:

✠ ALBERTUS G. MEYER
Archiepiscopus Milwauchiensis
February 26, 1957

PRAYERFULLY
FOR MY MOTHER
AND
FOR THE SOUL OF MY DAD

PREFACE

An explanation is needed to justify the addition of one more textbook in Aristotelian logic to the imposing list of volumes already in the family.

The present work has two modest ambitions: The first is to make logic come more alive for students by presenting it in terms of case histories of logical operations. The other emphasis is to move considerably beyond the purely formal treatment of the syllogism and to confront students with some modern applications of logic and the scientific method. For a course of one semester, both of these techniques must make the inevitable compromise imposed by having only forty-odd hours of teaching time available.

In presenting logic through exercises in terms of case histories, my first preference as a teacher was to choose examples mostly from the commonplace world of newspapers and of popular magazines. However, this ambition was superseded by another one. Instead of dissecting the logic of ordinary day-to-day journalism for students who (we can always hope) will not settle into ordinary day-to-day lives, it seemed more appropriate to choose case histories of logic chiefly from the learned world itself and, while teaching logic, also introduce the student to great arguments about great issues. In the present book, the second approach has been followed, even though there had to be a restriction of material to stay within the background of underclassmen. Arguments and other logical operations in areas like metaphysics or higher mathematics would, for the most part, be meaningless in content to underclassmen. However, the reader may find in these pages an introduction to what Robert M. Hutchins has termed the great conversation — questions that have been crucial in our Western intellectual culture such as the problem of God's existence, of man's dignity, of our power to know, of the movement of the heavens, the fall of bodies, the origin of life, the nature of law, determinism in history, and so on. Moreover, since the primary business of logic is to conduct the mind to science and finally to wisdom by a proper ordering of reason's own instruments, I have paid more attention to scientific procedures than to some other logical forms.

In addition to its general emphasis on case histories, the present book, with the restrictions again imposed by an audience of under-classmen, takes account of modes of reasoning which occupy a peculiar eminence in present-day scholarship, such as the scientific method and mathematical logic.

In order to achieve the objectives I have mentioned, some topics properly emphasized in other textbooks in Aristotelian logic have had to be shortchanged, and when some teachers object to this misfortune, I will be the first to share their regret. Thus, there is no discussion of analogy in connection with the first act of the mind, and there is no treatment of supposition or the moods of the syllogism. My only plea is that with thirty-five chapters distributed in the ratio of about one chapter per lecture hour, something had to give, and what is deleted or de-emphasized owes its fate to the compromises which a practical teacher must make in order to get into a course or a book items which somehow seem more im-portant than others.

In view of the foregoing apology, it may seem contradictory to find in these pages a chapter on the nature of history. Its inclusion is justified by the fact that in Part V there is a treatment, from the viewpoint of material logic, of the basic disciplines of the college curriculum, and students might after all want to know where history stands in the hierarchy. Did not Aristotle treat of the nature of history in the *Poetics** which St. Thomas Aquinas claims to be a part of logic?**

The author makes no pretense of capturing into written words the vital process which is teaching by a case-history method. This book is strictly a tool to facilitate the dialectical exchange between teacher and learner. It is suggested that the explanatory matter be assigned for outside reading so that classroom time can be spent largely in working on the practical exercises with a minimum of straight lecturing by the teacher. The book can be abridged, e.g., by omitting Part VI; or supplemented, e.g., by restoring the treat-

---

* *Poetics*, Ch. 9, 1451a36–1451b31; Ch. 23, 1459a21–40.

** *Exposition of the Posterior Analytics of Aristotle*, Bk. 1, Lesson 1, n. 6; translated by Pierre Conway, O.P. (Quebec: Librairie Philosophique M. Doyon, 1956), p. 6.

ment of analogy. The exercises have been organized in structure and in number within the sound educational perspective that in learning the learner must do the work and that some learners will learn more because they work more.

In view of blunders that have remained uncriticized even in the so-called great books, our college students cannot get enough logic in the full amplitude that Aristotle and Aquinas gave to the term. In this respect, I hope that the following pages will move at least a little way toward Newman's ambition when he wrote: "Suffice it, then, to say here that I hold very strongly that the first step in intellectual training is to impress upon a . . . mind the idea of science, method, order, principle, and system; of rule and exception, of richness and harmony."*

My thanks are due in a special way to my wife, Virginia, for her constant encouragement and understanding during the writing of this book; to the Dominican Fathers at the Albertus Magnus Lyceum for Natural Science on whom I tested its principles; to my former students on whom I tested its practicality; and to Dr. Donald A. Gallagher, of Marquette University, who helped on both counts. Finally, I wish to express my gratitude to Mr. William E. May, of the Bruce Publishing Company, who gave immeasurable aid in tracking down quotations and obtaining the necessary permissions to reprint them.

V. E. S.

---

* John Henry Newman, *The Scope and Nature of University Education*, Everyman edition (London and New York: J. M. Dent, Ltd., and E. P. Dutton, Inc., 1915), p. xliii.

CONTENTS

PART V: THE KINDS OF ARGUMENT

PART VI: SPECIAL QUESTIONS

PART VII: THE FALLACIES

THE ELEMENTS OF LOGIC

PART I: INTRODUCTION

Chapter 1:   THE WORLD OF LOGIC

Logic and argument. The study of logic is the study of how to reason well. The nature of logic can be brought to light if we analyze some samples of reasoning or argument. Three such examples are given below to show us that far from being a specialized subject, confined to a single department of human knowledge, logic is applied in all of learning. Hence no matter what field of knowledge we may enter we must first know logic in order to reason well within that field. After each of the three arguments is stated in the author's own words, the arguments will be explained and then analyzed to see what makes them examples of logic.

1.1.* Our problem is to find out what happens to bodies of different weight moving in a medium devoid of resistance, so that the only difference in speed is that which arises from inequality of weight. Since no medium except one entirely free from air and other bodies, be it ever so tenuous and yielding, can furnish our senses with the evidence we are looking for, and since such a medium is not available, we shall observe what happens in the rarest and least resistant media as compared with what happens in denser and more resistant media. Because if we find as a fact that the variation of speed among bodies of different specific gravities is more or less according as the medium becomes more and more yielding, and if finally in a medium of extreme tenuity, though not a perfect vacuum, we find that, in spite of great diversity, the difference in speed is very small and almost inappreciable, then we are justified in believing it highly probable that in a vacuum all bodies would fall with the same speed.

GALILEO GALILEI

---

* In numbering the case histories, what precedes the first period in a reference like 1.1 gives the chapter reference, and what follows refers to elements within the chapter. References will be found at the end of the book, p. 271.

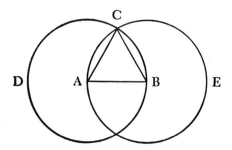

1.2. *To describe an equilateral triangle on a given finite straight line.*
   Let AB be the given straight line: it is required to describe an equilateral triangle on AB.
   From the centre A, at the distance AB, describe the circle BCD.
   From the centre B, at the distance BA, describe the circle ACE.
   From the point C, at which the circles cut one another, draw the straight lines CA and CB to the points A and B.
ABC shall be an equilateral triangle.
Because the point A is the centre of the circle BCD, AC is equal to AB.
And because the point B is the centre of the circle ACE, BC is equal to BA.
But it has been shown that CA is equal to AB;
Therefore CA and CB are each of them equal to AB.
But things which are equal to the same thing are equal to one another.
Therefore CA is equal to CB.
Therefore CA, AB, BC, are equal to one another.
   Wherefore *the triangle ABC is equilateral, and it is described on the given straight line AB.*

                                                                    EUCLID

   1.3. This [living in society] is clearly a necessity of man's nature. For all other animals, nature has prepared food, hair as a covering, teeth, horns, claws as means of defence or at least speed in flight, while man alone was made without any natural provisions for these things. Instead of all these, man was endowed with reason, by the use of which he could procure all these things for himself by the work of his hands. Now, one man alone is not able to procure them all for himself, for one man could not sufficiently provide for life, unassisted. It is therefore natural that man should live in the society of many.

                                                        ST. THOMAS AQUINAS

   It will be useful for us to inspect these three passages in their turn in order to see what it means to argue and hence what logic is about. Each of these passages comes from a different field of human knowledge, but they all have something in common which makes them arguments and therefore examples of logic.

As recorded in 1.1, Galileo clocked the speed with which various bodies of different weights descended through various solutions of different resistances. In thick media, he observed, heavy bodies fall faster than light ones, but the more the medium is thinned, the more all bodies, heavy and light, approach the same rate of descent. Galileo therefore concluded that in a vacuum, or a medium devoid of resistance, all bodies would probably fall at the same speed.

It is quite apparent that Galileo was dealing with bodies existing in the physical world such as gold, lead, and copper and with certain physical media in which he dropped the bodies, such as quicksilver, water, and air. Because he studied physical bodies and physical motions, Galileo is called a physicist.

But there is another dimension in Galileo's work. He reasoned or argued. He was trying to prove something. He was dealing also in a logical world. His sample of reasoning can be formulated in a more precise way.

> **1.1a.** *If,* as a medium becomes thinner and thinner, various bodies of different weights fall more and more with the same speed, *then* in a vacuum all bodies would probably fall at the same rate.
> But, as a medium becomes thinner and thinner, various bodies fall more and more with the same speed.
> Therefore, in a vacuum various bodies would probably fall at the same rate.

Relations, real and logical. Although bodies and their motions are realities in the world outside thought, the relation between the *if*-clause and the *then*-clause is not a physical quality. It is a relation that does not exist in the physical world. Galileo could see and touch the things represented by the words *bodies* and *media,* the gold, copper, or quicksilver. But he could never put his finger on something in the real world represented by the expressions *if* and *then.* The relation between the heaviness of a falling body and the thickness of a medium is a real, physical relation that can be varied as the medium is thinned. But the relation between *if* and *then* does not pertain to the physical universe. It is a logical relation.

Moreover, this relation between *if* and *then* has its own laws.

As shown in 1.1a, Galileo first affirmed the *if*-clause and thereupon affirmed the *then*-clause. Let us examine an argument in which the order of affirming would be the reverse of the one Galileo used:

> **1.1b. If John Jones is governor of Massachusetts, he resides in New England.**
> **But John Jones resides in New England.**
> **Therefore, he is governor of Massachusetts.**

Here the argument affrms the *then*-clause and goes on to affirm the *if*-clause. It violates a law of reasoning, to be studied later, and is a bad argument. Were it valid, then everyone living in New England would be the governor of Massachusetts. To be correct the concluding parts of the argument would have to read:

> **But John Jones is governor of Massachusetts.**
> **Therefore, he resides in New England.**

As in the case of Galileo's reasoning, our corrected argument involves a certain real situation. There is a man, an office of governor, and geographical places like Massachusetts and New England. But there is another and nonphysical order involved, the relation between the *if*-clause and the *then*-clause. This is a special kind of relation, unlike the relation between Massachusetts and New England and between being a man and being a governor. This special relation is brought about when John Jones and governor and Massachusetts and New England are taken not in their physical existence but in their positions within an argument.

To study relations of this nonphysical type and the laws which govern such relations is the business of logic.

In **1.2** (the argument from Euclid) there are two cases of the if-then relation:

> **1.2a. If AC and AB are radii of the same circle, they are equal.**
> **But they are radii of the same circle.**
> **Therefore, they are equal.**
> **1.2b. If BC and BA are radii of the same circle, they are equal.**
> **But they are radii of the same circle.**
> **Therefore, they are equal.**

Case **1.2** has a third stage where AC and BC are compared to a third line, AB, and, because AC and BC are found equal to this third line, they are declared equal to each other.

Once more, there are different orders, one real and one not real. *AB*, *BC*, and *AC* are real lines, and there is a real relation of equality between them. *BCD* and *ACE* are both circles. All of these realities are mathematical facts.

But there is another kind of order involved here to the extent that *AB*, *BC*, *AC*, equality, *BCD*, and *ACE* are not parts of the mathematical world but parts of an argument formed by the mind. Mathematics is interested in lines and circles as parts of the mathematical universe. Logic is interested only in the parts of an argument.

In the third stage, where *BC* and *AC* are found equal to each other because they are each equal to *AB*, the lines are mathematical realities; but for *AB* to be a medium for the comparison of two other lines is not a mathematical property. That is to say for *AB* to be a line is geometrical; for *AB* to be a medium involves this other kind of property which things acquire to the extent that they have place in argument.

Finally, there is 1.3 (the argument of St. Thomas Aquinas). Here two realities, man and *a being that is naturally ordered to live in society*, are compared with a common third thing, *a creature that depends on his fellows for the necessities of life*.

> 1.3a. A creature that depends on his fellows for the necessities of life is a being naturally ordered to live in society.
> Man is a creature that depends on his fellows for the necessities of life.
> Therefore, man is a being naturally ordered to live in society.

Now man, *a creature that depends on his fellows for the necessities of life*, and *a being that is naturally ordered to live in a society* — all three items are physical realities. But they all own a set of properties or relations called logical forms because of their place in an argument. In the real world, for instance, man is a rational animal. In the foregoing argument he is a subject of a proposition. In the physical world a creature that depends on his fellows for the necessities of life has a social existence. In the argument of St. Thomas, a creature that depends on his fellows for the necessities of life has only logical existence. It is the medium for comparing two things with a third thing.

The subject of logic. These properties which things take on when they become parts of argument or discourse are logical relations or logical forms. To study them is the province of the science of logic. Logic is concerned to find the laws which govern these relations or forms or properties so that by obeying the laws human reason may proceed in an orderly, correct, and easy manner to reach truth.

Let us look back over the road at this point to draw distinctions more sharply. There are two kinds of reality that are of interest here. First, there are properties that things have in themselves. These are physical or natural characteristics. Lead and quicksilver, in the experiment of Galileo, are real things in the real world; they have characteristic weights, colors, and electrical and magnetic properties. But in Galileo's argument, considered precisely as an argument, lead is a *subject* about which something is said or is *predicated*, e.g., *lead falls at a certain rate.* This is the second kind of property, that of lead as a subject, a property which lead receives when thought about. To be a solid is a physical property of lead. To be a subject about which something is said by human reason is a logical property or logical form, which lead assumes when part of an argument.

That about which something is said in examples like those above is called a *subject*, e.g., *John* or *Mary*. That which is said about the subject is called a *predicate*, e.g., *man*. The joining of subject and predicate through a connective like *is* forms a proposition, e.g., *John is a man.* To be a subject or predicate or proposition is not a physical thing like John or Mary. It is a logical property, and subject and predicate, like the *if-then* relation, are likewise called logical forms or properties or relations. There are many such logical forms. An argument, for instance, is not a physical reality but has only logical existence. In logic, man is a *species*. In the real world, he is a rational animal. When a disease is investigated, nothing physical is added to or subtracted from the disease itself. *To be under investigation* is a logical property only. When a number of cases of juvenile delinquency are examined to determine their cause, the delinquency and the cause are both realities outside our thought. But to be a *case* or an *example* or a *specimen* is a logical reality only.

The examples at the beginning of this chapter consisted of a physical, a mathematical, and a political-science argument. To the extent of being physical, mathematical, or political, they pertain to the respective sciences involved. But to the extent that the physical, mathematical, or political arguments are *arguments*, they belong to logic.

Distinct domain of logic. It is clear that logical beings are quite different from physical reality. They are not just unrealized possibilities that can some day come to be in the real world. An imagined flower that will at a later date grow from a seed is not a logical being like the *if-then* relation. Neither is a house that is merely in the planning stage. Logical relations do not, like a picture, resemble physical things. They can never exist in the real world. The order of logic is a quite distinct level of being.

Logic deals with properties that things acquire to the extent that they are considered by human reason. Physics, mathematics, biology, and numerous other studies are concerned with things as having a place in the real universe. Logic is concerned with things as having a place in the universe of human discourse.

This chapter has tried to indicate the kind of world with which logic is concerned and the kind of being that logic studies. A more precise definition of logic must await the discussion in the next chapter.

Problems

1. Show how in **1.1** and **1.2** there is a difference to the extent that one argument is physical and one mathematical but a likeness to the extent that they both are arguments.

2. Which of the following items are purely logical relations and which are real: a definition, our future life, signification, Julius Caesar, a proof, an angel, a metaphor? Give a reason for each answer.

3. Comment on the following statement: "Logical relations as such have no resemblance to physical things and can never exist in the real world."

4. Find an argument in a book, editorial, or advertisement, and analyze it to discover logical relations.

5. On the basis of the present chapter, how would you distinguish between logic and grammar?

6. In the following passages, indicate at least three items, mentioned or used, which belong to the world of logic and three items which do not:

1.4. There are three distinctions in the kinds of bodies, or three states, which have more especially claimed the attention of philosophical chemists: namely, those which are marked by the terms *elastic fluids, liquids,* and *solids.* A very familiar instance is exhibited to us in water, a body, which, in certain circumstances, is capable of assuming all three states. In steam we recognize a perfectly elastic fluid, in water a perfect liquid, and in ice a complete solid. These observations have tacitly led to the conclusion which seems universally adopted, that all bodies of sensible magnitude, whether liquid or solid, are constituted of a vast number of extremely small particles. . . .

JOHN DALTON

1.5. It is notorious that specific characters are more variable than generic. To explain by a simple example what is meant: if in a large genus of plants some species had blue flowers and some had red, the color would be only a specific character, and no one would be surprised at one of the blue species varying into red, or conversely; but if all the species had blue flowers, the color would become a generic character, and its variation would be a more unusual circumstance.

CHARLES DARWIN

7. Comment on the following passage:

1.6. The philosophical mathematician, Dr. Richard Dedekind, holds mathematics to be a branch of logic. This would not result from my father's definition, which runs, not that mathematics is the science of *drawing* necessary conclusions . . . but that it is the science which draws necessary conclusions. It is evident, and I know it as a fact, that he had this distinction in view. At the time when he thought out this definition, he, a mathematician, and I, a logician, held daily discussions about a large subject which interested us both; and he was struck, as I was, with the contrary nature of his interest and mine in the same propositions. The logician does not care particularly about this or that hypothesis or its consequences, except so far as these things may throw light upon the nature of reasoning.

CHARLES SAUNDERS PEIRCE

Chapter 2: LOGIC AS A LIBERAL ART

2.1. Here were these magnificent creatures of God, I mean the Alps, which now for the first time I saw from the heights of the Jura; and because they were fifty or sixty miles away, and because they were a mile or two high, they were become something different from us others, and could strike one motionless with the awe of supernatural things. Up there in the sky to which only clouds belong and birds and the last trembling colors of pure light, they stood fast and hard, not moving as do the things of the sky. . . . These, the great Alps, seen thus, link one in some way to one's immortality. . . . From the heights of the Weissenstein I saw, as it were, my religion. . . . This it is also which leads some men to climb mountaintops but not for me, for I am afraid of slipping down.

HILAIRE BELLOC

Logic can easily be confused with other subjects. It would be a good exercise to turn back to argument 1.2 of the past chapter (or to 1.6) and to ask how logic differs from mathematics. Mathematics and logic are often too closely identified with each other, and anyone who can differentiate the two from the discussion in Chapter 1 is on the road to understanding what logic is.

Logic and grammar. Meanwhile, there is another subject that should be compared and contrasted with logic. It is grammar. The passage quoted at the beginning of this chapter can bring logic and grammar into focus.

In the above example, Belloc is saying something. He is even presenting an argument, a weaker argument than any of those in the preceding chapter, but an argument nevertheless. He is giving reasons why the Alps symbolize the motionless character of eternal things that awaken the awe of the supernatural.

But there is also a grammatical, not to say literary, form in which this argument is expressed. Grammar has to do with the correct form of verbal expression. In grammar there are rules of language involving the use of words, like nouns and verbs; there are rules for spelling and punctuation. All such rules are familiar, and they resemble somewhat the logical relations described in Chapter 1.

But logic and grammar, in their narrower senses, are quite different. Logic is concerned with the relations among our ideas, grammar with the correct expression of those ideas first as spoken and secondly as written. Grammar thus depends on the logical world which it expresses, and in a real sense logic and grammar form one subject. However, throughout this book, logic will be taken as the study of what goes on in the mind alone, with grammar attending strictly to language. Grammar in our sense does not deal with the strictly logical relations discussed in Chapter 1 but with the consequences of these relations.

In another way, grammar has a likeness to physics. The grammarian is concerned with spoken sounds and written marks. But while the physicist is interested in the purely material make-up of these sounds and marks, the grammarian is concerned with ordering spoken or written characters in such a way that they correctly express his meaning.

In order to distinguish logic and grammar in their narrower senses, in which they are taken in this book, let us look again at the bad argument given as 1.1b in Chapter 1. There we read: *If John Jones is governor of Massachusetts, he resides in New England. But John Jones resides in New England. Therefore, he is governor of Massachusetts.* The verbal expression of this argument is grammatically correct, but the argument is not logically correct. The passage quoted from Belloc (2.1) is an excellent example of grammar; but as an argument it is weak, since it is not intended to be a scientific proof. It is also possible to have a good argument, from the logical viewpoint, even though, because of misspellings or errors of punctuation, the grammatical expression may be bad. Suppose that Belloc had said, in the second-last sentence of the passage quoted, "These, the great Alps, seen thus, link one in some way to one's immortality . . . from the heights of the Weissenstein. I saw, as it were, my religion." By thus changing the punctuation, Belloc would have expressed utter nonsense from the logical point of view, even though the insertion of the period would still leave the passage grammatically correct. Good grammar can express bad logic. Bad grammar can expresss good logic. Bad grammar can express bad logic. Or good grammar can express good logic.

But if there are differences between logic and grammar, there are some interesting similarities between them. The passage from *The Path to Rome* was not found by Belloc ready-made as the Alps were ready-made for him to see. He had to write the passage. He had to construct. He was a maker, an artist, and the passage is a product of his art.

Logic and art. In pure science the mind considers an order that is already made. It does not make the order. In the argument of Chapter 1 (1.3), St. Thomas did not make man or social life. Both realities were already in existence outside the mind, and St. Thomas found out what they were and what real relation exists between them. In art, however, man does not deal with an order already formed. He puts an order into things. He makes the order. For instance, in the so-called mechanical arts, knives and forks and shoes and automobiles are not produced by nature and simply discovered by man. Man makes them.

The making which takes place in logic and grammar is the reason why these two subjects are called liberal arts. Indeed, there are seven liberal arts, namely, logic, grammar, and rhetoric — which may be broadly grouped as the arts of expression — and arithmetic, geometry, music, and astronomy — which are all mathematical arts. In order to set logic in perspective, it will be useful to make a brief analysis of the liberal arts to determine, first, why they are arts and, second, why they are liberal.

Like all the other arts and unlike the pure sciences, the liberal arts do not deal with things that are formed in nature and merely discovered by man. They involve construction or making. They deal with an order of things produced not by nature but by human reason. In grammar (2.1) Belloc made sentences and paragraphs. In mathematics (1.2) Euclid produced lines and figures. In logic, reason forms those properties which the previous chapter termed logical relations or logical forms.

Outside the mind, for instance, the Alps are mountains in their physical existence, but when thought about, the Alps become the subject of a proposition or an illustration of eternity. To be a subject or an illustration is not a physical property added to the Alps, a property like color or shape or size. To be a subject or an illustration is a logical property or logical form which the mind gives to the Alps by considering them. As known by the human intellect, things require our reason to construct such properties or forms as propositions, the *if-then* relationship, etc.

Logic is thus a genuine art because it involves making. By contrast, what we ordinarily call science does not make what it considers but discovers what is already made, e.g., the elements in the sun or the pull of gravitation. In logic, reason studies those properties which things as known require the mind to produce. To be a subject or a predicate or part of an argument is not a property which things have prior to our consideration of them and which we merely discover as we discover the cause of a disease. Logical properties are given to things by the mind in its act of considering them.

But if logic is an art, the question why it is liberal remains.

Logic as a liberal art. *Liberal* comes from the Latin word, *liber*, meaning "free." Just as a free man is a person operating for his own good and not, like a slave, for the good of a master, so liberal knowledge is knowledge that is good to have just for its own sake. Such knowledge has an intrinsic value, apart from any work produced. An automobile mechanic studies automobiles in order to repair them. His studies perfect not the mind but something outside it, namely automobiles. Whereas nonliberal pursuits are aimed at what is outside the mind, a liberal mind seeks truth because truth is a perfection of the mind itself. A liberal mind operates for its own good and not merely for the good of a product like an automobile or an airplane. In the mechanical arts which produce such tools as knives and shoes and airplanes, the mind is operating not for its own sake but for the sake of the body. But in liberal pursuits, the mind, like the free man, is operating for its own good, namely truth itself.

Definition of logic. Consequently, the liberal arts — and in a special way logic — have for their aim the good of the mind, namely the attainment of truth. In the liberal arts, the products are for the mind's own good rather than, as in the mechanical arts, for the sake of the body. The study of logic aims to analyze the relations produced by reason in thinking about things in order to set such relations in their proper order for the attainment of truth. Logic may therefore be defined as *the art which directs reason in its operations so that reason in turn may proceed in an orderly, easy, and correct manner and may avoid error.*

Logic is both an art and a science. Because it involves construction, logic is an art. But because it must analyze the relations which things as known compel us to form, logic involves study and has a scientific character. It is both an art and a science. As an art it constructs things which realities require us to produce in order to consider them, and as a science it studies such products of reason in order to analyze the rules for reasoning well.

A review of examples 1.1 and 1.2 in Chapter 1 reveals that they involve relations expressed grammatically by *if-then,* and, as **1.1a** and **1.1b** indicated, there are rules involved by such logical relations. As a science logic studies these rules so that by obeying them and avoiding their violations reason may have the proper means to proceed from the known to the unknown or from one truth to another truth.

Logic and reality. Logic, however, should not be overestimated. Of itself, logic cannot put the mind in possession of truth. It studies only logical relations, not the things outside the mind which are set into logical relations by other sciences.

Logic might be compared in this respect to the scanning systems of poetry. The form for writing heroic couplets is iambic pentameter:

$$\cup \acute{-} \mid \cup \acute{-} \mid \cup \acute{-} \mid \cup \acute{-} \mid \cup \acute{-}$$

But a scheme of this sort fails to reveal anything about content. Of itself, it will not enable us to write lines like the following from Alexander Pope:

> 2.2. **A little learning is a dangerous thing;**
> **Drink deep, or taste not the Pierian spring.**

Somewhat like the metric scheme for writing heroic couplets, logic is not about content. It is not about physical subject matter. It is uniquely concerned with logical structure or logical form. Given two propositions, A and B, logic can name the conditions for concluding to a third proposition C, but logic itself cannot guarantee whether A and B are true to begin with. Such a task belongs to other sciences.

Logic may be compared to the wooden frames prepared for the pouring of concrete in the construction of a building. The molds or frames are necessary, but unless the right kind of concrete is used in them, the final product will be bad. In a similar manner, the scheme for writing heroic couplets is no assurance that a versemaker who writes according to this form will produce a good poem.

The forms considered by logic are empty of physical content. If there is an *if-then* relation in physics or biology or mathematics, logic can indicate how such a relationship must be ordered to proceed to a conclusion. Whether the content expressed within the logical form is a truth of fact logic cannot say. Such a truth of fact can be established only within physics or biology or mathematics. Turning back again to **1.1**, logic cannot determine whether balls or gold or lead fall fast or slow in air. This is a problem for physics. In **1.2**, logic cannot determine whether AB and BC are radii of ACE and whether all radii of the same circle are equal. This is a problem for mathematics. Nor can logic judge whether man depends on his fellows for the necessities of life. This is a problem of political science.

But given a proposition or propositions as true, logic can determine what consequences can be drawn from them. When lead or man or the radii of a circle are subjects of propositions, logic can determine their properties as subjects, though not as lead or man or quantities which have a real existence. In this sense, physics and mathematics are sciences of truth. Logic is the science of validity. The first two sciences deal with matter. Logic deals only with form. It should be clear by now that logic is not mathematics or grammar in its narrow sense, but an original liberal art.

Universal value of logic. Logic is not just the private property of philosophers. Like grammar, which is used in all human sciences, logic is a universal art. It is applied in all human discourse, even, as Belloc shows, in literature.

Like grammar too, logic does not have to await a college course in the subject in order to be used. All men have the power of speech, and minds that are relatively unschooled often attain a remarkable proficiency in the use of grammar. But ordinarily, if the mind is to have control of its verbal expression, it must attain the power of knowing why this or that expression is correct, and it must be able also to defend a given expression when it is criticized.

So it is with logic. All men have reason. But without logic, they will not be sure of their reasoning. In science, for instance, it is not enough to know the truth. We must also know why we hold the truth, and we must be able to defend our reasoning process when it is challenged. To aim at science without knowing logic is like desiring to write literature without studying grammar.

The unlearned, natural reason of man has the gift for verbal expression. Grammar does not destroy this gift. It builds upon it; it refines and perfects it. In the same way, logic extends and strengthens the native work of reason. Logic is the best example of an art that imitates nature. Natural reason can get along without logic just as man could get along without machines. But nature, perfected by art, is better than nature in the raw.

Problems

1. Can you formulate into an *if-then* relation any of the ideas expressed or implied in the passage quoted from Belloc (2.1)?

2. What is meant by saying that grammar is closer to physics than logic is? Is grammar concerned with logical relations? What is the difference between a grammatical noun and a logical subject?

3. Why is logic an art? Why is it liberal?

4. Name several items, either mentioned or used in the lines from Pope, which were constructed by the poet. Name several items mentioned or used which Pope did not construct.

5. In what sense is the study of grammar not necessary? In what sense is it necessary? Now answer these two questions with regard to logic.

6. Do you have any notions about the method of dividing up a subject into its parts so that the subject may be covered in an orderly way?

7. In the light of your knowledge of the difference between grammar and logic, write a brief essay on the relation between language and logic as suggested by one or both of the following passages:

2.3.   Words in prose ought to express the intended meaning; if they attract attention to themselves, it is a fault; in the very best styles you read page after page without noticing the medium.

SAMUEL TAYLOR COLERIDGE

2.4.   The ordinary objection to Browning, the charge of needless obscurity, is just in a certain degree, yet requires a serious qualification. Browning is the simplest and most manly of poets in his message and intention. It is only his speech that is rough and quaint. There are writers of great depth and delicacy, such as Mr. Henry James, against whom the charge of obscurity is brought, but here the sense is very different. The writings of Mr. Henry James are obscure even when we understand them. They have to do (even as they are seen by the eyes of the author) with dim and fugitive and anomalous sentiments.

GILBERT KEITH CHESTERTON

Chapter 3: THE DIVISIONS OF LOGIC

3.1. All things that exist, therefore, seeing that the Creator of them all is supremely good, are themselves good. But because they are not, like their Creator, supremely and unchangeably good, their good may be diminished and increased.

ST. AUGUSTINE

The foregoing argument, which is explained and justified in a science called metaphysics, offers a splendid example of an effort of the human mind to reason from certain facts and principles to a definite conclusion in such a way that the conclusion defended will be accepted by other minds.

Primary interest of logic. Logic is aimed principally at a study of arguments in order to determine whether or not the process of reasoning involved takes place in an orderly way, following definite laws which regulate the relations between the various elements of the argument.

The logician wants to understand arguments. As a result of studying logic, the mind should reason better and be more capable of a critical acceptance or rejection of arguments presented by others. But in order to achieve such aims with regard to arguments as wholes, there must first be an analysis of the simplest ingredients of an argument.

The logician's position is analogous to that of a builder. The builder is not interested in a foundation for its own sake. His main concern is the building as a whole, just as the logician's main concern is with the argument as a whole. Yet, if the superstructure of a building is to be supported, the foundation must be correspondingly strong. In a similar way, the mathematician does not stop with the arithmetic learned in the first grade. Yet, without first analyzing the unit of number, namely "1" and the simplest equation, $1 + 1 = 2$, a mathematician could never establish a more complicated equation like $25^2 = 625$.

The elements of an argument. So it is with the logician. He must first study the elements of an argument before he can analyze how they are put together to argue well. What are those elements?

There are two arguments in the passage from St. Augustine (3.1). We shall consider the first.

> 3.1a. Whatever comes from the Creator is good.
> 3.1b. All things that exist come from the Creator.
> 3.1c. Therefore, all things that exist are good.

At least three parts can be found in this argument. Each of the statements, **3.1a, 3.1b,** and **3.1c,** expresses a truth. Such statements are called *propositions.*

The propositions in turn are composed of parts. These parts are represented by the expressions, *whatever comes from the Creator, good,* and *all things that exist.* There is another part in each proposition represented by the word *is.* The word *is* is called the *copula.*

In each statement what is expressed by the words preceding the copula is called the *subject* of the proposition, and what follows the copula is called the *predicate* of the proposition.

The subject and predicate stand for single notions, even though they may be expressed grammatically by several words or even by several clauses and phrases. In an affirmative proposition, the two single notions are joined by the copula; in a negative proposition, subject and predicate are divided. An example of the negative proposition — one in which the copula is negative — is *Man is not a machine.*

A proposition is a logical compound in which a subject and predicate are joined by the copula *is* or divided by the copula *is not.* Whatever can stand as a subject or predicate of a proposition is called a *term.*

An argument, then, can be broken down into *propositions;* and propositions, in their turn, are formed of a *subject* and *predicate* as their simplest *terms,* and the relation between them is expressed by a *copula.*

The three acts of the mind. The subject and the predicate, it was observed, are simple notions by comparison with the proposition which is their logical compound. The subject and predicate are each grasped without affirming or denying anything about them. For example, the proposition, *All things that exist come from the Creator*, says something about all things that exist; it says that they come from the Creator. But the expression, *All things that exist*, neither affirms nor denies anything. To grasp something without affirming or denying anything about it is called the *first operation of the mind*.

In the proposition, the predicate is affirmed (or denied) of the subject. This is an operation quite different from the mere grasp of the subject alone or of the predicate alone. In a proposition, the subject and predicate are set in relation with each other. The act of the intellect joining or dividing a subject and a predicate is called the *second operation of the mind*.

Finally, in the argument as a whole, two propositions are combined with each other so that a third proposition can be formed. This act of the intellect, proceeding from two propositions to a third one, is called the *third operation of the mind*.

In the first operation of the intellect, the subject and predicate are each grasped alone. In the second act of the intellect, the subject and predicate are combined to form a proposition. In the third operation of the mind, propositions are put together to form an argument.

These three operations of the intellect will be considered in some detail throughout the next three parts of this book, Parts II, III, and IV.

Types of argument. Arguments are not always of equal value. Sometimes an argument is convincing, as in **1.2** or **3.1**. At other times only probable conclusions can be reached, as in **1.1**. At still other times, an argument may fail to convince us but nevertheless persuade us, like a political speech or a billboard advertisement. Finally, as in **2.1**, an argument may appeal to us by a pleasing or unpleasant representation of its subject.

To consider such problems, there is another part of logic, Part V in this book, which has for its purpose to name the conditions for each of the various kinds of argument: science, opinion, persuasion, or literature. An argument leading to science is said to be *demonstrative*; an argument leading to opinion is called *dialectic*; an argument leading to persuasion is called *rhetorical;* an argument that is *literary* is, of course, literature.

These are the four fundamental kinds of human discourse. To be able to discriminate among such types of argument is a mark of an educated man. In this respect, the following passage from Aristotle sets down the ambition for an undergraduate program in logic:

> 3.2. Every systematic science, the humblest and noblest alike, seems to admit of two distinct kinds of proficiency; one of which may be properly called scientific knowledge of the subject, while the other is a kind of educational acquaintance with it. For an educated man should be able to form a fair off-hand judgement as to the goodness or badness of the method used by a professor in his exposition. To be educated is in fact to be able to do this; even the man of universal education we deem to be such in virtue of his having this ability. It will, however, of course, be understood that we only ascribe universal education to one who in his own individual person is thus critical in all or nearly all branches of knowledge, and not to one who has a like ability merely in some special subject. For it is possible for a man to have this competence in some one branch of knowledge, without having it in all.
>
> ARISTOTLE

Undergraduate logic should enable a student "to form a fair off-hand judgement as to the goodness or badness of the method" of anyone presenting an argument. Any educated person should be able to identify a piece of argumentation as science, opinion, rhetoric, or literature and "be able to form a fair off-hand judgement" of whether the argument has been done well or poorly according to the rules which each kind of reasoning should follow.

After Part V, certain special questions will be considered in Part VI.

Part VII will form a special treatment of certain common mistakes in logic. It will concern illogical or fallacious argumentation.

In summary, the parts of this book are:

V. The Kinds of Argument
VI. Special Questions
VII. The Fallacies

Problems

1. Why could propositions be called the *proximate* parts of an argument, while the subject and predicate could be called *remote* parts?

2. Define *subject, predicate, term, copula, proposition, argument.*

3. Between which of the following pairs is the greater difference: (a) the first and second acts of the mind; and (b) the second and third acts of the mind?

4. Appearing in a London newspaper early in our century, the following paragraph, intended to recruit members for an Arctic expedition, has been called the most successful advertisement ever written. The day after it appeared, 5000 men answered it. Analyze it to show why, though primarily concerned with argument, logic must attend to the first operation of the mind.

3.3. MEN WANTED — for dangerous undertaking. Poor working conditions, bad food, long hours, constant and great danger. Survivors, if any, are guaranteed lasting fame. Apply . . .

5. Show why a study of the first and second operations of the intellect is important, using the following paragraph:

3.4. I recommend the following exercise: When, in a sentence expressing political opinion, there are words that arouse powerful but different emotions in different readers, try replacing them by symbols, A, B, C, and so on, and forgetting the particular significance of the symbols. Suppose A is England, B is Germany, and C is Russia. So long as you remember what the letters mean, most of the things you will believe will depend upon whether you are English, German, or Russian, which is logically irrelevant.

BERTRAND RUSSELL

6. The first two propositions in St. Augustine's second argument (3.1) will be formulated below. Can you supply the third and concluding proposition?

Things that are not supremely and unchangeably good may have their good diminished or increased.
Creatures are things that are not supremely and unchangeably good.
Therefore,

PART II: THE FIRST ACT OF THE MIND

Chapter 4: THE CONCEPT

4.1. "There will be striking phenomena in sun and moon and stars; on the earth throes will grip the nations, perplexed by the roar of sea and surge; men will faint away from fright and expectation of what is yet to befall the world; for the foundations of the universe will rock. At last they will see the Son of Man riding upon a cloud with great might and majesty. When these phenomena are well underway, raise your heads and look up, for then your redemption is close at hand."

He also told them a parable: "Look at the fig tree, or any of the trees: the moment they begin to shoot, you need but open your eyes to know that summer is near. Apply this to yourselves: as soon as you see these events in progress, you know that the kingdom of God is at hand."

ST. LUKE

In this passage, Christ is describing events that will precede the end of the world. He is revealing that the sun, the moon, the stars, and the seas, together with afflictions of the human heart, will indicate His second coming. Christ tells us that the unusual behavior of the heavens will be "striking phenomena," that the strange behavior of both nature and men "means" that the end of the world is approaching. In other words, Christ is revealing some "signs" that indicate the end of time.

What are signs? Examples will help to reach a definition: (1) A diploma is a sign of a college education. (2) Groaning is a sign of pain. (3) A red light is a sign of danger. (4) Dark clouds are a sign of an approaching storm. (5) A word, spoken or written, is a sign of what we are thinking. (6) A footprint in the snow is the sign of the animal that made it. (7) A salute is the sign of respect

23

for a superior. (8) Radioactivity is the sign of uranium or some similar substance. (9) A wedding ring is a sign of marriage. (10) An idea is a sign of what we are thinking about, and a sense image of what we are sensing. Like the portents of the end of the world, all these signs represent to us something other than themselves. A diploma is not an education, but it indicates or signifies an education. Groaning in itself is merely a sound that can be measured by physics, but it represents something else, namely pain. For a thing to indicate something other than itself is to be a sign.

College education is greatly concerned with signs. Words signify ideas. Ideas or concepts signify things. Diagrams in geometry or physics signify objects in the real world that are studied by the various sciences. The sacraments are signs. In all such cases, signs are things that represent to us something besides themselves.

An idea, or a concept, as produced by the first operation of the intellect is a sign of a thing. The idea of the Supreme Intelligence is not God, but represents God to our minds. It signifies God for us. When we write the written symbols, "Supreme Intelligence," our words are signs of the idea we have. A word is thus a sign of another sign. It is the sign of a concept.

Signs, artificial and natural. Before going further into the nature of words and of ideas or concepts, it will be useful to divide signs into their various kinds. Inspection will show that all of the odd-numbered examples in our list of signs are alike in that they are man-made. They are *artificial* or conventional. They are made by arbitrary human agreement. Salutes are different in different countries, but they all signify respect. Some nations, like ours, signify applause by clapping the hands, others by stamping the feet or snapping the fingers. All of these signs of applause are different, but they indicate the same thing. Man is signified by *anthropos* in Greek, *homo* in Latin, *l'homme* in French, *l'uomo* in Italian, *Der Mensch* in German. The expression in each case is the result of an arbitrary agreement that the written or spoken symbol concerned will stand for the reality, man. There is no natural connection between a word and a thing. As Shakespeare said, a rose under any other name would smell as sweet.

All of the even-numbered examples are *natural* signs. They are not man-made, but involve an essential or natural connection between the sign and what is signified. The artificial name for groaning will differ in various languages, but groaning has a natural connection with pain.

Among the natural signs, the one that is of interest here is the idea or concept, which forms the subject and predicate of a proposition. In the first act of the mind, the natural sign called the concept is formed. Sense impressions of things are also natural signs, but will be differentiated from concepts in Chapter 5.

Why is an idea a truly natural sign and not a man-made artifact like a diploma or a salute or a spoken or written word? The answer is that there is a natural and necessary connection between an idea and what it represents. Man is free to vary his traffic signals, making green to mean stop and red to mean go. But he has no such liberty with regard to concepts or ideas. To have an idea of man is necessarily to have an idea of a rational creature. The concept of a dog must be that of a four-footed animal that barks. The concept of a rose must always be that of a certain kind of flower. An idea is not a work of art in the sense in which art has been previously defined. A concept is dictated by the nature of things, by what things actually are. We can call a horse by different names in different languages, but our concept or idea of horse must always be the same, or else we are not thinking of a horse.

A concept, the product of the first operation of the intellect, is therefore a *natural* sign.

Signs, instrumental and formal. In addition to the division of signs into artificial and natural, there is another distinction of signs that bears in a special way on our study of the concept.

A reinspection of the ten examples of signs together with a rereading of the passage from St. Luke will disclose that all of the signs except concepts and sense images have two aspects: they are something in themselves and they indicate something other than themselves. The groan and salute are something in themselves. One is a sound that can be measured by a physicist, and the other is a movement of the hand. In addition to being something in themselves, they signify what is other than themselves, pain in the one case and respect in the other. Their reference to what they signify is superadded to what they are.

That is not true of the idea or concept or of sense images. Here the whole essence of the sign is to signify. The whole reality of a concept or image is to be about something else. Apart from its meaning or signification, the idea is nothing. It does not, like a dark cloud, have a character of its own apart from what it means or stands for. The concept is a pure sign. That is in its definition. A footprint can be described in terms of geometry, without referring to the animal that made it. But a concept cannot. Its essence consists in the reference or relation it bears to the object that it represents, and as a means of knowledge it consists in nothing else.

The concept and the sense image are called *formal* signs because their whole nature or form is to signify or mean something else. All other signs, natural as well as artificial, are called *instrumental* signs. Like a chisel or a hammer, they have a reality in themselves, but in addition, they are tools or instruments directed to something else.

There is another distinction between the formal and instrumental sign. The instrumental sign is always known first and what is signified is known only afterward. Smoke is recognized, when we see it, before we are directed to the fire by the sign-character of the smoke. We think of rain only after we have observed the dark clouds.

In the formal sign, however, what is signified is always known first. The sign is recognized only afterward. Only after knowing an object do we discover that we knew the object by means of ideas. People can go through life knowing many things about the physical world without ever pausing to consider that they knew such things by concepts or ideas. In looking at the sun, our attention is directed at the object, at the sun, not at the idea we are forming of the sun. Without reflecting upon our mind's work, we are not aware that we have ideas or concepts; we are simply aware of the objects that they represent. Only later do we discover and analyze the means by which we represent such objects.

Although formed in the mind, ideas are nevertheless not purely logical relations. An idea is not an arbitrary and artificial sign like a word or a salute; it is a natural sign and is not open to human convention. There is, therefore, a real and natural relation between the idea and what it represents. As being essentially about something outside the mind, an idea is really related to that something.

It is related to what it signifies by what is called a psychological relation. The logical properties which ideas acquire will be considered during the remaining chapters of Part II.

Problems

1. Characterize the signs in the passage from St. Luke's Gospel as being either natural or artificial.

2. Name two differences between the instrumental and formal signs.

3. Explain why a concept considered in itself is not a logical relation.

4. Without repeating examples mentioned in this chapter, make a list of ten artificial signs and ten natural signs.

5. Relate the notion of a sign to burning a person in effigy.

6. Discuss the importance of signs in social life, in business, in athletics, in education, in transportation, and in art.

7. Using your knowledge of natural and artificial signs and instrumental and formal signs, write a brief report on one of the following paragraphs:

4.2. Beasts do not read symbols; that is why they do not see pictures. We are sometimes told that dogs do not react even to the best portraits because they live more by smell than by sight; but the behavior of a dog who spies a motionless real cat through the window glass belies this explanation. Dogs scorn our paintings because they see colored canvases, not pictures. A representation of a cat does not make them conceive one.

SUZANNE K. LANGER

4.3. In the very beginnings of modern physics, in Galileo, we find the metaphor that the "book of nature" is written in mathematical ciphers. And since then, the entire development of exact natural science shows that every step forward in the formulation of its problems and concepts has gone hand in hand with the increasing refinement of its system of signs.

ERNST CASSIRER

4.4. Some persons would unhesitatingly say that blushing is a sign, others not. There are mechanical dogs which will come out of their kennels if one claps one's hands loudly in their presence. Is such clapping a sign? Are clothes signs of the personality of those who wear them? Is music a sign of anything? Is a word such as "Go!" a sign in the same sense as is a green light on a street intersection? Are punctuation marks signs? Are dreams signs? Is the Parthenon a sign of Greek culture?

                                                    CHARLES MORRIS

(NOTE: Can you answer Morris' questions?)

8. Read one of the following and discuss it in the light of what you know about signs:

"I See His Blood Upon the Rose," by Joseph Mary Plunkett

"The Parable of the Sower," St. Matthew's Gospel, Chapter 13

Chapter 5: THE UNIVERSAL

5.1. We live in two different worlds — the world of facts and that of their symbols. In order to acquire knowledge of ourselves, we utilize both observation and scientific abstractions. But the abstract may be mistaken for the concrete. In such an instance, facts are treated as symbols and the individual is likened to the human being. Most of the errors made by educators, physicians, and sociologists come from such confusion. Scientists, accustomed to the techniques of mechanics, chemistry, physics, and physiology, and unfamiliar with philosophy and intellectual culture are liable to mingle the concepts of the different disciplines and not to distinguish clearly the general from the particular. However, in the concept of man, it is important to define exactly that part of the human being and that of the individual. Education, medicine, and sociology are concerned with the individual. They are guilty of a disastrous error when they look upon him only as a symbol, as a human being. Indeed, individuality is fundamental in man. It is not merely a certain aspect of the organism. But it permeates our entire being. It stamps its mark on the whole of body and consciousness, and, although remaining indivisible, on each conponent of this whole. It makes the self a unique event in the history of the world.

ALEXIS CARREL

The concept, seen in the previous chapter as a natural, formal sign representing an object outside our minds, is given a logical property by our reason. The idea of human being, for instance, is related by the mind to many individuals, Mary and Joe, Betty and Bill, Rita and George. The property which our mind gives to a concept like *human being* in order to relate it to various individuals is the property of universality.

In order to gauge the relevance of this property to the study of logic, let us return to the notion of an argument. As shown in Chapter 1, a typical argument, that of Euclid in case history **1.2,** compares two things with a common third thing and then compares them with each other. Using symbols for concepts, A in an argument is compared with B, and C is compared with A. Then C and B, because of their relation to A, can be compared with each other. In logic, we have to make comparisons.

But Carrel reminds us that our physical world is made up of particular things — individual men, this or that dog, the various planets, this particular pane of glass in the north window and that one on the southern side of the room. If atomic theory is right, there are billions upon billions of individual atoms in this world. Each one is an individual, and as an individual each is unlike any other atom in existence. Individuals, in short, are unique, each in itself. Precisely as individuals, they do not have anything in common with other individuals. One individual is not comparable to another.

Necessity for universal concepts. Here then is a problem. If there is to be argument, comparisons must be made between things. But what we find in the physical world are particulars that, as particulars, do not admit of being compared. In a proposition, for instance, two things must be compared to a common third thing. If the mind is to make such comparisons, then, in considering things, it must leave aside what makes them individuals and attend only to what they have in common.

Jerry is an individual, and so is Dorothy. But each is also a human being. They have in common an essence or nature which makes them members of a common kind and allows us to term each of them a rational animal. Attention only to what is individual in things does not entitle us to compare them. Things can be related to each other through concepts only because the mind attends to the common, general, or universal character of the things in question and relates this common character to the particulars within its range. This common character constitutes the abstract and symbolic world. All men, for example, are alike to the extent of being human beings but differ as individuals.

The same relation of the general and particular pervades other realms. This piece of glass is different from that piece, since both are individuals. But insofar as both are glass, they are alike. In order to frame general laws about glass, e.g., all glass is fragile, the mind confronted with *this* or *that glass* must leave aside the *this* and the *that* and consider only the *glass*. Scientific reasoning, and indeed all forms of argument, aims at general or universal truth. Consider, for example, Newton's famous law of inertia:

5.2. **Every body continues in its state of rest, or of uniform motion in a straight line, unless it is compelled to change that state by forces impressed upon it.**

Newton here proposes a general truth of mechanics. Galileo does the same thing in 1.1; though examining individual bodies, he attempts to reach a general law regarding all bodies and their time of fall.

The concept then can take its place in an argument only because it is made universal and hence extends to many cases of a certain kind. Such a concept penetrates to what the cases have in common, what makes them comparable to each other, and what makes them share in the same nature or essence.

Real, extramental basis for universals. Carrel is right in reminding us that individuality is fundamental in our world. The universal as such exists nowhere except in our human minds. There is no separate thing called man-in-general or copper-in-general, no universal dog or abstract tree that enjoys a physical existence. Universality is in thought and thought alone.

Nevertheless, there is a foundation for generality or universality in things outside the mind. If this were not so, we could never explain why the universal applies to its many members, why for instance *man* can be said of any man, wherever or whenever he exists. But although it has a basis in reality, universality as such exists only in the thinking mind. It is a quality that pertains to the concept.

In terms of our discussion in Chapter 1, universality is a logical relation that a nature or essence, like a human being, acquires as the mind considers that nature or essence with reference to the actual cases in which it is found, such as Ann or Jack. A universal concept, therefore, represents one essence as being in many things, one type as having many members, one kind of thing as having many cases or instances. This logical relation adds nothing new to the content of the concept. Nothing really new is added to the essence of man as a rational animal when we think of human nature as universal in its relation to individual men. Man is neither more nor less of a rational animal by being universalized. Man, as universal, has merely a new logical relation to the individuals in which human nature is found.

Logical superior and logical inferior. In the usual terminology of logic, the members of a universal kind are called *inferiors* with respect to the universal or *superior* type to which they belong. It should also be noted that there are grades of universality. Thus, animal is more universal than man, living being more universal than animal, and mineral more universal than living being. In the first case, animal is a logical superior of man, and man a logical inferior of animal. In the second case, animal is now an inferior with living being a superior.

Universals differ from collectives. It is easy to confuse a universal or general concept with a collection. Thus the present student body of Notre Dame, while including many individuals, is not a universal concept; all members do not bear the same relation to the whole. Of no member can it be said, *he is the present student body of Notre Dame.* In the case of the universal, however, all inferiors bear the same relation to the whole. John is a man. So are Tom, Dick, and Harry, and all other human beings.

Having seen the property of universality as being of special interest in logic, it is now fitting to move on to the subdivisions of universality.

Problems

1. Why is it necessary to have universality in argument?

2. What is a universal? Where does it exist? Why is universality a logical relation? What would happen if universality added something real to a nature, say, man?

3. What is the relation of the universal to the individual? Why can it be said that the universal is founded in reality?

4. What is the meaning of the term *inferior* in logic? Would fiction and nonfiction be logical inferiors with respect to book? Can you show how fiction and/or nonfiction might be logical superiors in another context?

5. In the following examples, pick out those nouns in the nominative case that stand for universals, particulars, and collections: (a) John Paul Jones' Navy; (b) the president of the United States from 1952 to 1956; (c) the editorial staff of this year's annual;

(d) the nature of a dog; (e) the archangel Michael; (f) our solar system; (g) the reigning pope; (h) the Queen Mary's present crew; (i) the father of Rita and Mary; (j) justice; (k) the essence of a triangle; (l) the Holy Family; (m) causality; (n) the Milky Way.

6. Comment on the relation of individual to universal as suggested by the following passages:

5.3. My convictions are equally strong that great advantages result from the separation of the equity from the law jurisdiction, and that the causes which belong to the former would be improperly committed to juries. The great and primary use of a court of equity is to give relief in extraordinary cases, which are exceptions to general rules. To unite the jurisdiction of such cases with the ordinary jurisdiction must have a tendency to unsettle the general rules, and to subject every case that arises to special determination; while a separation of the one from the other has the contrary effect of rendering one a sentinel over the other, and of keeping each within the expedient limits.

ALEXANDER HAMILTON

5.4. Socrates: And you would admit that when you perceive through one faculty you cannot perceive through another; the objects of hearing, for example, cannot be perceived through sight, or the objects of sight through hearing?

PLATO

5.5. If you endeavour to trace in your mind the image of a tree in general, you never attain to your end. In spite of all you can do, you will have to see it as great or little, bare or leafy, light or dark, and were you capable of seeing nothing in it but what is common to all trees, it would no longer be like a tree at all. Purely abstract beings are perceivable in the same manner, or are only conceivable by the help of language. The definition of a triangle alone gives you a true idea of it; the moment you imagine a triangle in your mind, it is some particular triangle and not another, and you cannot avoid giving it sensible lines and a colored area.

JEAN-JACQUES ROUSSEAU

5.6. When memory begins to decay, proper names are what go first, and at all times proper names are harder to recollect than those of general properties and classes of things.

WILLIAM JAMES

7. What is wrong with the following analysis of the universal?

5.7. Whereas, in truth, there is no such thing as one precise and definite signification annexed to any general name, they all signifying indifferently a great number of particular ideas. All which doth evidently follow from what has been already said, and will clearly appear to anyone by a little reflection. To this it will be *objected*, that every name that has a definition, is thereby restrained to one certain signification. For example, a *triangle* is defined to be *a plain surface comprehended by three right lines,* by which that name is limited to denote one certain idea and no other. To which I answer, that in the definition it is not said whether the surface be great or small, black or white, nor whether the sides are long or short, equal or unequal, nor with what angles they are inclined to each other; in all which there may be great variety, and consequently there is *no one settled idea* which limits the signification of the word *triangle.*

GEORGE BERKELEY

Chapter 6: EXTENSION AND COMPREHENSION

A universal concept is one idea referring in the same way to a number of things. It is the one related to the many. What is it that determines the range of things to which it extends? What is it that makes one idea more universal than another? *Man* can be said only of men. But *animal* can be said not only of men but of dogs, cats, birds, etc.

Let us listen to a different example, as the Stranger, in Plato's dialogue *The Statesman*, is trying to classify the nature of clothing with respect to other, more universal concepts:

> 6.1. All things which we make or acquire are either creative or preventive; of the preventive class are antidotes, divine and human, and also defenses; and defenses are either military weapons or protections; and protections are veils, and also shields against heat and cold; and shields against heat and cold are shelters and coverings; and coverings are blankets and garments. . . .

Some concepts are more universal than others. Plato's Stranger continues this division into various subdivisions of garment, but the principles he is applying are clear enough to interrupt the dialogue and raise the question why his superior concepts are more universal than the inferior ones. Clearly the logical superior *preventive* has a greater generality than *garment*.

It is apparent from an inspection of the foregoing passage that the concept of *garment* is much richer in content than the corresponding concept of *preventive*, or, to put it in reverse, the superior is vaguer in content than the inferior. *Preventive*, to begin with, is vague enough to include both *antidotes* and *defenses*. That is to say, *preventive* includes less in the way of content than, for instance, *defenses* and, to use a common term, is less specific.

Defense adds to the content of the notion of *preventive*; it is a preventive against external harm whereas *antidote* is a preventive against internal harm. In following Plato's division, the vague idea of preventive is clarified by adding a number of qualifications to it until finally it becomes the notion of a garment; and all of these modifications, absent from the concept of preventive, are present in the idea of garment. The notion of garment adds to that of preventive the idea of a defense, protection, shield, covering, etc. To use the opposite approach again, the concept of preventive represents fewer actual characteristics than does the concept of defense, and the latter idea embraces fewer objects than the notion of a protection. By the time the division extends to garment, more characteristics or qualifications are designated in the object of thought than appear in any previous item of the quoted paragraph.

Comprehension and extension defined. The number of characteristics or qualifications which determines the content of a concept constitutes the *comprehension* or *intension* of that concept. The idea of a preventive has less comprehension than the concept of clothing. Being vaguer, it simply has less content.

On the other hand, the number of inferiors to which the concept applies forms the *extension* of the concept. The concept of preventive extends to all the individuals included under both antidotes and defenses. The concept of clothing obviously includes fewer inferiors than the notion of preventive and as a result has less extension.

To return to the earlier and simpler example, *rational* and *animal* are two characteristics included in the comprehension of man. All men, Jack and Joe, Ann and Mary, form the extension of the concept.

From the foregoing examples, it can easily be seen that the greater the extension of a concept the less its comprehension and vice versa. The notion of preventive, poor in content and hence less in comprehension than the idea of clothing, applies to more things than does clothing. The notion of clothing, while less in extension than the concept of preventive, has a greater comprehension, i.e., fuller content. *Rational animal*, it was said, forms the comprehension of the concept, *man*, which in turn extends to all individual men. If the *rational* in *rational animal* is dropped, thereby decreasing the comprehension of the concept concerned, the extension increases to take in not only all men but all irrational animals as well.

Comprehension is logical basis for extension. It is the comprehension of a concept then that determines its extension or logical universality and thus answers the question raised at the beginning of this chapter. The issue here is not whether comprehension is known first and extension only afterward, or vice versa; that is another problem and one for more advanced study. Our problem is to find out what determines the extension of a concept, and the answer is its comprehension.

Comprehension and extension are examples of those logical forms or relations discussed in Chapter 1. The various parts of the concept, considered in its comprehension, are related to each other by relations that are merely logical and not real. To be a part of the comprehension of defense adds nothing real to the concept of preventive. Indeed, to be a comprehension itself is not to be anything real but only to be a logical relation. To be a protective is, of course, to be real; but for protective to have a comprehension does not add to the concept of preventive as we add, for instance, stitches to clothes.

It is because of comprehension that a universal is not merely a collection of the inferiors to which it extends. There is a common nature, present as a foundation for universality, in all individual inferiors and represented by the mind as the comprehension of the universal concept in question. Comprehension is thus the logical ground for extension.

Like comprehension, extension is also a logical form. To apply *rational animal* to its inferiors does not, we have argued, either add to or subtract from the content of the concept itself.

Modern logicians have tended to substitute the terms "denotation" and "connotation" for *extension* and *comprehension*, but there is so much confusion about the meaning of these new terms that it would not be wise to use them as equivalent to the traditional words. In general, this modern logic has usually been a form of nominalism, refusing to admit that there is rooted in things a common nature represented by such names as man, dog, horse, etc. The new logic often takes all universals to be collections. Many modern logicians recognize extension only.

Logical forms and reality. Our list of logical forms or relations is steadily growing. To be an argument, a proposition, a subject, a predicate, a middle term — to be any of these is to be a logical form. To arguments and their parts, as logical forms, we must now add comprehension and extension or universality. Neither of these has a counterpart in reality. *Rational animal* in logic is the comprehension of man. In the world outside logic it is a real nature. Outside the mind, rational animal has physical attributes like size and shape and black hair and a scar from an operation. In logic, *rational animal* has logical qualities or attributes like comprehension and extension. No logical form is a physical thing that can be seen and felt, that causes motion or rest or life or death. A logical form is a merely logical relation, that, as logical, exists in the mind alone.

As shown in Chapter 2, logic is concerned with the ordering of logical forms. While the ordering of such forms can be seen most readily in a full-blown argument, there is an ordering that goes on in all the operations of the intellect. In the law governing the relation between comprehension and extension we meet our first rule for ordering the first operation of the mind.

Problems

1. Make an outline in diagram form of Plato's division of things we make or acquire.

2. Explain comprehension and extension and show, from the outline, their inverse relationship.

3. Explain why comprehension and extension are logical forms.

4. Show why comprehension is the ground for extension and why it prevents a universal from being a mere collection or sum.

5. In your opinion, do we know comprehension before extension or vice versa?

6. Give at least two examples of the extension of each of the following concepts considered as logical superiors: athlete; bird; school; horse; element; planet; nation; money; paper; vegetable.

7. Give, in whole or in part, the comprehension of each of the following concepts, considered as logical inferiors: the mosquito and the fly; the Secretary of State and the Secretary of Defense; hydrogen and oxygen; the rose and the violet; the magazine and the newspaper; the circle and the square; red and blue; the house

and the church; a black dress and the crepe on the door; a gun
and boxing gloves; an airplane and an automobile.

8. Show the relation between extension and comprehension, in
the following passage, among *man, animal, living, body, substance.*

6.2. Of the complex ideas signified by the names *man* and *horse,*
leaving out but those particulars wherein they differ, and retaining
only those wherein they agree, and of those making a new distinct complex idea, and giving the name *animal* to it, one has a
more general term, that comprehends with man several other creatures. Leave out of the idea of *animal,* sense and spontaneous motion, and the remaining complex idea, made up of the remaining
simple ones of body, life, and nourishment, becomes a more general
one, under the more comprehensive term, *vivens* [living]. And, not
to dwell longer upon this particular, so evident in itself; by the
same way the mind proceeds to *body, substance,* and at last to
being, thing.

JOHN LOCKE

9. Using *social group* as the logical superior, show, in terms of
comprehension and extension, its relation to the logical inferiors,
community and *society.*

6.3. A preliminary distinction must be made, namely between
community and *society.* . . . [It] is also licit — and proper — to
assign them to two kinds of social groups which are actually different
in nature. . . . Both community and society are ethico-social and
truly human, not mere biological realities. But a community is more
of a work of nature and more nearly related to the biological;
a society is more a work of reason, and more nearly related to the
intellectual and spiritual properties of man.

JACQUES MARITAIN

10. Using *friendship* as the logical superior, show, in terms of
comprehension and extension, its relationship to the three logical
inferiors mentioned in the following passage.

6.4. Since the act of friendship is love, there are thus three kinds
of friendship, according to the three objects of love: (1) friendship
because of virtue, which is true and essential good; (2) friendship
because of something pleasing to the senses; (3) friendship because
of utility.

ST. THOMAS AQUINAS

Chapter 7: THE FRAMEWORK FOR DEFINITION: I, GENUS, SPECIES, AND SPECIFIC DIFFERENCE

7.1. We can understand why a classification founded on any single character or organ — even an organ so wonderfully complex and important as the brain — or in the high development of mental faculties, is almost sure to prove unsatisfactory. This principle has indeed been tried with . . . insects, but when thus classed by their habits or instincts, the arrangement proved unsatisfactory. Classification may, of course, be based on any character whatever, as on size, colour, or the element inhabited; but naturalists have long felt a profound conviction that there is a natural system.

CHARLES DARWIN

These lines are taken from a famous book, *The Descent of Man*. Like any man of science, Darwin wants to know what things are. To achieve this aim, he has to gain a knowledge of the natures or essences of the various things he studies and of the ways in which such various things differ from each other in kind. What is a radish? An apple tree? A chipmunk? Copper? An electron? When we answer such questions, we make definitions. As an expression of the comprehension of a universal concept, definition is the most important work of the mind's first operation, and to it, either in its perfect form or in its various preparations, the remainder of our study of the first act of the intellect will be devoted. Does any characteristic of a thing enable us to define it? Can we define things best by structure or by function? Can all things be defined? What is the "natural system" recommended by Darwin? Are definitions merely arbitrary and verbal?

General function of definition. A full-dress discussion of definition must be deferred until Chapters 11 and 12, but in order to make the preliminaries of definition more meaningful in our study of them, it will be useful to anticipate those chapters in some general way. A definition expresses the kind or species to which a given thing belongs. Our best definition is that of man. He is defined as a *rational animal*. Individual men, we have seen, differ from each other; as individual, each man is unique. But there is something common to all men, not as individuals but as men. They are members of the same kind. They have a common human nature. They all belong to the same species, *rational animal*. When we know man's species or kind, we define man.

Genus, species, and specific difference. Now species, as shown by the familiar example of *man*, is made up of two parts. There is a general part called the *genus*, which the species under consideration shares in common with other species. Man belongs to the genus *animal*. Other species belonging to this genus, *animal*, include the horse, cow, butterfly, etc. A definition expresses the genus to which a species belongs and also states how the species under consideration differs from all other species in the same genus. It is not enough, in defining man, to say that he is an animal. There are many other animals besides man. Our definition must reveal how man differs in his species from other species of the same genus *animal*. This second part of the definition is called the *specific difference*. In the definition of man, *rational* is the specific difference.

It is time now to say more precisely what we mean by genus, species, and difference.

A genus is *that which is predicated essentially of several things that differ in species.*

A species is *that which is predicated essentially of several things that differ individually.*

A specific difference is *that which makes one species different from another within a genus.*

A look at some examples will show that our notions of genus, species, and specific difference are correct.

Animal, as a genus, is predicated of several things that differ in species, e.g., man, horse, dog, and fruit fly. It is predicated of each one of these species essentially as opposed to being predicated nonessentially. To say that a man is fat or bald or fleet-footed is to predicate what is likewise common to many species. But this does not make *fat* or *bald-headed* or *fleet-footed* a genus. *Fatness* or *fleet-footedness* do not belong to the essence of man or of other animals of which they are predicated. They are nonessential, not essential, predicates. They are not part of the essence of man. There could not be a man without the power of reason. But there could be (and are) men who are not *fat* or *bald-headed* or *fleet-footed*. Yet there is a serious difficulty about our definition of a species. Indeed, a genus is also predicated essentially not only of species — *man is a rational animal* — but also of individuals — *John is an animal, Mary is an animal*. It would look as though our definition of a species applies also to genera, because a genus is also an essential predicate of things differing individually. In reply to this difficulty, it should be conceded that a genus can be predicated of an individual — *this man is an animal; that dog is a physical body*. However, the genus is predicated of the individual only by virtue of the species to which the individual belongs. *Animal* is predicated of John or Mary only because they are members of the species, *rational animal*. Hence, the proper subject of a predicate that is a genus is a species; and the proper subject of a predicate that is a species is an individual.

The specific difference makes one species in a genus different from another species in the same genus. *Rational*, the specific difference in the case of man, makes the species *rational animal* different from other species of the genus *animal*, such as the blackbird or the jack rabbit.

The species of a thing expresses the complete essence of the thing. The genus and specific difference each expresses the essence in "part," the genus revealing a general "part" where the thing defined is like other species and the specific difference revealing the special "part" where the thing defined is unlike any other species in the genus.

Any general "part" of an essence, whether proximate or remote with respect to the species, is a genus. Thus, bird is not a species of animal but rather a more proximate genus having under it a number of species like redbird, duck, etc. Animal is a more remote genus. The general essential predicates, at least those applying to the material world, are each composed of a number of "parts" or "layers," one more universal than another. Each such "part" is a genus, proximate or remote. However, there is no such thing as a proximate or remote species or specific difference.

Genus, species, and specific difference are predicables. The aim of the first act of the mind is to reach good definitions. Definitions will be considered separately several chapters hence. Here we are concerned with building a framework for definition, and among the most important parts of that framework are the genus, species, and specific difference. They are three of the so-called predicables. As their name suggests, predicables have to do with the predicate in a proposition. They express the relation of the predicate to the subject. If a predicate expresses the whole essence of the subject, it is a species; if the predicate expresses part of the essence of the subject, it states either the genus, a general part, or the specific difference which marks the subject off from all other species. Two other predicables will be treated in the next chapter.

Logic is not concerned with such questions as whether a rose is a species of plant or not and whether the halogen family is a genus or not. Such problems belong to biology on the one hand and chemistry on the other. Logic is concerned to name the conditions whereby a character in a thing under consideration is a species, specific difference, or genus.

Biological approaches to definition. Darwin, in the passage quoted, offers a good example of the confusion among biologists of modern times who have neglected the logical rules for identifying various organisms. Biologists usually define things in terms of one of two principles: their structure or their genesis. Darwin brings this out. The classification of organisms by structure or morphology describes living things in terms of "character or organ," and in this fashion we obtain the various kingdoms, orders, families, etc., familiar to the freshman student of biology. But morphology, though of undoubted value, as will later be seen, is not the basic key to differentiate one thing from another. By bodily structure, you could never discover that man is rational, nor even that any living thing, human or otherwise, contains a principle of life. A purely structural approach to the problem of how one kind of living thing differs from another "is," to quote Darwin, "almost sure to prove unsatisfactory."

Since classification of organisms by "habits or instincts," to quote

Darwin again, is no longer considered a primary means of defining the various types of living things, we may pass it over in order to mention what Darwin calls the "natural system" of classification. This is the genetic method used widely as a result of Darwin's theory of evolution. In this method of defining, organisms are put into various genera and species on the basis of their common origin in the evolutionary development of living things.

But if the structural or morphological approach, taken alone, cannot give knowledge of the species and genera of organisms, the evolutionary or genetic method of definition is an even greater failure for other reasons. In the first place, the theory of evolution, however probable, will always remain a theory because anyone who could have checked it would be dead by millions of years. In the second place, the genera and species of living organisms cannot be established merely by studying their origins. To account for a fork by saying that it was produced by a metalworker tells us hardly anything about the intrinsic nature of the fork itself. We get a much better knowledge of the metalsmith by examining the fork than of the fork by examining the metalsmith. What made a thing and how it was made are questions that come after we know what the thing is. The origin, evolutionary or otherwise, of various forms of life is a question that follows our study, in some non-evolutionary way, of what these forms are. Evolution cannot be the organizing principle of our system of definition, however probable evolution may be.

Present-day taxonomy (the study of the classification of organisms) usually combines both the structural and evolutionary approaches. But if neither, taken singly, can give us a logic for identifying what organisms belong to this or that species or genus, the merely mechanical sum of the two approaches can fare no better. Modern biology still awaits a satisfactory principle for assigning organisms to their species and genera. The way out of the problem is not easy, but some degree of light may be shed upon the answer in the next chapter.

Problems

1. Define genus, species, and specific difference. Why are they important? Why are they called predicables?

2. Explain how there can be a common predicate which is not a genus.

3. Explain the inadequacy of a purely structural or purely evolutionary approach to the problem of classification.

4. The following are names for genera. Name one species in each genus: Fish, Bird, Triangle, Rodent, Number, Metal, Rectangle, Acid, Fruit, Insect.

5. The following are names for species. Name a genus for each species: Monkey, Maple, Square, Oxygen, Tomato, Skylark, Gold, Fifteen, Wool, Mosquito.

6. Analyze the following passages to find what is sound and what is unsound concerning the concepts of genus, species, and specific difference.

7.2. In the natural order of ideas, the name of the class or genus is that which expresses a quality common to a great number of individuals; the name of the species, on the contrary, expresses a quality peculiar to certain individuals only.

ANTOINE LAVOISIER

7.3. A scientist is one who, when he does not know the answer, is rigorously disciplined to speak up and say so unashamedly; which is the essential feature by which modern science is distinguished from primitive superstition which knew all the answers except to say, "I don't know."

HOMER SMITH

7.4. Although man has many points of resemblance with the brutes, one trait is peculiar to himself — he improves: they are incapable of government.

ALEXIS DE TOCQUEVILLE

7.5. But it can nowise be maintained that, in the words of M. Arnauld, body is related to mind as genus is to species; for, although the genus can be apprehended apart from this or that specific difference, the species can by no means be thought apart from the genus.

RENÉ DESCARTES

Chapter 8: THE FRAMEWORK FOR DEFINITION: II, ACCIDENT AND PROPERTY

8.1. Number is limited multitude or a combination of units or a flow of quantity made up of units; and the first division of number is even and odd. The even is that which can be divided into two equal parts without a unit intervening in the middle; and the odd is that which cannot be divided into two equal parts because of the aforesaid intervention of a unit.

NICOMACHUS

8.2. Bowed by the weight of centuries he leans
Upon his hoe and gazes upon the ground. . . .

EDWIN MARKHAM

Essential and nonessential predicables. In the preceding chapter, the three predicables considered — species, genus, specific difference — relate the predicate of a proposition to the subject as either the complete essence of the subject of as part of the essence. When the complete essence of the subject is revealed by the predicate, the predicate represents the species of the subject. When only part of the essence of the subject is revealed by the predicate, the predicate then represents a genus to which the subject belongs or the specific difference characterizing the subject. In all three cases, the predicable involves the essence of the subject.

The final two predicables are not essential, to the extent that they do not make up the essence of their subject in whole or in part. To be *fat* or *bald-headed* is not part of the essence of being a *rational animal*. There could be men even if no one was ever *fat* or *bald-headed*. To have a sense of humor or to be capable of learning grammar are also outside the essence of man. This can be seen by looking at the species, *rational animal*. *To be able to laugh or to communicate by artificial signs* is not a part of man's essence, even though both abilities are implied by his possession of reason. What an essence implies is not part of that essence, any more than a statue which implies a sculptor is part of the sculptor or vice versa. Nevertheless, there is no man who is without a sense of humor or the capability of learning grammar, even though there are men who are not fat or bald-headed. Hence, though both kinds of nonessential predicates are outside the essence of man, it is clear that the two kinds are quite different from one another.

Property and accident defined. *To be capable of laughter or of language* is called a property of man. A property is not part of the species of a thing but is found *always and only in* that species and in each and every member of the species. It is implied by the species as, to use an analogy, a statue implies a sculptor. *To be fat* is called an accident of man. It is that which can either be or not be without a change in the subject in which it is. A man can grow *fat* or *lean*; but under either aspect he is still a man.

Property and accident, while not parts of an essence, inhere in the essence. *Fatness*, for instance, is not man. But it inheres in man. The boiling point of water is not water. It is an attribute or quality that exists in water. It is an attribute that flows from the nature of water but is not the water itself.

Difference between property and accident. Here we are approaching a principal difference between a property and an accident. A property, although not part of the essence of a given species, flows necessarily from that essence. *To be capable of laughter or of grammar* is not the same thing as *to be rational;* but reason is the root or cause of such abilities. They flow necessarily from our nature as rational. Reason implies them, but once more we ought to remind ourselves that what a thing implies is not what the thing is. Man implies God, but he is not God. Reason implies the ability to speak but it is not the ability to speak. The cause of an effect is not the same as the effect.

But an essence, while implying its properties, does not imply accidents. They are incidental. It is incidental for a dog to be in the living room. It would be the same animal if it were in the kitchen. It is accidental to a man to be sunburned. He would be the same man if his skin were pale.

Properties of a species are found only in the species. A property, then, as opposed to an accident, flows necessarily from the essence of a thing. But the really crucial nature of a property remains to be explained. A property of a species, in the strict sense, is found only in that species. To have weight or to be capable of eating flow from man's essence. An animal requires a body and therefore weight; it also requires food and therefore eating. In a wide sense of the word, weight and nutrition could be called properties of man. But in the stricter sense, a property is peculiar to a given species. To have weight or to need food could be said of a great number of things besides man. *To be able to laugh* or *to use language* is proper to man alone. That is why we call it a *property.*

Illustrations of properties and accidents. Nicomachus, in the passage at the beginning of our chapter, gives an illustration of properties. He characterizes even number as (a) "that which can be divided into two equal parts without a unit intervening in the middle," and odd number as (b) "that which cannot be divided into two equal parts because of the aforesaid intervention of a unit." Does (a) represent the essence of even number and (b) the essence of odd number? Or do they each represent a property or, possibly, an accident?

No doubt the suggestion that (a) and (b) are accidents can be ruled out at once. What Nicomachus is describing is necessarily associated with each of the kinds of number under consideration. The two possibilities remain then that (a) and (b) represent either essences or properties. Inspection will show that Nicomachus is characterizing the two kinds of numbers in terms of the different effects produced when we operate upon each of the two kinds. Since these are effects flowing from the numbers as a result of our operations of dividing them, they must be properties which, we saw, are effects flowing necessarily from an essence that is their root and cause. The essence of an even number is what it is in itself, not what can be done with it. All numbers have certain properties by which they can be combined and divided with respect to other numbers. But these are properties of the numbers in question, not their essences.

Markham, in the lines from his "Man With the Hoe," is describing accidents. *To be leaning upon a hoe or to be gazing upon the ground* are in no way connected with the essence of man. If they flowed from the nature of man, as his ability to laugh does, there could never be a man who was not leaning on a hoe and gazing upon the ground. In Markham's lines, then, there is mention of accidents to man's nature. Man would still be a man if they were not present. They are not required by human nature as is man's ability to laugh or to use language.

Approaching definition through the examination of properties. In the last chapter, we faced the problem of classifying organisms into their proper genera and species. Naturally the problem of classification is important in any scientific enterprise. The chemist must classify substances; an excellent example of classification in chemistry is the periodic chart. The physicist must, of course, arrange his subatomic particles in some systematic way. The astronomer classifies the stars; the geologist, strata of rocks; the sociologist or ethnologist, various races and groups; the economist, resources and demands; the political scientist, the various forms of government and subdivisions within government; the literary critic, the numerous varieties of literature; the geographer, the different bodies of land and water with all their subdivisions. It is not a problem in logic to achieve these various classifications but only to name the rules for identifying in any specimen of interest what constitutes a species and a genus and a specific difference and a property and an accident.

A learned mind using the rules of logic can identify rather easily the genus and difference in artificial species, e.g., in things we make, like hammers or shoes or race tracks. It is also possible to find species in the mathematical world, e.g., various kinds of triangles. But natural species, on the other hand, present great difficulties in the search for definition, and the biologist, chemist, and physicist — to mention only these three — will find no easy formula to solve their problems of classification.

In the world of nature, as opposed to that of the various arts, we can give a complete definition only of man. From our own personal acts of sensing and understanding, we learn man's genus, and we learn his species, whereas we have no such internal experience of other things. We have no perfect essential knowledge of the fox by contrast to the wolf, of silver as different from gold, and of water as opposed to sulphuric acid. We have a rich knowledge of the material world, but the difficulty is to formulate such knowledge into accurate definitions, in terms of genera and specific differences.

There are two ways of achieving exact, scientific definitions of material things: *through a description of properties* and *structural analysis*. In the first place, properties, according to our analysis, are not merely incidental possessions like being fat or bald-headed, in the case of man. They flow necessarily from the essence. They are necessary effects of the essence, and hence, by learning about properties we learn something about the species which is their cause. The boiling point of water is 100 degrees Centigrade. This is a characteristic peculiar to water. Hence by knowing such a property we are able to discern something about the nature of water itself. As necessary and unique to every essence, a property is a natural and instrumental sign of the essence. It signifies or reveals the essence to us as smoke signifies fire.

As in the case of water, so with other elements and compounds. Their boiling points, melting points, specific heat, complete spectral lines, and other such characteristics are properties peculiar to the essence which bears them and hence are capable of marking off that essence from others in the same genus. In the biological world, it is a property of a species to be fertile only within itself. Consequently, interfertility is a property or a sign that two organisms belong to the same species. Interfertility is not the essence of a species. It is a power that an essence has and, among other things, it reveals an essence to us, as a sign of the essence or species. Taxonomy, though favoring structural or evolutionary approaches to classification, usually employs the test of interfertility to decide in the end what organisms actually belong to the same species.

Approaching definition through structure. But the more general method of classification in vogue among biologists is morphological, the description of structures, like organs and even tissues. For instance, the possession of a backbone marks off a subphylum called vertebrates. The class of fishes is characterized by gills. Chemistry and physics also employ to a large extent the structural method of classifying things. Hydrogen, for instance, is distinguished from helium by the possession of a single proton as a nucleus; helium has two protons and usually two neutrons. Protons and neutrons are particles or structures, and the physicist describes the difference between one element and another by the structure of the nucleus in terms of particles.

In our struggle to assign the genus and specific difference of the living and nonliving world, what is the value of the structural approach? We have seen that in dealing with infrahuman reality, where precise knowledge of essences is so difficult, we can still use the properties of things as signs of their essences and hence learn something of the essences which the properties naturally signify. Is structure also a sign of essence?

It is clear that in natural species structure is not essence. A dog or a cat is not the mere sum of the organs and tissues which anatomy reveals to us. Nor is an element like helium a mere sum of nuclear structures and electrons outside of them. But like a property, structure is an effect of species. The soul of a dog or of a cat requires that each animal have certain structures. If a principal structure, like the heart or brain, is removed, the dog or cat can no longer exist. The same truth holds in regard to elements like helium. Remove a proton, and helium changes into hydrogen. Hence, structures can reveal essences to us. When we attain knowledge of the structures peculiar to this or that type of animal, a cat or a dog, for example, or to this type of atom, like helium, we get some insight into the essence of the thing in question.

It cannot be repeated often enough that structures are not essences. A dog that has just died has the same visible structures as the dog when living. But the dead dog is no longer a dog. It is the remains of the dog. It is no more a dog than a dog's picture would be.

Yet while not the essence of natural things, living or lifeless, structure, like property, is the sign of an essence. It is the effect of an essence. When we understand what structures are peculiar to a dog or to helium we can define dog or define helium. The mistake of modern taxonomy is oftentimes to regard a living thing as nothing but its structures, just as physicists and chemists sometimes identify an atom or a molecule of a substance in terms of structure alone. Structure, as signifying an essence, is no more the complete essence than a groan, signifying pain, is the pain itself. Classification in biology and physics requires a knowledge of signs.

By way of drawing this chapter to a conclusion, it may be useful to point out that a property, unlike an accident, flows necessarily from the essence and is found in that essence only. Hence, a knowledge of property gives proper knowledge of an essence. Even in the case of man, the definition *rational animal* is known by analyzing the activities proper to a rational and an animal nature. Properties are natural signs of the essences which are their causes. So too are structures.

An introductory book of this sort is hardly the place to engage in a long discussion of the differences between property and structure. One rule of thumb for distinguishing between them is that properties in the natural world are always dynamic whereas structural analysis, as in anatomy, considers things only statically.

Essences in the natural world are not completely hidden from us. They are revealed by properties and structures.

The five predicables are genus, species, specific difference, property, and accident. Structure, however, is not a predicable. What it is will be discussed in Chapter 11.

Problems

1. Differentiate between a property and an essence; between a property and an accident.

2. Show how property would be important in achieving a definition. Show how structure is related to the problem of definition. Explain how property and structure are signs.

3. Comment on the following passages in the light of the problems discussed in the past two chapters:

8.3. To say, then, that shape and colour constitute the animal is an inadequate statement, and is much the same as if a woodcarver were to insist that the hand he had cut out was really a hand.
ARISTOTLE

8.4. For, as to be extended, divisible, possessed of figure, etc., are the forms or attributes by which I recognize that substance called *body*; so, to be a knowing, willing, doubting being, etc., are the forms by which I recognize the substance called *mind*; and I know that thinking substance is a composite thing, no less than that which is extended.
RENÉ DESCARTES

Natural Divisions Among Animals

8.5. *Branches* or *types* are characterized by the plan of their structure;

Classes, by the manner in which that plan is executed, as far as ways and means are concerned;

Orders, by the degrees of complication of that structure;

Families, by their form, as far as determined by structure;

Genera, by the details of the execution in special parts; and

Species, by the relations of individuals to one another and to the world in which they live, as well as by the proportions of their parts, their ornamentation, etc.

LOUIS AGASSIZ

(NOTE: This passage should be discussed as an example of structural analysis and also as an example of proximate and remote genera.)

8.6. Next: how shall we define the whale, by his obvious externals, so as conspicuously to label him for all time to come? To be short, then, a whale is *a spouting fish with a horizontal tail.* There you have him. However contracted, that definition is the result of expanded meditation. A walrus spouts much like a whale. But the walrus is not a fish, because he is amphibious. But the last term of the definition is still more cogent, as coupled with the first. Almost any one must have noticed that all the fish familiar to landsmen have not a flat, but a vertical, or up and down tail. Whereas, among spouting fish the tail, though it may be similarly shaped, invariably assumes a horizontal position.

HERMAN MELVILLE

8.7. Species may be properly regarded as natural units in that they are groups which a) have a geographical distribution area; b) are self-perpetuating as groups; c) are morphologically (or in rare cases only physiologically) distinguishable from other related groups; and d) normally do not interbreed with related groups, in most cases showing partial or total infertility on crossing with them (though neither the lack of crossing nor of fertility is universal).

J. S. HUXLEY

8.8. But the properties of atoms are mainly determined by their mass or weight, and are in dependence upon it. Only in this case there is a peculiarity in the dependence of the properties on the mass, for this dependence is determined by a periodic law. As the mass increases, the properties vary, at first successively and regularly, and then return to their original magnitude and recommence a fresh period of variation like the first. Nevertheless here as in other cases a small variation of the mass of the atom generally leads to a small variation of properties, and determines differences of a second order. The atomic weights of cobalt and nickel, of rhodium, ruthenium, and palladium, of osmium, iridium, and platinum, are very close to each other, and their properties are also very much alike — the differences are not very perceptible. And if the properties of atoms are a function of their weight, many ideas which have more or less rooted themselves in chemistry must suffer change and be developed and worked out in the sense of this deduction. Although at first sight it appears that the chemical elements are perfectly independent and individual, instead of this idea of the nature of the elements, the notion of the dependence of their properties upon their mass must now be established; that is to say, the subjection of the individuality of the elements to a common higher principle which evinces itself in gravity and in all physico-chemical phenomena. Many chemical deductions then acquire a new sense and significance, and a regularity is observed where it would otherwise escape attention.

DMITRI I. MENDELEYEV

4. In the following propositions, state the relation of subject and predicate in terms of the predicables:
  a) Hydrogen has an affinity to combine with oxygen to form water.
  b) A triangle is three-sided.
  c) Peas are green.
  d) Some men are married.
  e) The bobwhite makes a noise that sounds like its name.
  f) All bears have fur.
  g) Water expands at 4 degrees Centigrade.
  h) Red is a color.

Chapter 9: THE MATTER OF DEFINITION: THE CATEGORIES

9.1. Of those expressions which in no way signify composition, each signifies either *substance*, or *how much*, or *of what kind*, or *being related to something*, or *where*, or *when*, or *to be in a posture*, or *to be equipped*, or *to act*, or *to receive*. For there is *substance*, in the common understanding of the term, such as man or horse; *how much* [e.g.] as being of two or three cubits; *of what kind* [e.g.] as being white or being grammatical; *being related to something* [e.g.] as double, half, or greater; *where* [e.g.] as being in the grove or market place; *when* [e.g.] as tomorrow or the day before yesterday; *having a posture* [e.g.] as one is reclining or standing; *to be equipped* [e.g.] as one is shod or armed; *to act* [e.g.] as a thing cuts or burns; *to receive* [e.g.] as a thing is cut or burned.

ARISTOTLE

The content of definition. Definitions, the most important work of the first act of the mind, not only require a certain form but content as well. It is important that a definition, in addition to expressing a relation to the thing defined in the fashion that a species represents an essence, be about something, for instance, about man or water or a color, like red or blue. Having found in the predicables the form or framework in which a definition takes place, we may now inquire about the material which takes on the form. Having seen the tools of definition, we can ask what things can be defined.

Aristotle, in the passage above, has answered our questions for us. He names and exemplifies the ten categories, sometimes called the ten predicaments. They are the ten general kinds of predicates or the ten supreme genera of what we think about: substance, the quantified, the qualified, to be related, where, when, to have a posture, to be clothed, to act, and to receive.

The mere mention of these categories raises a number of questions: What is the relation of the categories or predicaments to the predicables? Why are the categories of interest to a logician, and why are they not considered by sciences dealing not with logical relations but with the real world? How do the various categories differ from each other? What are the rules for assigning objects of our thought to the categories?

Relation of categories to predicables. In replying to the first question, it will be useful to consider an example. Suppose that we are defining a foot measure. We must first give its genus — a unit of length — and then its specific difference — containing twelve inches. The category in which we are working is that of the quantified, and the predicables — genus and specific difference — express the different parts of a species (the foot) within that category. In terms of the predicaments, the colored is in the category of the qualified. In terms of the predicables, it is a genus, having for its species various members like blue or yellow. To be visible is a property of color. That color appears in an orange is an accident to color, since color could exist even if no oranges existed.

The predicables then are the relations for achieving divisions within the predicaments or categories. They are the key to the co-ordination and subordination of concepts within each category. The categories are, so to speak, the matter or content divided by the predicables. Thus, substance can be divided into species like *man* or *horse*. To be related, where, having a posture, having clothing, to act — all are divided by genus, specific difference, species, property, and accident. For instance, *next week* is a genus of *when* and a *day* within that week is a species in the same category. *To be married* is a genus of *being related*, divided into two species, *to be a husband* and *to be a wife*. *Being cauterized*, in the category of *affection* or *reception*, is a species of *being medicated*.

Categories, reality, and logic. Concerning our second question, it is true that the categories are kinds of real things and that they are studied by sciences that, unlike logic, have to do with the real world. But the logician does not consider the categories as kinds of things. He considers them only as objects of thought and as taking on logical relations. He is interested in them only as they are represented by concepts and capable, as concepts, of being ordered by predicables. Concepts, we saw, are signs that refer to real things as signified. Sciences of the real world study the categories that are signified by concepts. Logic studies the signs themselves. These ten different categories of things are studied by various sciences of the real world. Paralleling in the logical order the ten categories of the real order, there are ten different kinds of natural, formal signs by which the ten real categories are represented. The logician is interested in the categories, not as signified and as content of reality, but as signs and as content of concepts, bearing those logical relations or logical forms described in Chapter 1.

Everything that we can represent in a concept falls within the ten categories in some way. Aristotle is careful to note that the categories are in no way composite, i.e., they do not involve the second operation of the intellect where concepts are joined by "is" or divided by "is not"; they involve only the first operation of the intellect, where concepts are considered without being compounded into propositions.

Differences between the various categories. Aristotle has given examples of each of the ten categories. It will be helpful now, in answer to our third question, to elaborate some definitions. To simplify the project, the individual categories will be considered only as they fall within the interest of the logician, by contrast to the scientist of the real.

Substance is defined as that which does not exist in anything else, as in a subject, but is nevertheless capable of being predicated of something else. In this respect, substance is contrasted with accident. An accident exists in something else and is predicated of something else. Man and horse are substances; they do not exist in anything else as in a subject. The height of a man or the color of the horse are accidents; they require a subject in which to exist. There is no pure height; there is always a something, called a subject, which has height. There is no pure color but only colored things, the subjects in which color inheres.

Such examples may serve to distinguish substance and accident, but they do not necessarily clarify the description of substance itself. To explain what substance is in the world of logic, let us consider the following propositions: *Fido is a dog* and *Jerry is a man*. Now *dog* or *man* are not accidents, like color or shape. Fido is not accidentally a dog nor is Jerry accidentally a man. But while dog and man do not exist in anything else, as in a subject, they can be predicated of other things like Fido or Jerry, and under this aspect, as a predicate, substance is a category. Other examples of substance are copper, cat, grass, water, table salt, eagle, grasshopper, sugar.

The quantified is that which has parts each one of which is capable of being a whole. To exemplify this, let us first make a division into discrete quantity like number and continuous quantity like lines, planes, and solids. Both number on the one hand and lines, planes, and solids on the other are composed of parts that upon division become wholes in their own right. Ten is divisible into at least two parts, namely, fives, each of which, on the division of ten, becomes a whole. Similarly, each half of a line can be a complete line, a whole, and each part of a solid can become a solid itself. All numbers belong to the category of the quantified, so do the points, lines, planes, and solids of geometry. As in the case of substance, the category of the quantified is divided by the predicables. There, curved and straight are species of the line. Two and four are species of number.

The qualified is that which, already being a substance, is further determined to be such and such. The most common qualities are in the sensible order, the colors, sounds, tastes, smells, the hotness or coldness of things, their hardness or softness, their wetness or dryness. Qualities do not make a substance to be what it is, e.g., they do not make iron to be iron. As accidents, they make a substance to be such and such a substance, i.e., red or green apple, hot or cold iron.

Another important kind of quality is figure, by which a substance having quantity is terminated. Under figure would be included all shapes, regular or irregular, which are studied in geometry or merely observed in nature without being reducible to geometrical laws. By figure, substance having quantity is limited to this or that shape, like a sphere or a cone. Figure thus is not quantity. The quantity of a geometrical object is the plurality of its parts. Figure gives to quantified substance the proper termination or boundary.

But qualities in things outside us are only one type of quality. Another important type includes habits — habits of mind like the possession of this or that science or habits of the will like the moral virtues of justice, temperance, and fortitude. To be geometrical, literary, logical, to be a theologian, a scientist of the natural world — to be any of these is to have a quality called an intellectual habit. Prudence, justice, fortitude, and temperance are likewise habits and therefore qualities. Geometry is a quality determining man to be geometrical and justice is a quality determining man to be just. Intellectual and moral habits thus fit our definition of quality.

Sensible qualities, figures, and habits are the most obvious among the qualities. There are other types also, but they need not be mentioned here.

To be related is to make reference to something else. Examples are to be a mother, son, equal, congruent, chairman, present, proportional. The whole reality of a relation consists in the reference or respect which one thing has to another. To be related, as in the case of the other categories, is divisible according to the predicables. To be a member of the cabinet, for instance, is subdivided into being secretary of state, secretary of defense, etc. These are species with the genus of cabinet membership. It is an accident that such a relation belongs to this or that particular individual like Mr. Brown or Mr. Jones. The office would still go on without them, and someone else would take their places.

Being related can easily be confused with being qualified. They are distinct, however, since quality exists *in* substance, whereas relation exists *between* things. To be president of the United States is a relational being existing *between* the chief executive and the people he heads. His qualities like complexion or height are *in* him.

Place and time are measures. The place of anything may be thought of as a container. In this respect, the earth is a container for everything present in it or on it. The sky overhead or the various levels of the earth underfoot are also places. The proper place of anything is the innermost immobile surface of the body surrounding that thing. Thus, the innermost surface of a glass is the proper place of the liquid contained in the vessel. The room, the building, the city, the state, etc., would be common or more generic places of the water. But place for a logician is not a category. The logical category is *where*, an accident possessed by a body by virtue of its presence in place. Thus room is not the logical

category of *where* but *in the room* is the logical category, *where.*
Other examples of where are *on earth, at the airport, in the sock.*
Time is a measure of motion according to a before and after.
Taking the *now* as a reference point, we number or measure the
motion of anything before and after the *now,* thereby becoming
aware of the past and the future. Time may be subdivided into
any unit of interest, the year, the month, the week, the day, the
hour, etc. To define the year as a time-interval composed of 365
(and a fraction) days is to give the species of a year in the usual
terms of genus and specific difference. As place is not a logical
category, neither is time. The category is *when, the present century,
next Christmas, in 1984.* It is these that are predicated of subjects
and these that, for the logician, are predicaments.

To have a posture is to have a disposition of parts in a whole.
One may remain in the same place, as in a chair, but change
position, now reclining, now hunching forward, now leaning to
this side, now to that. According to modern physicochemical theory,
our body contains molecules which are in constant motion even
while we are at rest or asleep. Such changes would be changes of
the disposition of our parts with respect to each other. The motion
of the parts could go on without requiring the whole to change
its place. *To be sitting, standing, lying, crouching,* etc. — all are
predicates in the category of position or posture.

There is a special accident that exists in man by virtue of his
wearing clothes. This accident forms the category usually termed
to be clothed. To it are reduced such predicates as *to be armed* or
ornamented. Hence, the category has been here called *to be
equipped.* Animals, of course, have horns and hair and hooves
and feathers. But these are parts of the natural bodies of the animals
and belong to the category of substance. *To be equipped* is an
accident produced by the addition of a covering, weapon, or decora-
tion to man's natural body. As place and time are not logical
categories but the causes of the predicates *where* and *when,* so
clothing or equipment itself is not a category. The category, resulting from equipment or clothing, is *to be equipped or clothed.*
It is this that we predicate.

Finally, there are the two correlative categories of *to act* and
to receive. To act is to do something to something else, while to

receive is to be affected by something else. Usually when using the passive voice, we are referring to the category of reception. *To kill, to plant, to hit, to pull* or *push* — all belong to the category of action; *to be killed, to be planted, to be hit, to be pulled* or *pushed* — all belong to the predicament of reception.

Further clarification of the relations between the categories and the predicables. Of the ten categories, the first is substance, that which does not exist in anything else as in a subject, and the last nine are accidents, which can exist only in a substance. There may be some confusion in our study of the categories between substance and essence on the one hand and on the other hand between the predicamental accidents studied in this chapter and the predicable accident studied in the last.

By way of clarifying the issue, it should be pointed out that essences exist in all the categories. Substances, like man or horse, have essences. So does the colored in the genus of the qualified; to be a general in the genus of to be related, etc. The predicables, we have seen, divide the categories according to genus, specific difference, species, property, and accident. There are species in every category and hence there are essences there also and not merely in the category of substance.

In the case of the predicamental accident, we are dealing with accident as a kind of being; in the case of a predicable accident, we are concerned with the mode of a predicate's connection with the subject. Predicamental accident is contrasted with substance; predicable accident is contrasted with essence. Just as essence appears in all of the categories, so does the predicable accident. The predicamental accident, it was observed, is divided, just as substance, by the predicables. To be president of the United States is to be a predicamental accident. That it should be vested in this or that man is a predicable accident; since the presidency would be the same office in any man, it is not essentially connected with any one individual. That it should be predicated of any individual is a predicable accident. The office itself is a predicamental accident in the genus of *to be related.*

Rules for assigning objects of thought to the categories. A final question concerns the rules for determining what a predicate must be in order to belong to a category.

First of all, it must not be a composite concept, like *fragrant flower* or *brave husband*, in which an accident is combined with a peculiar species of subject. In such a case, two categories are represented. The *fragrant* is in the genus of the qualified, *flower*, of substance; the *brave* is also in the genus of the qualified, being a *husband*, of being related. Any of these four concepts can be in a predicament, but no two of them together can be. In the case of man, *rational* and *animal* belong to the same category; so do *isosceles* and *triangle*. The rule is that where an idea is composed of two or more categories, the resulting concept cannot belong to any one of them. Any one of the last nine categories, like the quantified or the qualified, expresses the general relation of an accident to a substance but does not imply any particular species of a subject.

Second, only a univocal concept — a concept whose meaning is fully and identically realized in every subject of which it is predicated — can be in a category. What may be ambiguous cannot be put in a predicament. Thus, *red* can designate a color in the genus of the qualified or Communistic in the genus of being related. *Red*, therefore, may be equivocal. It cannot be used unless it is clearly specified which of its meanings is involved. By this rule also, figures of speech cannot be used in strictly scientific arguments.

A third rule states that only something predicable of something other than itself is in the categories. John Jones can be predicated of nothing else except John Jones. This rule means that only a universal can find place in a predicament, since a singular, whether it be a substance, like *this* man, or an accident, like *this* redness or *this* loudness, can be predicated of nothing other than itself. Singulars are always subjects, hence not predicates and not predicaments.

A fourth rule is that only what is finite is capable of being in the categories. God, for instance, is not in a genus, since He is wholly simple and not composed even of a genus and a specific difference.

With this chapter, our study of the mind's instruments for definition is complete. In the preceding two chapters, the predicables were analyzed. They constitute the form of definition. A definition, for instance, will be required to be in the *form* of genus and of specific difference. The present chapter has been concerned with the *matter* or content that goes into the *form* prescribed by the predicables.

Problems

1. What are the categories, and how do they differ from the predicables?
2. If the categories are kinds of real being, how and why are they studied in logic?
3. Name the ten categories and define each of them.
4. Compare essence with substance, predicable accident with predicamental accident.
5. What are the rules to determine what belongs to a category?
6. How does a knowledge of the categories help us to understand the parts of speech in grammar where our concepts are represented by language?
7. To which of the categories do the following predicates belong? (1) in the present millenium; (2) being a leader; (3) being uniformed; (4) to sing; (5) statue; (6) kneeling; (7) rectangle; (8) to be aroused; (9) mile; (10) in the desk; (11) neutron; (12) midpoint; (13) in the Christmas season; (14) to swim; (15) coal; (16) wearing a watch fob; (17) sidewise; (18) being a Christian; (19) to be humiliated; (20) metal; (21) being bemedalled; (22) standing at attention; (23) being oval; (24) wearing lipstick; (25) the number "pi"; (26) to get a hair-cut; (27) middle-C; (28) on the wall; (29) being a mayor; (30) upside-down; (31) being logical; (32) being angered; (33) to shoe a horse; (34) being beribboned; (35) at midnight; (36) a symphony; (37) to fake; (38) in the phonebook; (39) being silent; (40) x^2.
8. In the following three passages, a number of objects are mentioned that belong to this or that category. Name the object and identify the category to which it belongs. (In order to familiarize yourself with the kind of object that belongs in each category, you may disregard the rule that only universals can be placed in a category, and you may mention individual things, that, if considered at a universal and abstract level, would belong in a category. You may also break down any compound concept and put the component parts into the proper categories.) You should find at least five distinct categories in each passage for a good answer.

9.2. **I had three chairs in my house: one for solitude, two for friendship, three for society. When visitors came in larger and unexpected numbers, there was but the third chair for them all,** but they generally economized the room by standing up. It is surprising how many great men and women a small house will contain. I have had twenty-five or thirty souls, with their bodies, at once under my roof, and yet we often parted without being aware that we had come very near to one another.

HENRY DAVID THOREAU

9.3.   So when they had armed themselves on either side in the throng, they strode between Trojans and Achaians, fierce of aspect, and wonder came on them that beheld both in the Trojans tamers of horses and on the well-greaved Achaians. Then took they their stand near together in the measured space, brandishing their spears in wrath each against other. First Alexandros hurled his far-shadowing spear, and smote on Atreides' round shield; but the bronze brake not through, for its point was turned in the stout shield. Next Menelaos son of Atreus lifted up his hand to cast, and made prayer to father Zeus: "Kind Zeus, grant me revenge on him that was first to do me wrong, even on goodly Alexandros, and subdue thou him at my hands; so that many an one of men that shall be hereafter may shudder to wrong his host that hath shown him kindness."

HOMER

9.4.   Next day he waked up late. Going over the impression of the past, what he recalled most vividly was that he was to be presented to the Emperor Francis; he remembered the minister of war, the ceremonious adjutant, Bilibin, and the conversation of the previous evening. He dressed for his attendance at court in full court dress, which he had not worn for a long time, and fresh, eager, and handsome, he walked into Bilibin's room with his arm in a sling. Four gentlemen of the diplomatic corps were already there. With Prince Ippolit Kuragin, who was a secretary to the embassy, Bolkonsky was already acquainted; Bilibin introduced him to the others.

LEO TOLSTOY

9. Comment on the following passage:

9.5.   And what did it profit me that when I was barely twenty years old there came into my hands, and I read and understood, alone and unaided, the book of Aristotle's Ten Categories — a book I had longed for as for some great and divine work because the master who taught me Rhetoric at Carthage, and others held learned, mouthed its name with such evident pride? I compared notes with others, who admitted that they had scarcely managed to understand the book even with the most learned masters not merely lecturing upon it but making many diagrams in the dust: and they could not tell me anything of it that I had not discovered in reading it for myself. For it seemed to me clear enough what the book had to say of substances, like man, and of the accidents that are in substances, like the figure of a man, what sort of man he is, and of his stature, how many feet high, and of his family relationships, whose brother he is, or where he is placed, or when he was born, or whether he is standing or sitting or has his shoes on or is armed, or whether he is doing something or having something done to him — and all the other countless things that are to put either in these nine categories of which I have given examples, or in the chief category of substance.

ST. AUGUSTINE

(Note: Check to see whether St. Augustine has mentioned all of Aristotle's categories.)

Chapter 10: DIVISION: THE WAY TO DEFINITION

General function of division. The predicables and the categories have furnished us with the two most important instruments for organizing the first operation of the mind. To organize logical relations so that reason may proceed in an easy, orderly, and correct manner is the purpose of logic. The most important result of our study of the first operation of the intellect should be a knowledge of definition. Prior to the formal study of definition, however, there remains one more consideration. It is a study of the logic of division, where concepts are put in a preliminary order so that definition may, when achieved, be itself properly ordered. Division thus prepares the way for definition.

Let us observe a case of division in action, as the Stranger and Theaetetus, in Plato's dialogue, *The Sophist*, divide human art.

10.1. *Str.* Seeing then, that all arts are either acquisitive or creative, in which class shall we place the art of the angler?

Theaet. Clearly in the acquisitive class.

Str. And the acquisitive may be subdivided into two parts: there is exchange, which is voluntary, and is effected by gifts, hire, purchase; and the other part of acquisitive, which takes by force or word or deed, may be termed conquest?

Theaet. That is implied in what has been said.

Str. And may not conquest again be subdivided?

Theaet. How?

Str. Open force may be called fighting, and secret force may have the general name of hunting?

Theaet. Yes.

> Str. And there is no reason why the art of hunting should
> not be further divided.
> Theaet. How would you make the division?
> Str. Into the hunting of living and lifeless prey.

The hunting of living things is further divided and subdivided, as a reading of the *Sophist* will show, but we have followed Plato's method sufficiently to determine the direction of his logical operation. Logical division, which Plato did so much to perfect, is the arrangement of the extension of a logical whole into all of its subordinated parts. If a diagrammatic outline were made of the division quoted above, it would show more forcefully how division works and what it is.

Division is a very common operation in all learning. It is important in biology for the classification of living things. Chemistry employs division in the periodic chart. Physics employs division, e.g., positive and negative electricity, kinetic and potential electricity, uniform and accelerated movement. Division is important in the organization of a business into its parts, of a government into various agencies, of an army into its branches, of a college into departments, and of a departmental program into its courses.

Division is essential in writing a novel or a play, so that the various parts are organized with respect to one another as chapters, acts, or scenes. Even a smaller composition like an essay must employ logical division to be organized properly into paragraphs, and the paragraphs must be divided within themselves according to the logical co-ordination and subordination of ideas. That is why an outline, mental or written, is important for the composition of literary pieces.

Rules for division. There are three rules for good logical division. In order to understand them, let us call that which is divided the *logical dividend*. Thus, animal is a dividend when broken down into rational and irrational. The parts of a dividend, e.g., rational and irrational, will be called *members*. Art, in Plato's example, is the logical dividend. Acquisitive and creative are members in the division. Acquisitive arts form the dividend for a further division in which exchange and conquest are now members.

Rule I: *Each member must have less extension than the dividend.* If a member had an extension equal to or greater than the dividend, a part would be equal to or greater than the whole. Thus you cannot divide nouns into proper nouns, common nouns, and names. The third member in this instance has an extension equal to that of the dividend; every noun is a name. Hence this division has not clarified anything, and we would have to begin our division all over again by dividing names. Even stronger criticisms could be made of it.

Rule II: *All of the members, taken together, must be equal to the dividend in extension.* This rule insures that our division is exhaustive or complete. The hunting of living and of lifeless prey, taken together, are equal, in extension, to hunting. There are no other possible objects of hunting to be mentioned. But suppose we are dividing the parts of speech and include as members the noun, the verb, and the preposition. Obviously, our list is incomplete. There is no mention of the article, the adjective, the adverb, the conjunction, the interjection.

Rule III: *There must be an opposition between the members.* If they are not opposed, they may be either identical or unrelated. To divide the states of water into liquid, gaseous, solid, and frozen is not a good division. *Solid* and *frozen* in the case of water would be identical. To divide the states of water into liquid, gaseous, solid, and salty does not properly divide water either. *Salty* is not opposed to the other three states but is unrelated to them. Salt water has for its opposite fresh water.

For the most certain kind of logical division, it is best to use contradictory opposition employing a positive term to designate one member and the negation of that term by *non-* or *not* to designate the other. Thus, substance can be divided into material and non-material; material substance or body is divided into physical and nonphysical; physical is divided into living and nonliving. The use of *non-* or *not* makes sure that our division is complete and exhaustive and excuses us from the worry that there may be other alternatives not mentioned among our members. Such a division in terms of the positive and negative is a simple dichotomy, easy to handle and not likely to lead us into error.

Instead of dividing body into physical and nonphysical, we could have divided it into physical and mathematical. But to say physical and nonphysical implies a stronger kind of opposition than to say physical and mathematical. Physical, we subdivided into living and nonliving. This is stronger than saying living and mineral. For anything living has, in addition to its qualities of life, the characteristics of the mineral world. What is living includes the mineral and adds something to it. Living and nonliving is a clearer kind of opposition than living and mineral.

As another aid in observing our three rules, the same principle of division must be employed whenever we divide a logical whole. This conclusion can be understood in terms of another example. If, for instance, we are dividing the states of the United States, we can use several principles. We can divide them into those north and those south of the Mason-Dixon line, into those east and those west of the Mississippi, into those that are predominantly agricultural and those that are predominantly industrialized, into those that were the thirteen original states and those entering the Union later, into those having a population of 15,000,000 or more and those having less than 15,000,000 inhabitants. But once we have chosen to divide the states in one way, we must follow the same principle of division in deriving our members. For instance, we cannot divide the states into those west of the Mississippi, like Colorado and California, and those east of the Mississippi, like Indiana and Ohio and then suddenly introduce New York on the grounds that it has a population of more than 15,000,000. Such a procedure would violate Rule III. We had initially chosen to divide the states by their geographical relation with respect to the Mississippi River; logically we cannot, in the middle of the division, suddenly shift our ground and start dividing the states according to a quite different principle, that of population. Two different principles of division would thereby be mixed.

A subdivision need not follow the same principle of division as the division preceding it. But once a principle is selected for the subdivision, it must be used, without alteration, through the subdivision itself.

The difference between division and definition. Division is a preparation for definition. It is a way of seeing what things have in common and how they differ from each other, and such a procedure is an important step in defining things. The logical mind, attempting to make definitions of the fox as opposed to the wolf, of silver as contrasted with gold, and of water as different from sulfuric acid, must first be able to make good divisions, listing, with respect to two similar kinds of thing, what they have in common and wherein they differ. Division is the way to definition. In division, the mind orders the extension of universal concepts; in definition, we organize universals according to their comprehension.

In seeking to know, for instance, what a virtue is, the first step must be a listing of the various cases to which the term extends. Then we are on the road to finding out what such cases have in common and hence what virtue in its comprehension really is. Mendeleyev classified the elements in his periodic chart according to their weights. This helped chemistry and physics discover that a particular atomic structure is peculiar to each element; the weights of different species of atoms are now associated with the numbers and kinds of particles they contain. Here, classification or division led the way to a knowledge of the intrinsic constitution of matter and in some oblique way, as we saw in Chapter 8, to a knowledge of essences. The nature of heavenly movements began to be clearer when astronomers learned to divide celestial bodies into fixed stars and planets.

Intrinsic logical value of division. There is a sense, however, in which division is not merely a step toward definition. It has a certain logical value of its own. Conclusions can be made from a good division, according to the following rules:

Rule I: *Whatever is said about the dividend, e.g., triangle, can also be affirmed about the members, e.g., isosceles, scalene, and equilateral, and what is denied of the dividend can be denied of all the members.* If it belongs to the nature of a triangle to have the sum of its interior angles equal to 180°, such a characteristic belongs to isosceles, scalene, and equilateral triangles. If it is denied that a triangle is a curvilinear figure, such a denial also holds for the various kinds of triangles.

Rule II: *If contradictory opposition, through the use of the "non-" or "not" prefix, obtains between the members of a dividend, where one member is affirmed the other is denied, and where one member is denied the other is affirmed.* If physical things are divided into living and nonliving and if the slime molds of the sea are living, it can be denied that they are merely nonliving substances. If it turns out that the children inoculated with the Salk vaccine do not get polio, the Salk vaccine can be safely classified as a polio preventive. Such a rule may not seem very valuable in ordinary affairs. Nevertheless, it is extremely useful in exploring areas that are too small in size or too distant in space to be open to our direct observation and measurement. If, then, we can set up contradictory alternatives in our division and affirm one of them, we can deny the other; and in denying one, we can affirm the other. The sciences afford many examples of applications of this rule.

Problems

1. Explain what is meant by division. How is division related to extension?

2. Explain each rule for division and give examples of your own to illustrate each rule. What is meant by the principle of division?

3. In the rules for drawing conclusions from a division, what would be wrong with the following proposition: What is affirmed of any member can be affirmed of the dividend, and what is denied of any member can be denied of the dividend. Explain your answer in terms of examples.

4. Outline in a diagrammatic form all divisions and subdivisions in the following and evaluate each division as being good or bad in accordance with the rules:

10.2. Gaul as a whole is divided into three parts. The Belgians inhabit one part, the Aquitanians another, and those who call themselves Celts — in our language, Gauls — inhabit the third.

JULIUS CAESAR

10.3. Democracy has, therefore, two excesses to avoid: the spirit of inequality, which leads to aristocracy or monarchy; and the spirit of extreme equality, which leads to despotic power, as the latter is completed by conquest.

MONTESQUIEU

10.4. The study of radioactivity includes the study of the chemistry of the radioelements, the study of the rays emitted by these elements, and the conclusions to be drawn from such studies relative to the structure of the atom. The radioelements can be defined as particular elements from which there emanate, spontaneously and atomically, rays designated as *alpha, beta* and *gamma.* . . .

MARIE CURIE

10.5. Now order can be compared to reason in four ways. There is a certain order which reason does not make but only considers, such as the order of natural things. There is another order which reason in carrying on its considerations makes in its own proper act, as when, for example, it orders its own concepts and the signs of these concepts in so far as these are significant sounds. There is a third order which reason makes in the operations of the will. There is a fourth order which reason makes in external things of which it is the cause, as for example in a chest or in a house.

ST. THOMAS AQUINAS

10.6. Before the end of the present century, unless something unforeseeable occurs, one of three possibilities will have been realized. These three are:

I. The end of human life, perhaps of all life on our planet.
II. A reversion to barbarism after a catastrophic diminution of the population of the globe.
III. A unification of the world under a single government, possessing a monopoly of all the major weapons of war.

BERTRAND RUSSELL

10.7. The various phenomena exhibited by electricity may, for the purposes of comparison, be arranged under two heads: namely, those connected with electricity of tension, and those belonging to electricity in motion. This distinction is taken at present not as philosophical, but merely as convenient. The effect of electricity of tension, at rest, is either attraction or repulsion at sensible distances. The effects of electricity in motion or electrical currents may be considered as 1st, Evolution or heat; 2nd, Magnetism; 3rd, Chemical decomposition; 4th, Physiological phenomena; 5th, Spark.

MICHAEL FARADAY

5. Name the principle of division for each of this series of objects: (a) paragraph; sentence; chapter; (b) Louisiana; Florida; Maine; (c) line; plane; solid; (d) virtue; figure; color; (e) mathematics; grammar; rhetoric; (f) hammer; clock; fork; (g) snowflake; air; smoke; (h) weapons; shoes; wedding ring; (i) being on the campus; being on the seashore; being in an airplane; (j) to be sitting; to be standing; to be scratching the head; (k) sun tan oil; ear muffs; shatter-proof glass; (l) Caesar; Constantine; Charlemagne; (m) to be tossed about; to be frostbitten; to be humiliated; (n) logical universal; argument; comprehension; (o) maternity; equality; legality; (p) storm warning; a blueprint; the idea of a cow.

6. Organize a game of twenty questions in which the student-

moderator tells the class only the category to which the thing he has in mind would belong. The student tells the teacher the name of the thing, and the class has twenty questions in which to work by an orderly division from the more extensive to the less. E.g., the irrational number "pi" is in the genus of the quantified; knowledge of physics is in the genus of the qualified; the folding (of hands in prayer) is reduced to posture; to be in polo players' uniforms is in the genus of to be clothed; to be magnetized is in the category of reception, etc.

7. What is wrong with the following divisions: (a) men divided into bright, dull, colored; (b) number divided into even, odd, fractions; (c) reality divided into mass and energy; (d) commodities divided into products and men; (e) the value of a product divided into labor ability and labor time; (f) the marks of civilization divided into bathtubs, electrical power, and mechanized farming; (g) governments divided into those which leave men free and those where man obeys authority; (h) the liberal arts divided into grammar, logic, rhetoric, mathematics, history, and science; (i) facts divided into true, false, and probable; (j) spirits divided into ghosts, souls, alcohol.

8. Show the relation between division and definition as illustrated by the following passage:

10.8. Suppose we see together a Dog, a Cat, a Bear, a Horse, a Cow, and a Deer. The first feature that strikes us as common to any two of them is the horn in the Cow and Deer. But how shall we associate either of the others with these? We examine the teeth, and find those of the Dog, the Cat, and the Bear sharp and cutting, while those of the Cow, the Deer, and the Horse have flat surfaces, adapted to grinding and chewing, rather than cutting and tearing. We compare these features of their structure with the habits of these animals, and find that the first are carnivorous, that they seize and tear their prey, while the others are herbivorous or grazing animals, living only on vegetable substances, which they chew and grind. We compare further the Horse and Cow, and find that the Horse has front teeth, both in the upper and lower jaw, while the Cow has them only in the lower; and going still further, and comparing the internal with the external features, we find this arrangement of the teeth in direct relation to the different structure of the stomach in the two animals — the Cow having a stomach with four pouches, adapted to a mode of digestion by which the food is prepared for the second mastication, while the Horse has a simple stomach. Comparing the Cow and the Deer, we find that the digestive apparatus is the same in both; but though they both have horns, in the Cow the horn is hollow, and remains through life firmly attached to the bone, while in the Deer it is solid and is shed every year. With these facts before us, we cannot hesitate to place the Dog, the Cat, and the Bear in one division, as carnivorous animals, and the other three in another division as herbivorous animals, — and looking a little further, we perceive, that, in common with the Cow and the Deer, the Goat and the Sheep have cloven feet, and that they are all ruminants, while the Horse has a single hoof, does not ruminate, and must therefore be separated from them, even though, like them, he is herbivorous.

                                                    LOUIS AGASSIZ

Chapter 11: THE AIM OF THE MIND'S FIRST OPERATION: DEFINITION

11.1. Hence it is, that it is almost a definition of a gentleman to say that he is one who never inflicts pain. This description is both refined and, as far as it goes, accurate. He is mainly occupied in merely removing the obstacles which hinder the free and unembarrassed action of those about him; and he concurs with their movements rather than takes the initiative himself.

JOHN HENRY NEWMAN

Nature of definition. These are the opening lines of a long passage from the *Idea of a University*, on the qualities of a gentleman. Whether Newman intended his remarks, in whole or in part, to form a definition may be an open question. But the passage at issue does seem, at least at first sight, an attempt to answer the question of what a gentleman is, and if so, it is an attempt to define. For the definition of a thing is the answer to the question of what that thing is. Definition is the expression of the essence of a thing.

Intended as a definition or as something else, Newman's lines, in spite of his logic in thought and brillance of expression, underline the difficulties of reaching good definitions. From what has already been said, it should come as no surprise that a definition must express the genus and specific difference of what we are defining; and moreover, the genus and specific difference must fall within the same category. For a definition is an expression signifying what a thing is, and we know what a thing is only when we know its genus and how it differs intrinsically from other species in the same genus.

Two broad types of definition. There are two kinds of definition that can be immediately distinguished: The *nominal* and the *real*. In the nominal definition, we simply say what we mean by our words, and in this respect, our definition is about names rather than things. One kind of nominal definition is simply the synonym, found for instance in a dictionary, for the term to be defined. To define a spinster as an unmarried woman is to give a nominal definition. Such a definition, though extremely common and of great interest in the liberal art that we call grammar, is less important for our present purposes than the real definition expressing what a thing is in terms of its real components. In this context we almost always have to see a term used in a sentence to know whether it is a definition of words or a definition of a real, existing thing. The use of a term in a proposition is technically called the supposition of that term.

Difficulty of definition.   Definition is to comprehension as division is to extension. A definition expresses the essence of a thing, and to know the real definition of anything is to know its species. Our best definition is that of man; he is defined as a *rational animal*. But what is the specific difference between a cat and a dog? A mind with a moderate fund of experience does not mistake one for the other in actual life, but when it comes to setting down precisely how the two species differ, there are serious problems. It is likewise possible, at least in principle, to distinguish the gentleman from his opposite, but when we try to formulate our distinction in clear concepts, could we do any better than Newman?

Value of definition.   The importance of real definition can hardly be overestimated. Unless we know what things are in the first operation of the mind, how can we predicate about them in the second or reason about them in the third? Whenever a scientist asks what things are, he is looking for definitions. In recent years, a bill was introduced into a state legislature to license psychologists in a fashion similar to the licensing of doctors; the issue concerned the kind of service a psychologist renders; it concerned what a psychologist is. In the election campaign of 1954, it was argued that a candidate for a state governorship had voted in another state at a previous election, and having surrendered residency in his own state was not eligible to run for its governorship. Here too the issue depended on definition: what is residency? Thus, not only in the pursuit of science but even in practical affairs like legal decisions, real definition is of great moment.

Definition and structure. A definition is not the essence of what is being defined. It is not properly speaking even our knowledge of the essence. It is our way of formulating knowledge of essences. Such knowledge is gained, in the case of natural things, from operations and structures which are signs of the essences under consideration. Since all, or at least nearly all, of our real definitions are in terms of signs, there may be a question of why so much attention is paid to the perfect definition which is given in terms not of properties and structures but of genus and specific difference. Would it not be more appropriate to neglect the perfect definition and to concentrate, instead, on the imperfect type so common in intellectual life?

The answer to this difficulty, if difficulty it is, lies precisely in the doctrine of the sign itself. Imperfect definitions, such as those which express property or structure, are definitions precisely to the extent that they signify the species in the perfect definition; and unless we know what the signs signify, there may be a temptation to stop our considerations with instrumental signs themselves, without going on to regard the signs in relation to the essence they reveal to us. To study species in terms of structure only would be to consider species as nothing but its instrumental signs — as though we would take smoke to be not the sign of fire but fire itself.

Types of real definition. There are three broad divisions of the real definition: the *logical*, or, as it is sometimes called, the metaphysical definition; the *physical* definition; and the *descriptive* definition. The logical definition is the perfect type, expressing the nature of a thing by a genus and specific difference belonging to the same category. The physical definition is a definition through causes which are signs of the essence being defined. The descriptive definition is a definition by property which is likewise a sign of the essence but as an effect rather than as a cause. These three kinds of real definition will now be discussed in their turn.

Enough has been said in Chapter 7, which dealt with the predicables, to explain the logical definition. If a real definition is an expression indicating what a thing is, it can readily be concluded that our best definitions would be cast in the form of genus and specific difference. In this manner, the mind is able to express the complete essence of a thing, its general "part" and its special "part." The genus indicates what an essence has in common with other essences and the specific difference indicates how the essence in question differs from others. To express how an essence is like other essences and how it is unlike these others by what it contains of its own is surely to define the essence in question by setting it apart from all others. Further discussion of how genus, difference, and species relate to essences need not be undertaken in an introductory book.

In approaching the physical or causal definition, it is first necessary to indicate what a cause is. A cause is that on which another thing depends in order to be or to come to be. To most of us, a cause is an agent producing something else — a sculptor making a statue, a cow giving birth to a calf, dynamite producing an explosion. But cause has a wider meaning. In the light of our proposition that a cause is that on which something depends in order to be or to come to be, there are four kinds of causes in the material world.

There is first of all the *material cause* — the marble out of which a statue is made or the material in the body of the calf. Philosophers usually refer to the *material cause* as matter, but such an expression in ordinary language has a different meaning. Matter or the material cause is the subject of change. In the fall of a snowflake, the snowflake is matter or the material cause. In the reddening of an apple or the growth of a dog, the apple is matter in the one case and the dog is the material cause in the other. In any change, then, there is a subject remaining throughout the change, and this is all that a philosopher means by matter or material cause. The *formal cause* or form is that which determines matter to be this or that, e.g., a statue or a cow. The shape given to the marble would be the formal cause of the statue, and the soul of the cow is the formal cause why this animal is a cow. In the reddening of an apple or the growth of a dog, the new color and the new size are the formal causes or simply the forms. When the cow dies, the matter in the body loses the form it had, and the result is merely an aggregate of chemical elements, each with its own form and no longer having as a whole that form which we call the cow's soul, its life principle. A potato, when eaten, does not remain a potato, but something of the original does remain; from it we gain nourishment and strength. After digestion, the matter in the potato has lost its form but remains under a new form, that of man. Everything in the physical world, living or not, has matter, the raw stuff out of which it is made, and everything material also has form which makes the matter to be this or that, cow, man, potato, silver, dynamite. Both matter and form are causes, since any material thing depends on its matter and its form in order to become and to be.

The third kind of cause is the agent, the producer of something; it is that which, by its activity, does something or makes something extrinsic to itself. Such an agent is called the *efficient cause*. A carpenter is the efficient cause of a house; rain is the efficient cause of the hollowing out of a rock; the mother cow is an efficient cause of a calf. The fourth kind of cause is the *final cause*, which is the aim or purpose of the thing made. A knife is for cutting; cutting is, therefore, its final cause. The eye is for seeing, the spring rain for fertilizing the plant life of the world, the acorn for the production of an oak tree.

To summarize the notions of the four causes: matter or the material cause is that out of which a thing is made. The formal cause determines the matter to be this rather than that. The efficient cause is the producer or agent. The final cause is the goal or purpose of a thing.

Much will be said in the philosophy of nature concerning the four causes which are found in all physical things. But some brief introduction has been necessary here in order to explain the various kinds of causal or physical definition. A few examples will help to explore the causes as they appear in definition.

11.2. All atoms consist of very small solid nuclei (diameter 10^{-12}cm) and extended outer shells (diameter about 10^{-8}cm).

C. F. VON WEIZSAECKER

11.3. The extremities of a line are points.

EUCLID

11.4. Accordingly, when a man is said to have the grace of God, there is signified something supernatural bestowed on man by God.

ST. THOMAS AQUINAS

11.5. The basic idea which gives to the word "democracy" its original and latent meaning is the idea of a social group organized and directed by all of its members for the benefit of all its members.

RALPH BARTON PERRY

In 11.2, the definition is in terms of the material cause. The morphological descriptions in modern biology and the structural approach to matter in chemistry and physics are reducible to definition by material cause. What we observe when we see a potato, for instance, and what we envision when we reflect upon the particle structure in a helium nucleus are the effects of the form on the matter, the structural determination produced in the matter by the formal cause. The human body has the structural appearance we observe because of the soul's causality in the matter. The same matter, on death, will become organized differently because of the different form it will take after the loss of that human form which is the soul. To define by structure is to define in terms of the effect produced in matter by the form, and the resulting definition is called a definition by material cause.

Case 11.3 in defining a point is a definition in terms of formal cause. That which determines a line to be this or that line and not any other are the points terminating the line in question. Other points would make a different line. Nearly all definitions in mathematics are in the order of formal causality. But as previous examples showed, there is a form in all material things. The soul of man is our form and to define man in terms of his spiritual soul is to define him in terms of his formal cause.

Case 11.4 is a definition principally by efficient cause, namely God. Such definitions are especially common in the modern physical and biological sciences. Indeed, the genetic approach to classification lays great stress on efficient causality. Definitions by efficient cause are also quite common in defining the various functions or offices in a government, a business, a branch of the military service, or in any other large organization where a division of labor is required.

Case 11.5 emphasizes the final cause or purpose, although the material cause, namely the social group, and the efficient cause, the members, are also part of the definition. To define things by final cause or purpose is especially important in the study of nature, particularly the living world, and the mind must be content with descriptive or causal definitions that substitute for logical definitions. The substitutes are not definitions in themselves but only as related to the genus and specific difference on which they throw light as natural, instrumental signs. Causal definitions are more perfect in signifying essences to the extent that all four causes are taken into account.

Definition by property is a descriptive definition. Because a property flows from a specific essence as an effect from a cause, property becomes an important means for knowing what things are.

Newman's definition of a gentleman expresses the properties of what he is defining. Such definitions are also possible in our study of the world of nature. But in physics, biology, and the social studies causal definitions are also prominent, as shown especially by the structural approach. Such an approach yields knowledge in the order of material causality.

Definition is the highest achievement of the first act of the mind. Division prepares for definition. In his own mind, Newman no doubt listed the qualities of a gentleman and the qualities of the opposite kind of man. By dividing we see the differences among things as well as their likenesses. Finally we put differences and likenesses together to reach our definition. By listing what man can do and what lower animals cannot, we can reach a definition of man as a rational animal. From a list of the four causes of various other organisms, we can, at least in principle, learn the causes specific to each one. In the inorganic world, our definitions of each of the various elements by the particle structure of their respective nuclei was suggested by the division of the elements according to the periodic chart. Division starts us in quest of the causes and reasons why the members differ from each other and to find such causes and reasons is to give explanations by definition.

Problems

1. What are the substitutes for perfect definition? Why is it important to know that these substitutes are signs of perfect definition?

2. What are the four causes? What is a causal definition? What is the most perfect form of causal definition?

3. Looking back over our whole study of the concept, what is the relation between definition and (a) the sign; (b) the universal; (c) comprehension and extension; (d) the predicables; (e) the predicaments; (f) division?

4. Consider the following definitions and mark them as nominal or real and if real as logical, descriptive, or causal, and finally if causal, to which cause or causes is the definition reduced: (a) Man is a worrying animal; (b) Man is an animal that can ask itself what it is; (c) Man is a rational animal; (d) Man is a composite of body and a spiritual soul; (e) Man is a creature whose form was especially created by God; (f) Man is a visible creature whose end is happiness; (g) Man is any member of the human race; (h) Man is a talking animal; (i) Man is a tool-using animal; (j) Man is a religious animal; (k) Man is an argumentative animal; (l) Man is a political animal.

5. Show the relations of definition and division in the following and characterize the definition which is at least implied:

11.6.   If I begin chopping the foot of a tree, its branches are unmoved by my act, and its leaves murmur as peacefully as ever in the wind. If, on the contrary, I do violence to the foot of a fellowman, the rest of his body instantly responds to the aggression by movement of alarm or defense. The reason of this difference is that man has a nervous system, while the tree has none; and the function of the nervous system is to bring each part into harmonious cooperation with every other.

WILLIAM JAMES

11.7.   Let me ask you now: — How would you arrange goods — are there not some which we welcome for their own sakes, and independently of their consequences, as for example, harmless pleasures and enjoyments, which delight us at the time, though nothing follows from them?

I agree in thinking that there is such a class, I replied.

Is there not also a second class of goods, such as knowledge, sight, health, which are desirable not only in themselves, but also for their results?

Certainly, I said.

And would you not recognize a third class, such as gymnastic, and the care of the sick, and the physician's art; also the various ways of money-making — these do us good but we regard them as disagreeable; and no one would choose them for their own sakes, but only for the sake of some reward or result which follows from them?

There is, I said, this third class also. But why do you ask?

Because I want to know in which of the three classes you would place justice?

In the highest class, I replied, — among those goods which he who would be happy desires both for their own sake and for the sake of their results.

PLATO

11.8. Certain objects, such as the sun, a flame, or glowing iron, are observed to be *visible* in themselves, whilst others, such as a piece of chalk, wood, (cold) copper, are visible only in the presence of the former. We call the first class of objects *self-luminous*, or for short *luminous*, the second class, *dark*. A dark body, then, *becomes luminous* in the neighborhood of a luminous one. . . . The illuminated object can again *illuminate* a third (in itself dark) object by reflected light, and so on. We call the sum total of the physical relations between one object and another, determined by the feature of the visibility of the first object, the condition of *illumination*. The *mechanism* imagined to be involved, conditioned by the first object, is designated briefly as *light*.

ERNST MACH

6. Define in either a descriptive or causal way: (a) hammer; (b) education; (c) slander; (d) a book review; (e) sacrament; (f) hydrogen; (g) airplane; (h) justice; (i) water; (j) spider.

7. Discuss the importance of definition in connection with the following items:

a) As a sequel to the Supreme Court decision outlawing segregation, the state of Georgia empowered the state treasury to allot sums of money to *private* schools which would continue segregation policies.

b) In the United States Senate, Senator Chavez declared that John Paton Davies was just as *loyal* as Senator McCarthy.

c) Catholic missionaries, imprisoned in Red China, were tried by *People's* Courts.

d) At the end of World War II, a special tribunal was constituted by the conquerors of Germany to try Nazi war criminals for *crimes against humanity.*

e) The neutral meson (a tiny subatomic particle) has been said to exist on the *border line between space and time.*

f) The United States Air Force has set up a special command unit to investigate *flying saucers.*

g) The National Educational Association has issued a pamphlet claiming that private schools are *divisive and hence un-democratic.*

Chapter 12: THE RULES OF DEFINITION

12.1. By liberty is understood, according to the proper signification of the word, the absence of external impediments . . .

THOMAS HOBBES

12.2. Science is organized knowledge.

HERBERT SPENCER

12.3. With regard to the concept of "mass," we remark first
that the formulation of Newton which defines mass to be the
quantity of matter of a body, as measured by the product of volume
and density, is unfortunate.

ERNST MACH

12.4. Numbers are classes of classes, namely of all classes similar
to a given class.

BERTRAND RUSSELL

12.5. We are willing to treat the term "religious sentiment" as
a collective name for the many sentiments which religious objects
may arouse.

WILLIAM JAMES

Rules for definition. Although some of these examples would
not be regarded by their authors as definitions, each illustrates in
one way or another what the logician would consider a bad definition. They all violate certain rules that a good definition must obey.
Such rules are not man-made recipes but laws that flow from the
very nature of a definition. The mind must obey them if it is to
put in order those logical relations which it is the aim of logic to
organize. Such rules apply to all definitions, logical, causal, and
descriptive.

Rule I: *A definition ought to explain its object in terms of what
it has in common with other things and of what it has that is*

proper to itself. This is indeed almost a paraphrase of what a definition is.

In the light of this rule, a definition, truly indicating what a thing is, cannot, for instance, be purely negative, saying what a thing is not. Reference should be made at this point to Newman's notion of the gentleman in 11.1. By the same rule, it should be observed that in 12.1 and 12.2, the objects under definition are not suitably distinguished from other things. Liberty, for example, is not characterized by the mere absence of restraint. If this were so, bodies falling in so-called free space would possess liberty. We know that they are not truly free since they cannot help doing what they do; yet Hobbes's definition would permit us to ascribe liberty to them as well as to many other material things.

Example 12.2 is an admirable statement on science, but it is not a definition. A great deal of knowledge is organized — as in a telephone book or chronicle of historical events — without being scientific. Spencer's definition does not adequately distinguish what is being defined, namely science.

Rule II: *The definition should be clearer than the thing defined.* If a definition is to express the essence of a thing, it can do so only in terms of what is more familiar to us. What is unknown cannot be explained by what is equally and perhaps even more unknown.

Newton's definition of mass, as cited by Mach in 12.3, turns out, on closer inspection, to disobey this rule. For what is meant by matter in the definition? Though using *matter* in a sense quite different from that of Chapter 11, Newton apparently assumes that matter is somehow clearly known when actually it is not. Here is a comment by a physicist on the fundamental equation in Newtonian physics that force is equal to mass times acceleration:

. . . every freshman is told the formula $F = MA$ and immediately is shown problem solutions and then required to work other problems himself, using this relationship. This continues until the student "believes" the relationship "because it works." Few freshmen are ever induced to wonder whether or not they understand the meanings of the concepts of force, mass, and acceleration. Indeed, few freshmen are aware that they do not understand what they are doing when they use these concepts.*

* R. Green, "Education in the Sciences," *The Scientific Monthly,* LXXIX (1954), 40.

In biology, it was observed, higher forms of living things are oftentimes defined in terms of their evolutionary descent from lower forms. But evolution is an hypothesis more obscure to us than the organisms it would explain. Finally, any use of figures of speech in definition disobeys Rule II.

Rule III: *The definition should not be circular as, for instance, by assuming and using what is to be defined; nor should it have a greater or lesser comprehension than what is being defined.* Put in a more positive way, this rule requires that the definition and what is defined should be just equivalent to each other.

Considering 12.4, many logicians would justify Russell's definition. But in contrast to this view, it could strongly be argued that Russell is using the notion of number in order to define number. Support for this charge can be found several chapters previously in Russell's work, where he says that "a class is a *numerical* conjunction of terms." A similar charge can be made against James in 12.5. A person not knowing what *religious* and what *sentiment* stand for would look in vain for a clarification of these two concepts into the words of James.

In a more positive way, Rule III says that a definition and its object are equivalent and hence provides an effective way to test a definition. If the definition can be substituted for what is defined in any proposition, the definition is satisfactory; otherwise, it is not. For instance, wherever the concept of man occurs in a discourse, the concept of rational animal can be substituted. But organized knowledge on the one hand and science on the other (12.2) cannot be used interchangeably.

Additional aids in formulating definitions. Our study of the categories warrants the following further observations concerning definition. A definition that takes place in the framework of the predicables — as opposed to substitute definitions through causes and properties — can involve only one category. A union of substance and accident does not admit of definition. For instance, there is no definition for the accidental union expressed by man-on-a-horse, lady-in-a-red-hat, or one-legged-hen. Man can be defined and so can having a posture; but objects within two categories cannot be defined together. Put even more strongly, accidental unities cannot be defined. In the light of Rule I, accidental unities do not form a single object.

Second, whether in a metaphysical or causal or descriptive framework, only the universal can be defined. A definition has to be a predicate in a proposition, and individuals cannot function as predicates in a meaningful sense of the word. Such predication will always be tautological, e.g., *John is John, this stone is this stone.* Furthermore, a particular thing is unique and, precisely as individual, it has no relations to a higher class. The definition of an individual could not fulfill Rule I.

As a third observation, a definition must be rendered in univocal terms. When Pascal referred to man as "a thinking reed," he was using figurative language that would be misleading in a scientific discourse. It would violate Rule II.

Finally, a definition must be in terms of what is proximate rather than what is remote. When Kilmer wrote, "only God can make a tree," he was not, of course, thinking of a scientific definition of a tree. Nor would this excerpt from his poem constitute such a definition. To be made by God does not distinguish a tree from other things, since all visible things are made by God. It would be a satisfactory definition by efficient cause to say that an oak tree is produced from an acorn. But to say that the acorn or the oak is produced by God, while true in itself, would not yield a knowledge of either the tree or the seed so that each could be marked off from other things. In the order of metaphysical definitions, we should use a proximate genus and the specific difference. If Pascal means by thinking reed that man is a thinking vegetable, he is using a remote genus. The definition should proceed in terms of the more proximate genus, animal. Such a definition, e.g., *rational animal* rather than *rational vegetable*, gives a more distinct idea of man, and a definition, if it is anything at all, should make that which we know in a confused way to become known in a distinct way. To insist on this is only to paraphrase Rule I.

Definitions are much easier to criticize than they are to construct. In the present chapter, we have explored a number of requirements that a definition must fulfill and hence a number of ways in which a definition can be criticized.

Whatever has been studied in this Part of our book, concerning the first operation of the intellect, has been aimed at understanding definition. The study of signs, of the universal, of comprehension and extension, of the predicables and the predicaments, and of division should assist us in making definitions and in understanding from a critical point of view the definitions proposed to us by others. Good definitions are the foundations of good logic. The person using logic in any field — mathematics, physics, chemistry, biology, theology, politics, and even literary and artistic criticism — will find his logic all the more effective the better he is able to make and to evaluate definitions.

Problems

1. Show how all of the rules of definition flow from the very nature of definition.

2. What is the importance of definition in human reasoning? Relate definition to all the other considerations concerning the first act of the mind and show, if you can, how definition would be important in argument.

3. In the following examples, characterize each proposed definition as being nominal or real and where the definition is real, characterize it further as logical, descriptive, or causal. If the definition is causal, what cause or causes are employed? Finally, evaluate each of the definitions in the light of the rules discussed in this chapter.

> 12.6.   A friend is a person with whom I may be sincere.
>
> RALPH WALDO EMERSON

> 12.7.   Life is the co-ordination of actions.
>
> HERBERT SPENCER

> 12.8.   [Matter] is the receptacle, and in a manner the nurse, of all generation.
>
> PLATO

> 12.9.   The most conspicuous of the sacrificial garments is the *chasuble*, as we say, from the Latin *casula*, a little house; so-called . . . because it covered the whole man.
>
> GERALD ELLARD, S.J.

> 12.10.   By utility is meant that property in any object, whereby it tends to produce benefit, advantage, pleasure, good, or happiness, (all this in the present case comes to the same thing) or (what

comes again to the same thing) to prevent the happening of mischief, pain, evil, or unhappiness to the party whose interest is considered: if that party be the community in general, then the happiness of the community: if a particular individual, then the happiness of that individual.

JEREMY BENTHAM

12.11. Love is nothing else but an insatiate thirst of enjoying a greedily desired object.

MONTAIGNE

12.12. An impressed force is an action exerted upon a body, in order to change its state, either of rest or of moving uniformly in a straight line.

ISAAC NEWTON

12.13. Law is whatever is boldly asserted and plausibly maintained.

AARON BURR

12.14. Rationalization may be defined as faulty thinking which serves to disguise or hide the unconscious motives of behavior and feeling.

PERCIVAL M. SYMONDS

12.15. Patience is the art of hoping.

VAUVENARGUES

12.16. What is the prime of life? May it not be defined as a period of about twenty years in a woman's life, and thirty in a man's?

PLATO

12.17. The nucleus of the hydrogen atom is called a *proton*. This particle has a positive charge equal numerically to the negative electric charge of the electron and is so small that it takes 2.72×10^{26} to make a pound. The nuclei of atoms of other substances contain a number of protons equal to the atomic number of the element.

UNITED STATES ATOMIC ENERGY COMMISSION

12.18. Law is . . . an ordinance of reason for the common good, promulgated by him who has the care of the community.

ST. THOMAS AQUINAS

12.19. A figure is that which is enclosed by one or more boundaries.

EUCLID

12.20. "Hair-splitting" is a colloquial term for making unnecessarily subtle distinctions.

MONROE BEARDSLEY

12.21. The whole of government consists in the art of being honest.

THOMAS JEFFERSON

4. Discuss the following definitions.

12.22. My friend, George Bancroft, defined democracy, in a lecture which I published in my *Boston Quarterly Review*, to be "eternal justice ruling through the people": I defined it in a series of resolutions adopted by a Democratic state convention, to be the "supremacy of man over his accidents" — meaning thereby that democracy regards the man as more than his possessions, social position, or any thing separable from his manhood — and got most unmercifully ridiculed for it; but the ridicule did not move me, and I held fast to the doctrine that the will of the people is the most direct and authentic expression of the divine will that can be had or desired.

ORESTES BROWNSON

12.23. A true classic is an author who has done something to enrich the human mind; who has really added to its wealth; who has caused it to take another step forward; who has discovered some incontestable moral truth, or caught sight in the human heart, where everything seemed known and explored, of some unrecognized but eternal human passion; who has expressed his thought, his observation, or his discovery, in some form, no matter what, which is at once large and grand, delicate and judicious, healthy and charming; who has addressed everybody in a style of his own, which is yet the style of everybody, — a style at once new and antique, and which may readily be current in all ages.

CHARLES AUGUSTIN SAINTE-BEUVE

12.24. Somehow, for me, the word *study* came to mean "Work hard at something in which you are not interested." Somehow *reading* came to mean "lose yourself in the scene of writers like Scott and Dickens and Cooper and Alger, or in the sun-and-tackle pages of a catalogue." Somehow I seemed to remember better what I "read" than what I "studied." I suspect that I remember better because the authors of the books I "read" lifted me out of the room in which I sat, lifted me out of myself, as the authors of books I "studied" never did.

WALTER M. MASON

12.25. Art may be defined as a single minded attempt to render the highest kind of justice to the visible universe, by bringing to light the truth, manifold and one, underlying its every aspect. It is an attempt to find in its forms, in its colors, in its light, in its shadows, in the aspects of matter and in the facts of life what of each is fundamental, what is enduring and essential — their one illuminating and convincing quality — the very truth of their existence. The artist, then, like the thinker or scientist, seeks the truth and makes his appeal.

JOSEPH CONRAD

12.26. But in practice a citizen is defined to be one of whom both the parents are citizens; others insist on going further back; say to two or three or more ancestors. This is a short and practical definition; but there are some who raise the further question: How this third or fourth ancestor came to be a citizen? Gorgias of Leontini, partly because he was in a difficulty, partly in irony, said — "Mortars are what is made by mortar-makers, and the citizens of Larissa are those who are made by magistrates; for it is their trade to make Larissaeans." Yet the question is really simple, for, if according to the definition just given they shared in the government, they were citizens. This is a better definition than the other. For the words, "born of a father or mother who is a citizen," cannot possibly apply to the first inhabitants or founders of a state.

ARISTOTLE

12.27. But children were allowed to leave school before that age to enter *beneficial* employment. Beneficial to whom, we should like to know. The children themselves? Or is it the parents, or the employer, or the community at large? It really *does* make a difference, does it not?

So when we hear of a *beneficial* or *desirable* scheme, we should ask "To whom?" When we hear of a movement called *subversive* or *revolutionary* or *destructive*, we are quite justified in inquiring what it is going to upset, or change, or destroy. If precise information is not forthcoming, we should probably not be far wrong if we suspected that all the speaker meant was that he personally approved of the scheme and disapproved of the movement.

R. W. JEPSON

12.28. Plato having defined man to be a two-legged animal without feathers, Diogenes plucked a cock and brought it into the Academy, and said, "This is Plato's man." On which account this addition was made to the definition, "With broad flat nails."

DIOGENES LAERTIUS

12.29.   When we talk of any particular sum of money, we sometimes mean nothing but the metal pieces of which it is composed; and sometimes we include in our meaning some obscure reference to the goods which can be had in exchange for it, or to the power of purchasing which the possession of it conveys.

ADAM SMITH

12.30.   A living creature might, indeed, be defined as a minor and subordinate piece of the Universe which, by a *tour de force*, has partially disengaged itself from the rest and has set itself up as an autonomous power that strives, up to the limits of its capacity, to make the rest of the Universe minister to its selfish purposes.

ARNOLD TOYNBEE

12.31.   Beauty is pleasure regarded as the quality of a thing.

GEORGE SANTAYANA

PART III: THE SECOND ACT OF THE MIND

Chapter 13: THE PROPOSITION

13.1 The proposition, *God is omnipotent*, contains two conceptions, which have a certain object or content; the word, *is*, is no additional predicate — it merely indicates the relation of the predicate to the subject.

IMMANUEL KANT

In the first act of the mind, the concept grasps something of the natures or essences of things. The concept is a formal sign of what things are, and it reaches its most perfect form in definition. Kant has given an example of the second act of the mind. How does this second operation differ from the first?

In the expression, *God is omnipotent*, it is apparent that concepts are present. *God* and *omnipotence*, to the extent that they are known by an earthly mind, are known by concepts. But it should also be apparent that in the intellect's second operation there is something in addition to concepts. There is a composition of concepts. In the expression, *God is not material*, concepts are divided from each other; there is a division of concepts.

These two cases are typical of the second act of the mind, where there is composition or division of concepts.

Distinction between propositions and composite concepts. However, not every compound expression belongs to the second act of the intellect. Thus, *gray fox, men in uniform, sons of Noah, soldiers who did not go overseas* — all are composite. Hobbes, in defining a just man as "he that in his actions observeth the laws of his country," also used a composite expression. Hence, to set off the second operation of the intellect from the first it is not enough to point to the composition or division of concepts.

But look at our examples, *God is omnipotent* and *God is not material;* both of these show a peculiar mode of composition and division. Concepts, like *gray fox* or *soldiers who did not go overseas*, neither affirm nor deny anything of a subject. However, in the composition, *God is omnipotent* and in the division, *God is not material*, there is affirmation on the one hand and denial on the other. The second act of the mind is an operation of the intellect composing or dividing by affirming or denying.

The proposition a natural, formal sign. From the logician's point of view, there is, in the first operation of the mind, a concept as the formal sign of a nature or essence either in whole or in part. It is fitting now to inquire about the name of the second act of the mind which corresponds, in the case of the first act, to the concept. That name is, as Kant reminds us, the proposition.

As the concept is the natural formal sign of an object outside thought, so the proposition is the natural, formal sign of the identity of two objects, where one is affirmed of the other, or of the non-identity of two objects, where one is denied of the other. As the verbal expression of a concept is usually a word or phrase, so the verbal expression of a proposition is a sentence. Sometimes both the mental composition and the verbal or grammatical composition are each called propositions. Indeed, it is not always easy to distinguish the logical order from the grammatical or linguistic order. However, unless otherwise indicated, *proposition* will be used in this book to mean the logical composition of concepts, and *sentence*, where used at all, will mean the expression of a proposition in oral or written form.

Proposition defined. A proposition is a logical reality in which there is either a composition of concepts through an act of affirmation, or a division of concepts through an act of denial. This is a definition in terms of the material and formal cause. The efficient cause of a proposition is the human mind thinking of the relations between concepts and thus bringing the proposition into existence. The most revealing causal knowledge of things is furnished by their ends, and fortunately a proposition can be defined in terms of its final cause or purpose. A proposition is a logical expression which signifies truth or falsity.

Truth and falsity are found only in the proposition. Concepts are neither true nor false. The same verdict holds regarding definition. *Rational animal* taken in itself is neither true nor false. Truth or falsity enter only where the definition is applied to a subject. Thus, *man is a rational animal* is true; *the horse is a rational animal* is false. If the object of one concept is affirmed of the object of another and these two objects are identified in reality, the proposition is true; if the object of one concept is denied of the object of another and the two objects are divided in reality, the proposition is likewise true. But when the objects of concepts are affirmed of each other in the logical order but divided from each other in the real order or when they are denied of each other in the logical order but united in the real order, the proposition in question is false.

Propositions can be stated verbally only in declarative sentences. As a logical expression indicating what is true or false, a proposition can be stated verbally only in declarative sentences. Questions, commands, exclamations, and other such expressions are not propositions. A proposition affirms or denies something of something else. That about which something is expressed is called the logical subject: in the proposition, *all matter is extended*, *all matter* is the subject. That which is affirmed or denied about the subject is called the predicate: in the foregoing example *extended* is the predicate.

In drawing a practical conclusion from this analysis, note that the logical subject is not always represented by the first grammatical nominative case occurring in a sentence. In the Shakespearean line, *Sweet are the uses of adversity*, sweet is not the logical subject. Shakespeare intended to express something not about *sweet* but about *the uses of adversity*. The logical subject is always that about which something is said.

A second practical observation concerns the copula. As Kant remarks, the copula expresses the relation between the subject and the predicate. This is true, of course, when the copula is positive and expressed by *is*. When the copula is expressed by *is not*, a relation between subject and predicate is denied. Quite frequently, however, the copula is implied rather than expressed by our language, and the resulting grammatical expression combines the logical copula with the logical predicate. Here are some examples:

> 13.2. A good talker, even more than a good orator, implies a good audience.
>
> LESLIE STEPHENS

> 13.3. The Puritan hated bearbaiting not because it gave pain to the bear but because it gave pleasure to the spectators.
>
> THOMAS BABINGTON MACAULAY

Propositions like these can be cast into rigorous logical form, and sometimes such a step is necessary in the interest of logical analysis. For instance, Stephens' proposition can be put: A good talker, even more than a good orator, is a man (or person, etc.) that implies a good audience. Macaulay's proposition, in strict logical form is: The Puritan was a man who hated, etc. Often the logical structure of a proposition is clear enough without putting it into stricter form involving *is* or *is not*, and in such cases the grammatical form can be treated as equivalent to the logical form.

Various kinds of propositions. A *categorical* proposition is one in which a single predicate is affirmed of a single subject. The propositions in 13.2 and 13.3 are categorical.

A *hypothetical* proposition is one in which there is more than one subject or predicate. It thus joins at least two categorical propositions in relations that may be designated grammatically by *if-then, both-and,* and *either-or* clauses. The conditional proposition is the most common of the three forms:

> 13.4. We make a ladder of our vices if we trample those same vices underfoot.
>
> ST. AUGUSTINE

Another form of hypothetical proposition is the conjunctive, of the grammatical form *both-and.*

> 13.5. The world is a looking glass and gives back to every man the reflection of his own face.
>
> WILLIAM MAKEPEACE THACKERAY

Putting this passage into strict logical form reveals Thackeray to be making two propositions: *Both the world is a looking glass and the world gives back to every man the reflection of his own face.* Sometimes the expressions *both* and *and* are omitted, and the conjunctive proposition is divided by a semicolon.

Finally there is the disjunctive proposition expressed grammatically by an *either-or* clause, or if the propositions are negative by a *neither-nor* clause.

> 13.6. **Either death is a state of nothingness and utter unconsciousness, or . . . there is a change and migration of the soul from this world to another.**
>
> SOCRATES

> 13.7. The moving finger writes; and, having writ
> Moves on: not all your piety nor wit
> Shall lure it back to cancel half a line,
> Nor all your tears wash out a word of it.
>
> EDWARD FITZGERALD

In the last three lines of this poem, the following disjunctive proposition can be found: *Neither all your piety shall lure the moving finger back to cancel half a line, nor shall all your wit lure the moving finger back to cancel half a line, nor shall all your tears wash out a word of the line.*

A categorical proposition is divided according to *quality* into affirmative and negative. In the first case, the predicate is affirmed of the subject; and in the second, the predicate is denied of the subject.

According to *quantity,* categorical propositions are divided into universal, particular, and singular. In the universal proposition, the predicate is affirmed or denied of the whole extension of the subject: *every man is rational; all men are capable of speech; whatever is human can err; no man has wings.*

In a particular proposition, the predicate is affirmed or denied of only a part of the extension of the subject: *some men are politicians; some men are not politicians.* In a particular proposition, the subject is expressed in terms of a word like *some, a few, certain.* In the universal proposition, the subject is expressed by a word like *every, all, no.* At times, the quantity of the subject is not expressed, and the resulting proposition is vague. Examples are: *knowledge is power; generals die in bed;* and *children believe in fairy lands.* Here the extension of the subject is unexpressed, and it is not clear whether *all* or *some* is meant. Propositions of this sort are used in ordinary discourse, but they should not be employed in a scientific argument unless their meaning is made more precise by a suitable prefix to the subject.

Finally, according to quantity, a proposition may be singular, applying only to one subject: *John is sick*. For purposes of this book, the particular and singular can be taken as equivalent. *Some*, the prefix to a particular subject, will be taken to mean that there is at least one case of the subject. *Some dogs are spotted* will be considered to mean that there is at least one spotted dog. Hence, divided according to quantity, propositions, as analyzed in this book, can be considered as universal or particular.

Problems

1. Distinguish between the first and second operations of the intellect.

2. Give two definitions of the proposition and explain the relation of the two definitions to each other.

3. What are the parts of a proposition and how are they related to each other?

4. Explain the relation between a sentence and a proposition and discuss the relation of grammatical form to logical form.

5. Divide the proposition and explain all of the divisions in accordance with the principles in Chapter 10.

6. In the following passages, (a) identify all propositions; (b) choose five propositions which are not in strict logical form and put them into such strict form; (c) state whether the propositions are categorical or hypothetical; (d) divide the categorical propositions according to quantity and quality.

13.8. If God did not exist, it would be necessary to invent him.
VOLTAIRE

13.9. Some people will never learn anything for this reason that they learn everything too soon.
ALEXANDER POPE

(HINT: This is a negative proposition. Show why.)

13.10. Never is there either work without reward nor reward without work being expended.
LIVY

13.11. To thine own self be true; and it must follow as the night the day, Thou canst not then be false to any man.

WILLIAM SHAKESPEARE

(HINT: Put this proposition into conditional form.)

13.12. Some books are to be tasted, others to be swallowed; and some few to be chewed and digested. . . .

FRANCIS BACON

13.13. Abandon hope all ye who enter here.

DANTE

13.14. All power of fancy over reason is a degree of insanity.

SAMUEL JOHNSON

13.15. Weather is a literary speciality, and no untrained hand can turn out a good article on it.

SAMUEL CLEMENS

13.16. Cleopatra's nose: had it been shorter, the whole aspect of the world would have been altered.

BLAISE PASCAL

(HINT: Put this proposition into conditional form.)

13.17. All happy families resemble one another; every unhappy family is unhappy in its own fashion.

LEO TOLSTOY

13.18. For all have not the gift of martyrdom.

JOHN DRYDEN

(HINT: Try putting this proposition into particular form.)

13.19. What is the use of running when you are on the wrong road?

JOHN RAY

13.20. Beauty draws more than oxen.

GEORGE HERBERT

13.21. Some men look at Constitutions with sanctimonious reverence and deem them like the ark of the covenant, too sacred to be touched.

THOMAS JEFFERSON

13.22. The only biography that is really possible is autobiography.

G. K. CHESTERTON

Chapter 14: THE OPPOSITION OF PROPOSITIONS

A. All animals are winged.
E. No animals are winged.
I. Some animals are winged.
O. Some animals are not winged.

The meaning of opposed propositions. Although these categorical propositions are all different from one another, they are all related. Because of their relations they are of great interest to the logician, and the rules which govern these relations are of great value in our reasoning.

First the standard abbreviations must be explained. The universal affirmative is always called an A proposition, while the particular affirmative is called an I proposition. To remember these two symbols for affirmative propositions, think of the first two vowels in *AffIrmo*, the Latin for "I affirm." The universal negative is called an E proposition and the particular negative is called an O proposition. These designations are taken from the first two vowels in *nEgO*, the Latin for "I deny."

When are propositions opposed to one another? Propositions are opposed when they have the *same subject* and the *same predicate* but differ in quantity, quality, or both. Propositions with different subjects and different predicates are not opposed to each other. They are simply unrelated.

In our study of opposition only the categorical proposition will be of interest.

Logical value of opposition. Let us examine in a preliminary way how reason can make use of the opposition between propositions. Suppose we know that the A proposition, *All animals are* winged, is false. If we know nothing else from biology about the opposing propositions, we can, nevertheless, infer that O is true. But we do not know merely from the falsity of A whether E is also false and whether I is false. For instance, an A proposition can be false: *All members of Congress are women*, and the corresponding E proposition can also be false: *No members of Congress are women*.

In short, there are rules or principles or logical laws governing propositions that are opposed to one another. We are now in a position to see more clearly what logic is all about. There are logical realities like propositions, just as there are physical realities like hydrogen. Just as the chemist studies the properties of hydrogen and the laws of its combination, so the logician studies the properties of logical relations and the laws governing their combination.

Kinds of opposition. Only opposed categorical propositions will be of interest throughout the rest of this chapter. For instance, *All animals are winged* is not opposed to *No animals are trees*. Not having the same predicate, these two propositions are unrelated. To be opposed, categorical propositions must have the same subject and the same predicate and must differ in quantity, quality, or both. Let us identify the four kinds of opposition.

The A and O propositions are *contradictory* to each other. So are the E and I propositions.

The A and E propositions are *contrary* to each other.

The I and O propositions are *subcontrary* to each other.

The A and I propositions are called *subalterns* and their relation is called subalternation. The same is true of the E and the O.

The oppositions between propositions are represented on a square in the following way:

The diagonals represent contradictory opposition.

The upper side represents contrary opposition.

The lower side represents subcontrary opposition.

The vertical sides represent subalternating opposition.

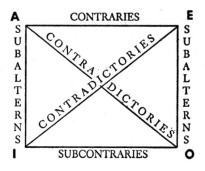

We can, of course, discover whether all or some or no animals have wings by examining animals in our experience. But it is possible by considering the merely logical relations among propositions, and hence without consulting experience, to know about the truth or falsity of one opposed proposition when the truth or falsity of another opposed proposition is given. In such a case we are proceeding from one proposition to another not through our knowledge of reality but by our knowledge of logical relations.

Let us now examine each pair of opposites to see what can be inferred about the truth or falsity of one member when the other member is known to be true or false. The relations of opposition will be illustrated by example rather than derived from abstract principles.

I. Contradictory opposition: Contradictory propositions cannot be either true at the same time or false at the same time.

a) A-O contradiction: If it is true that (A) *All men are mortal,* then it is false that (O) *Some men are not mortal.* If it is true that (O) *Some plays are not comedy,* then it is false that (A) *All plays are comedy.* If it is false that (A) *All teachers are mathematicians,* then it is true that (O) *Some teachers are not mathematicians.* If it is false that (O) *Some coal is not black,* then it is true that (A) *All coal is black.*

b) E-I contradiction: If it is true that (E) *No traitors are patriots,* then it is false that (I) *Some traitors are patriots.* If it is true that (I) *Some figures are triangles,* then it is false that (E) *No figures are triangles.* If it is false that (E) *No ponds are stagnant,* then it is true that (I) *Some ponds are stagnant.* If it is false that (I) *Some trees are animals,* then it is true that (E) *No trees are animals.*

Summary: When one of two contradictories is true, the other must be false, and when one is false, the other is true.

II. Contrary opposition: Contrary propositions cannot both be true at the same time, but both may be false at the same time.

If it is true that (A) *All insects are animals,* then it is false that (E) *No insects are animals.* If it is true that (E) *No oceans are small,* then it is false that (A) *All oceans are small.* However, if it is false that (A) *All houses are shingled,* it is still not true — and it may even be false — that (E) *No houses are shingled.* If it is false that (E) No fruit is round, it is still not true — and it may even be false — that (A) All fruit is round. From the falsity of (A) alone or of (E) alone, nothing can be inferred about the corresponding contrary.

Summary: When one of two contraries is true, the other is false; but when one is false, the other remains undetermined.

III. Subcontrary opposition: Subcontrary propositions cannot both be false at the same time, but both may be true at the same time.

If it is false that (I) Some roses are green, then it is true that (O) Some roses are not green. If it is false that (O) Some horses are not black, then it is true that (I) Some horses are black. If it is true that (I) Some governors are old men, it may nevertheless also be true that (O) Some governors are not old men. If it is true that (O) Some climates are not damp, it may also be true that (I) Some climates are damp.

Summary: When one of two subcontraries is known to be false, it can be inferred that the other is true. However, where we know only that one subcontrary is true, nothing can be inferred about the other. From the truth of one, the other is undetermined.

IV. Subalternating opposition: The particular is true if the universal is true. The universal cannot be true if the particular is false, but where the universal is false the particular may be true and where the particular is true the universal may be false.

If it is true that (A) All newspapers are printed, then it is also true that (I) Some newspapers are printed. If it is true that (E) No germs are visible, it is true that (O) Some germs are not visible. If it is false that (I) Some dogs are artists, then it is also false that (A) All dogs are artists. If it is false that (O) Some students are not rational, then it is false that (E) No students are rational.

If it is false that (A) All men are criminals, it may, from logical relations only, be true or false that (I) Some men are criminals. Knowledge of the falsity of (A) does not determine the status of (I). Similarly with (E) If it is false that (E) No icebergs are large, it may be true or false that (O) Some icebergs are not large. If the mere truth of (I) is known, nothing can be inferred about the truth of (A). Likewise, where the truth of (O) alone is known, the truth of (E) remains undetermined. If it is true that (I)

Some Americans are healthy, it may be true or false that (A) *All Americans are healthy.* If it is true that (O) *Some animals are not tame,* it may be true or false that (E) *No animals are tame.*

Summary: In subalternation, where the universal is known to be true, it can be inferred that the particular is true. Where the particular is false, it can be inferred that the universal is false. Where only the truth of the particular is known, nothing can be inferred about the universal. Where the universal is false, the particular likewise is undetermined.

In the following table, where propositions in the left hand column are given, the opposed propositions in the right hand column can be inferred as true, false, or undetermined. The reader is left to fill in the appropriate answers.

OPPOSITION	IF	THEN
Contradictory	A is true	O is ....
	O is false	A is ....
	E is true	I is ....
	I is false	E is ....
Contraries	A is true	E is ....
	E is true	A is ....
	A is false	E is ....
	E is false	A is ....
Subcontraries	I is false	O is ....
	O is false	I is ....
	I is true	O is ....
	O is true	I is ....
Subalternation	A is true	I is ....
	E is true	O is ....
	I is false	A is ....
	O is false	E is ....
	A is false	I is ....
	E is false	O is ....
	I is true	A is ....
	O is true	E is ....

The square of opposition is in general a useful logical instrument for extending our knowledge of one proposition to a knowledge of its opposite by the use of logical relations alone. Some of the relations catalogued on the foregoing pages are not too important, but many of the properties of opposition do help the mind, in a firm and sure way, to attain truth, avoid error, and defend itself against fallacies.

Problems

1. Explain the symbols for the four kinds of categorical propositions that are of interest in the study of opposition.

2. Name and identify the four kinds of opposition.

3. Give the rules in each kind of opposition for concluding to an opposite proposition when the truth or falsity of the other opposite is given.

4. Show how the laws of opposition among propositions reveal the nature of logic as opposed to the sciences that deal with the real world.

5. If you were told that it was false that (E) *No viruses are living*, in what two ways could you discover the truth of (I) *Some viruses are living*.

6. Criticize the following arguments in the light of your knowledge of the laws of opposition: In order to make the criticism more effective, rewrite sentences so that they clearly show the opposition between propositions.

> 14.1. After this I inquired in general into what is essential to the truth and certainty of a proposition; for since I had discovered one which I knew to be true, I thought that I must likewise be able to discover the ground of this certitude. And as I observed that in the words *I think, hence I am*, there is nothing at all which gives me assurance of their truth beyond this, that I see very clearly that in order to think it is necessary to exist, I concluded that I might take, as a general rule, the principle, that all the things which we very clearly and distinctly conceive are true, only observing, however, that there is some difficulty in rightly determining the objects which we distinctly conceive.
>
> RENÉ DESCARTES

(NOTE: Descartes's argument can be criticized in several ways. Here, he can be regarded as saying: One truth [that of my own existence] is clearly and distinctly known. Can he conclude that all truth is clearly and distinctly known?)

14.2.   The demand for certainty is one which is natural to man, but is nevertheless an intellectual vice. If you take your children for a picnic on a doubtful day, they will demand a dogmatic answer as to whether it will be fine or wet, and be disappointed in you when you cannot be sure.

BERTRAND RUSSELL

(Can Russell conclude that all men always demand certainty because the children in his example do?)

14.3.   When everyone is wrong, everyone is right.

LA CHAUSSÉE

(Taking the second proposition as a denial of the first, does it follow from the truth of the first?)

14.4.   The world is a wheel, and it will all come round right.

BENJAMIN DISRAELI

(If we grant Disraeli his implied thought that *all wheels come round right*, does it follow that *this one, i.e., the world will do so?* Explain.)

14.5.   Freeman and slave, patrician and plebeian, lord and serf, guild-master and journeyman, in a word, oppressor and oppressed stood in constant opposition to one another.

KARL MARX AND FRIEDRICH ENGELS

(Have Marx and Engels provided enough evidence to conclude that *all oppressors and oppressed in the history of man have stood in constant opposition to one another?*)

14.6.   None deserves praise for being good who has not spirit enough to be bad; goodness for the most part is nothing but indolence or weakness of will.

LA ROCHEFOUCAULD

(Even if we granted the second proposition which tells us that *some good is not praiseworthy* because it is allegedly due to ignorance, could we conclude to the first proposition that *no good is praiseworthy?* Why?)

7. If the propositions in column I are true or false as marked, what can be said about each of the opposing propositions in column II, in terms of being true (T), false (F), or undetermined (U)?

I	*II*
(T) Some tools are hammers.	1. Some tools are not hammers.
(F) All books are worth reading.	2. No book is worth reading.
(T) All sharks are scavengers.	3. Some sharks are not scavengers.
(T) All explosives are dangerous.	4. No explosives are dangerous.
(F) No bird is four-legged.	5. Some birds are four-legged.
(F) All climates are healthy.	6. Some climates are healthy.
(F) Some habits are virtues.	7. Some habits are not virtues.
(T) Some pets are domestic.	8. All pets are domestic.
(T) Some men are married.	9. No man is married.
(F) Some sciences are not teachable.	10. All sciences are teachable.
(T) Some students are not lazy.	11. No students are lazy.
(F) No comedians are funny.	12. Some comedians are funny.
(T) All trades are skilled.	13. No trades are skilled.
(T) Some men are orators.	14. No man is an orator.
(T) No pencils are mechanical.	15. Some pencils are not mechanical.
(T) No work is pleasant.	16. Some work is not pleasant.
(F) Some murders are justified.	17. No murder is justified.
(F) No lawyers are dishonest.	18. All lawyers are dishonest.
(T) No diamonds are fragile.	19. Some diamonds are fragile.
(F) No TV programs are educational.	20. All TV programs are educational.
(F) Some men are not equals.	21. All men are equals.
(F) All swans are white.	22. Some swans are white.
(F) Some grass is not green.	23. No grass is green.
(T) All music is harmonious.	24. No music is harmonious.
(F) All cities are large.	25. Some cities are not large.
(T) Some insects are dangerous.	26. All insects are dangerous
(T) Some stationery is lightweight.	27. No stationery is lightweight.
(F) Some planets are distant.	28. All planets are distant.
(F) All libraries are large.	29. No libraries are large.
(F) Some operations are not serious.	30. No operations are serious.
(F) All knives are sharp.	31. Some knives are not sharp.
(F) All birds are flying creatures.	32. No birds are flying creatures.
(T) Some doctors are licensed.	33. Some doctors are not licensed.

(T) All life on earth is
     perishable.

34. Some life on earth is
    perishable.

(F) Some laws are not binding.

35. Some laws are binding.

(T) No critic is objective.

36. All critics are objective.

(T) Some propaganda is
     successful.

37. All propaganda is successful.

(F) All of the Roman emperors
     were wise.

38. Some of the Roman em-
    perors were wise.

(F) No congressman is above
     the law.

39. All congressmen are above
    the law.

(F) All hunters are careful.

40. No hunters are careful.

Chapter 15: THE CONVERSION OF PROPOSITIONS

The relations of categorical propositions that are opposed to one another enable us to infer something about one proposition when the truth or falsity of an opposing proposition is given. There are some other properties in categorical propositions which enable the mind to perform additional operations upon the propositions themselves. Among these properties are the extension of terms. By studying the extension of the subject and predicate, logic is able to achieve what is called the conversion of propositions.

The problem of conversion. Conversion is the interchange of subject and predicate within the same proposition. Let us see what this means. Suppose we take an A proposition which says: *All X is Y.* Can we conclude from this that *All Y is X?* Or given the E proposition, *No X is Y,* can it be concluded that *No Y is X?*

If in the first case Y is universal in the original proposition, we can argue that since *All X is Y,* therefore *All Y is X.* If, however, Y is particular in the original proposition, then we cannot convert to *All Y is X* since Y in the converted proposition is universal. We are saying more in our conclusion than our original premise contained. If, in conversion, we go from a particular to a universal concept, we violate the same kind of rule which applied in subalternation. In other words, we can convert *All X is Y* to *All Y is X* only if Y is universal in the first proposition. We can convert *All men are animals* to *All animals are men* only if *animals* is universal in the first proposition. Otherwise, we would be putting more into our second proposition than the first one warranted. In a similar way *No X is Y* can logically be converted to *No Y is X* only if Y is universal in the original proposition.

The problem of conversion thus brings us to a study of the extension of terms in propositions. The laws governing conversion could also be discovered through a study of comprehension, but such a task, while more fundamental in itself, is more difficult for a beginner's purposes. It is easier to deal with conversion by a close analysis of the extension of the terms, provided we remember that universality does not consist in extension only.

It is a rule of logic that no concept in a converted proposition can have a wider extension than it had in the original proposition from which the conversion was made. Concepts may have the same or even less extension in the new proposition by comparison with the old. The point is that they may not have more extension in the second proposition than they had in the first. For the old proposition is the cause of the new one: hence, if a concept, particular in the old proposition, becomes universal in the new, there is more in the effect than in the cause. If we are talking about some X and make a conclusion about all X, there is something wrong in our procedure.

The problem of conversion is, therefore, squarely a problem concerning the extension of terms in the categorical proposition. In the various propositions, A, E, I, and O, what is the extension of the subjects and of the predicates?

It is fairly easy to settle the problem of the extension of subjects. The subjects of the A and of the E propositions are always universal. In *All men are mortal*, we apply the predicate, *mortal*, to all men. In *No man is irrational*, we deny the predicate, *irrational*, of every man. The subjects of the A and of the E propositions are, therefore, universal or distributed through the whole range of their extension.

The subjects of the I and of the O propositions are particular or undistributed as indicated by *some*: *Some men are Americans*, *Some men are not Americans*.

The extension of predicates. The determination of the extension of a predicate is more difficult. Let us take the familiar: *All men are animals*. It is evident upon analysis that *animals* here is particular, since the proposition obviously says *All men are some of the animals there are*. There are other animals besides men. Hence, *animals* in our example is not used in its universal sense. This fact can be represented diagrammatically by two circles. Let the large circle represent *animals* and the small circle represent *men*:

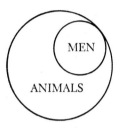

It is evident that only part of the large circle, representing *animals*, is taken up by *men*. *Animals* include more than *men*. Hence in *All men are animals*, the predicate is particular. The predicate of an A proposition, therefore, is particular or undistributed through the range of its extension.

Let us now examine the E proposition: *No man is irrational*. Here we are using *irrational* in its full extension, and we are saying that man falls nowhere within such an extension. *Irrational*, therefore, is universal or distributed. Let us go again to circle diagrams. Let the large circle represent *irrational* and the smaller circle represent *man*. Our E proposition uses irrational in its widest extension and says that no part of the extension of man is in it. The circles do not overlap.

The predicate of an E proposition is, therefore, universal or distributed.

The predicate of the I proposition resembles that in A. In

Some dogs are spotted, the *Some dogs* are only part of the things that are spotted. In terms of circles, let the large circle represent *things that are spotted,* while the small circle represents *dogs.*

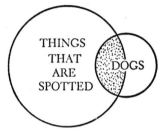

The shaded area represents the *Some dogs* that are in the predicate of spotted things; the unshaded area of the small circle represents the dogs that are not spotted. It can be seen at once that the shaded area represents only a small portion of the large circle of spotted things. Hence, in *Some dogs are spotted,* the *Some dogs* are clearly only some of the spotted things. There are many other spotted things besides dogs. Thus, in the *I* proposition as in the *A,* the predicate is particular.

The predicate of the *O* proposition resembles that in *E.* In *Some dogs are not spotted, spotted* is used in its widest sense, and it is denied that the *Some dogs* are included in this universal extension. The dogs that are not spotted are represented in the unshaded portion of the small circle above. The unshaded portion of the small circle is nowhere within the whole circle of spotted things. Hence *spotted* is used here in its widest extension, and it is denied that some dogs are in it. The predicate of an *O* proposition is always universal.

On the basis of our analysis of the subjects and predicates of the four categorical propositions, we have the following table:

Proposition	Subject	Predicate
A	Universal	Particular
E	Universal	Universal
I	Particular	Particular
O	Particular	Universal

In summary, universal propositions have universal subjects while particular propositions have particular subjects. Affirmative propositions have particular predicates while negative propositions have universal predicates. It should be obvious that it will often be desirable to put propositions into their strict logical form in order to convert them.

Conversion applied. Applying what has been said, can we in our introductory example convert *All X is Y* to *All Y is X?* No, for Y, a particular in the original proposition, has universal extension in the new proposition.

Can *No X is Y* be converted to *No Y is X?* Let us check. Y is universal in the old proposition and it is universal also in the new. The same is true of X. Thus the conversion is valid.

All X is Y must be converted to *Some Y is X. All men are animals* is validly converted only to *Some animals are men.* X in the new proposition is, of course, particular, whereas it was universal before. But this does not matter. The rule says that in conversion a concept may not have a wider extension, under the new proposition, than it had in the original. For a concept to have less extension in the new than it had in the old violates no logical law.

No X is Y can be converted to *No Y is X. No man is irrational* is validly converted to *No irrational beings are men.* The E proposition is converted simply. This means that the quantity of the new proposition is the same as the old. The E proposition is converted to another E. The A proposition is converted relatively, since the converted proposition has a different quantity. It is always an I proposition.

Some X is Y is converted to *Some Y is X. Some dogs are spotted* becomes *Some spotted things are dogs.* Both the old and new propositions have the same quantity. Both are I. The I proposition, like the E, makes a simple conversion.

The O propositions *Some X is not Y, Some dogs are not spotted* cannot be converted at all. The X, particular in *Some X is not Y,* would always become universal if the O proposition were converted, since X would then be a predicate of a negative proposition. Such predicates are universal.

The utility of conversion may not be evident at once. But the laws of conversion are quite useful. In writing or speaking we may wish at times to vary our expression in order to improve our style without changing the content expressed. Propositions, when converted, thus enable us to repeat a point without being monotonous.

Then too, the laws of conversion help us to order our own reason to truth and to detect the fallacies in the arguments of others. In conversion, there is always a temptation to make a simple conversion of the A proposition. Materialists do this implicitly when they argue: *All that I can see and taste and touch is real* and then conclude: *All (the whole of) reality is what I can see and taste and touch.* Some scientists have argued: *All that science can measure is meaningful,* therefore: *All that is meaningful is what science can measure.* Both of these arguments make a simple conversion of the A proposition, thereby violating the logical law which states that in conversion a concept may not have a wider extension in the new proposition than it had in the original.

Advertising often plays upon the temptation of man to make a simple conversion of the A proposition. This is apparent in some of the advertising which depends upon endorsements. Children are given the impression that all great athletes eat a certain kind of breakfast cereal, and there is a tendency to conclude that all who eat this brand of breakfast cereal will be great athletes. Or Hollywood movie stars give their endorsement, in an advertisement, to a certain kind of cosmetic. The impression is given that all beautiful women use this kind of cosmetic with the implication that all who use this cosmetic will be beautiful.

Problems

1. Explain the quantity in the subject and predicate of each of the four main kinds of categorical proposition.

2. What is meant by conversion? How are the A, E, and I propositions converted?

3. What is the relation between conversion and the principle of causality?

4. Using the comprehension of terms, show that the predicate of the A proposition is particular.

5. Convert the following propositions. It will be well to put them into strict logical form in order to identify the predicate and discover its quantity.

15.1.   [All] science is organized knowledge.
                                                    HERBERT SPENCER

15.2. No gifted eye can exhaust the significance of any object.

THOMAS CARLYLE

15.3. Some truths are clearly and distinctly known.

CF. 14.1

15.4. Every principle contains within itself the germs of prophecy.

SAMUEL TAYLOR COLERIDGE

15.5. No man is a hero to his valet.

MADAME DE CORNUEL

15.6. All men are weak.

W. S. LANDOR

15.7. Some [men] praise at morning what they blame at night.

ALEXANDER POPE

15.8. No [man] could foresee . . . that the "highbrow" conclusion that the earth is round, based on observations in pure astronomy, combined with farflung theorizing, would result in the discovery of America and Australia and the complete reorganization of world economy.

HERMAN J. MULLER

15.9. All good things which exist are the fruits of originality.

JOHN STUART MILL

15.10. Every science has been an outcast.

RALPH W. INGERSOLL

15.11. Art never expresses anything but itself.

OSCAR WILDE

(NOTE: Put this into the form of an E proposition.)

6. In the following conjunctive propositions, does the second follow logically, on logical grounds alone, from the first?

15.12. What's thine is mine, and all mine is thine.

PLAUTUS

15.13. What is fitting is honorable, and what is honorable is fitting.

CICERO

15.14. Beauty is truth, truth beauty.

JOHN KEATS

15.15. What is rational is actual and what is actual is rational.

GEORG HEGEL

7. In the light of your knowledge of conversion, criticize the following passages:

15.16.   The only proof capable of being given that an object is visible, is that people actually see it. The only proof that a sound is audible, is that people actually hear it; and so of the other sources of our experience. In like manner, I apprehend, the sole evidence it is possible to produce that anything is desirable, is that people do actually desire it.

JOHN STUART MILL

(NOTE: Start with the proposition, "Everything desired is desirable," and see whether Mill's conversion is valid.)

15.17.   You can say of it [an idea] then either that "it is useful because it is true" or that "it is true because it is useful." Both these phrases mean exactly the same thing, namely that here is an idea that gets fulfilled and can be verified.

WILLIAM JAMES

(NOTE: Start with the proposition "the true is useful," and see whether it can be converted into "the useful is the true.")

PART IV: THE THIRD ACT OF THE MIND

Chapter 16: THE NATURE AND DIVISIONS OF ARGUMENT

16.1. Since happiness consists in peace of mind, and since durable peace of mind depends on the confidence we have in the future, and since that confidence is based on the science we should have of the nature of God and the soul, it follows that that science is necessary for true happiness.

GOTTFRIED LEIBNIZ

16.2. Of those who see the essence of God, one sees him more perfectly than another. This does not take place as if one had a more perfect likeness of God than another, since that vision will not be through any likeness. But it will take place because one intellect will have a greater power or faculty to see God than another. The faculty of seeing God does not belong to the created intellect naturally, but through the light of glory. . . . Hence the intellect which has more of the light of glory will see God more perfectly.

ST. THOMAS AQUINAS

16.3. No man whatever believes, or can believe, exactly what his grandfather believed; he enlarges somewhat, by fresh discovery, his view of the universe, and consequently his theorem of the universe. . . .

THOMAS CARLYLE

16.4. As surely as there is a natural body, so surely is there a glorified body. So the Scriptures say: "The first Adam became a soul having life; the last Adam became a spirit imparting life."

ST. PAUL

16.5. A struggle for existence inevitably follows from the high rate at which all organic beings tend to increase. Every being, which during its natural lifetime produces several eggs or seeds, must suffer destruction during some period of its life, and during some season

117

or occasional year; otherwise, on the principle of geometrical increase, its numbers would quickly become so inordinately great that no country could support the product. Hence, as more individuals are produced than can possibly survive, there must in every case be a struggle for existence, either one individual with another of the same species, or with the individuals of distinct species, or with the physical conditions of life. It is the doctrine of Malthus applied with manifold force to the whole animal and vegetable kingdoms; for in this case there can be no artificial increase of food, and no prudential restraint from marriage. Although some species may now be increasing, more or less rapidly, in numbers, all cannot do so, for the whole world would not hold them.

CHARLES DARWIN

16.6.   Now it is scarcely possible to conceive how the aggregates of dissimilar particles should be so uniformly the same. If some of the particles of water were heavier than others; if a parcel of the liquid on any occasion were constituted principally of these heavier particles, it must be supposed to affect the specific gravity of the mass, a circumstance not known. Similar observations may be made on other substances. Therefore, we may conclude that *the ultimate particles of all homogeneous bodies are perfectly alike in weight, figure, etc.* In other words, every particle of water is like every other particle of water; every particle of hydrogen is like every other particle of hydrogen, etc.

JOHN DALTON

The common kind of argument.   In our analysis of the second act of the mind, we discovered that a proposition puts together concepts by affirmation or denial. There is a third act of the intellect which puts together propositions. The expression of this act of the mind is called an argument or a discourse.

The six examples of argument bear analysis. Our purpose in this chapter will be to determine not what makes them good or bad arguments but what makes them arguments at all.

In 16.1 Leibniz is saying something like this to us:

X   Y

16.1a.   (Whatever is required for peace of mind) is (necessary to true happiness.)

Z   X

(Science) is (required for peace of mind.)

Z   Y

Therefore, (science) is (necessary to true happiness.)

This argument, with letters representing what is in parentheses, has the form:

X is Y.
Z is X.
Therefore, Z is Y.

Here the mind proceeds to unite the objects of two concepts because each is united with the object of a third concept. To proceed in this way is to make an argument or logical discourse or syllogism.

Let us now look at the second case, 16.2. St. Thomas appears to reason here:

         X

16.2a. All (intellects glorified with a greater light for seeing

    Y

God) will (see God more perfectly than others).

    Z   X

16.2b. Some (intellects) will be (intellects glorified with a greater light for seeing God).

    Z   Y

16.2c. Therefore, some (intellects) will (see God more perfectly than others).

This argument, in symbols, has the form:

All X is Y.
Some Z is X.
Therefore, some Z is Y.

Carlyle in 16.3 reasons:

    X

16.3a. No (one who enlarges by fresh discovery his view of the

    Y

universe) is (a believer in exactly what his grandfather believed).

    Z   X

16.3b. Every (man) is (one who enlarges by fresh discovery his view of the universe).

    Z   Y

16.3c. Therefore, no (man) is (a believer in exactly what his grandfather believed).

Put symbolically:

No X is Y.
All Z is X.
Therefore, no Z is Y.

In all such cases, the mind compares the objects of two concepts to the object of a third, and then compares the first two objects to each other. To do this is to construct an argument.

The hidden propositions in the common argument. Almost always arguments involve hidden propositions, and seldom are all the propositions expressed in the grammatical form of *is* and *is not*. Where such conditions exist, a logician must do two things. He must first bring the hidden or implicit proposition into open and explicit form, and he must likewise express each proposition, when necessary, in strict logical form where the predicate is attributed to the subject by means of a copula.

Stalin was once asked about the possibility of bringing the Holy Father's representatives into international conferences. The remark attributed to him was: "How many legions does the Pope have?" This expression, though not even a proposition in its grammatical form, is a whole argument that may be phrased thus:

> Whoever has legions has bargaining power.
> The Holy Father has no legions.
> Therefore, the Holy Father has no bargaining power.

There is a serious error in this argument as we shall later see; the point is, however, this: it forms an argument nearly all of which, in its original grammatical expression, was left unstated but implied.

In mathematical discourse or in legal documents, arguments often occur in their pure or explicit structure, *All X is Y; all Z is X; therefore, all Z is Y.* However, in most arguments, one of the first two propositions, and sometimes the last one, is left unstated; moreover, what is actually stated does not have to correspond to the subject-copula-predicate structure by which every proposition must be finally judged. The arguing party believes that the suppressed proposition is so clearly involved in his argument that he lets the reader or hearer fill it in; and he may likewise take the liberty to combine the subject and predicate in such a way that the copula is included in the predicate itself.

But if logic is to analyze arguments, it must bring the hidden propositions into open form. Unless otherwise clear, each proposition should be expressed in simple logical structure where a predicate is applied to a subject by means of the copula.

The parts of the common argument. So far, our examples have been drawn from the simplest and most typical kind of argument. In each of our three cases, the first two propositions, called the premises, compare the objects of two concepts with the object of a third; then, in the third premise called the conclusion, the two objects are compared with each other. If in the premises, each of the two objects is identified with the third, the objects, in the conclusion, are identified with each other. But if one of the two objects is identified with the third and the other is not, as in 16.3, they are divided from each other in the conclusion by a negative proposition.

In the parts of an argument, such as the three cases so far analyzed, any concept that can stand as the subject or predicate of a proposition is called a term, at least according to the simplified usage of this book. Employing a language of terms rather than of concepts, the third term to which two others are compared in the premises is called the middle term. The term that is the predicate of the conclusion is called the major term. Major (the Latin for *greater*) is applied to this term because it is the term of widest extension as shown in the three arguments so far analyzed. The minor (*lesser*) term is the term of least extension. It is always the subject of the conclusion. The middle term, which occurs only in the premises, has an extension intermediate between that of the minor and that of the major. The premise containing the major term is called the major premise. The premise containing the minor term is called the minor premise.

All of the foregoing definitions apply only in an argument where all three propositions are categorical.

Another kind of argument. In 16.4, St. Paul argues to the existence of a spiritual body in this fashion:

$$X \qquad\qquad\qquad Y$$
16.4a.   If (there is a natural body), (there must be a spiritual body).

$$X$$
16.4b.   (There is a natural body), i.e., the original Adam.

$$Y$$
16.4c.   Therefore, (there must be a spiritual body), i.e., the new Adam who is Christ.

Symbolically:

> If X is, then Y is.
> X is.
> Therefore, Y is.

In 16.5, Darwin argues:

16.5a.   Either (the production of living seed becomes so great that no country can contain the product) or (there is a struggle for existence).

16.5b.   There is no (production of seed so great that no country can contain the product).

16.5c.   Therefore, (there is a struggle for existence).

Symbolically:

> Either X is or Y is.
> X is not.
> Therefore, Y is.

The five cases so far examined are examples of what is called a syllogism. A syllogism is an expression in which certain things being laid down, i.e., the premises, something else necessarily follows.

In the first three cases, 16.1, 16.2, and 16.3, both premises were categorical. Such a syllogism is called a categorical syllogism. In 16.4, one premise is a conditional proposition. Such a syllogism is called conditional. Finally, in 16.5, one premise is disjunctive. Such a syllogism is called disjunctive. Conditional and disjunctive syllogisms are called composite or hypothetical syllogisms. There are thus two genera of syllogisms: the *categorical* and the *hypothetical*; and the hypothetical may be divided into *conditional* and *disjunctive*. There is a third kind of hypothetical syllogism which is called *conjunctive*. It will be discussed in Chapter 34.

Up to this point, the arguments considered have all been very much alike. From two propositions or two premises, a third proposition, called the conclusion, necessarily followed. In the categorical syllogism, for example, the major and the minor terms were each compared to a third or middle term and then, in the conclusion, compared to each other.

Induction versus the syllogism. But the argument employed by Dalton in 16.6 is of a different type. There he argued in the following way:

16.6a. Every observed particle of water is like every other particle of water in weight, figure, etc.

16.6b. Every observed particle of hydrogen is like every other particle of hydrogen in weight, figure, etc.

16.6c. And so with the other elements and compounds.

16.6d. Therefore, the ultimate particles of every homogeneous substance are alike in weight, figure, etc.

This kind of procedure is called induction. In it, there is no middle term involved in the process, and more than two "premises" are certainly employed in drawing a conclusion.

Moreover, it is not so easy here, as in the case of the syllogism, to detect the hidden "premises" which the reader or hearer of the argument is left to supply on his own. Perhaps there are such premises, but the point here is to introduce induction rather than to analyze it.

The syllogism was seen to be an argument in which certain things being laid down something else necessarily follows. The best definition of induction is that it is the passage from particular facts or cases to some common or general truth without going through a middle term. Since induction does not proceed through a middle term, it cannot be called a syllogism. The inductions common to the various sciences surely involve reasoning, but the more precise determinations of what induction is can await later chapters. For the present, it is enough to note that "argument" or reasoning may be divided into two forms: syllogism and induction.

Identifying expressions as arguments. Not every combination of propositions is an argument. Where argument occurs, the conclusion must *follow* from what has been previously established. The premises of a categorical syllogism, for instance, express the causes or reasons why the conclusion must be accepted. In **16.3** Carlyle argues that no one can believe what his grandfather did *because* everyone enlarges his view of the universe. In **16.2** St. Thomas reasons that some intellects will see God more perfectly than others *because* they will have a greater light of glory. An argument must state *why* the conclusion is true.

The following lines from Walt Whitman, for instance, do not constitute an argument:

> 16.7.   Whatever may have been the case in years gone by, the true use for the imaginative faculty of modern times is to give ultimate vivification to facts, to science, and to common lines, endowing them with the glows and glories and final illustriousness which belongs to every real thing and to real things only.

It may be possible to draw a conclusion from what Whitman has said, but to do so another premise would have to be supplied.

As a preparation for the exercises and problems to follow, it should be repeated that arguments are rarely expressed in the full-blown and formal structure that they imply. The work of bringing an argument, with its hidden propositions, into an explicit form like *All X is Y, All Z is X, therefore, all Z is Y* is sometimes quite difficult. But unless such a work is done, an argument cannot be critically analyzed from the logician's point of view.

Finding the form of arguments.   There are several aids that can be given to translate a categorical argument from its grammatical brevity into its full and formal logical structure.

1. Find the conclusion before attempting to set forth the premises. The conclusion will usually not be a suppressed proposition, as all of the following exercises will show.

2. The conclusion can be found by asking what the author is trying to show. The premises will give the reason for the proposition he is trying to establish. The proposition to be established is the conclusion.

3. The conclusion can often be identified by looking for words like "therefore," or "hence." The conclusion will follow these words, if they occur.

4. If the grammatical expression of an argument contains conjunctions like "because" or "since" or "for," the conclusion will not be contained in clauses which open with such words. As giving reasons, a "because" or a "since" or a "for" clause will form a premise or premises.

5. With the conclusion isolated, the major and minor terms can now be identified. We will want to construct a major premise with the major term as either its subject or its predicate and a minor premise whose subject or predicate is the minor term. But

while looking to the major and minor term, we must also try to find the middle term, the one link in the argument not occurring in the conclusion.

6. Since our knowledge of the conclusion does not tell us whether the major and minor terms form the subject or predicate of their respective premises, the only thing to do is to try various combinations until we hit upon the proper sequence of terms that is in logical form but still corresponds to the original grammatical expression.

Problems

1. Give two definitions for the syllogism.
2. Divide the syllogism, carrying out the division to two subdivisions.
3. Define induction and show the difference between syllogism and induction.
4. Using, when necessary, the observations at the end of this chapter, put the following arguments into the formal structure of a categorical syllogism.

16.8. **Men act . . . by a rational judgment, for they deliberate about what is to be done.**

ST. THOMAS AQUINAS

(The two premises are: *Everything that deliberates about what is to be done acts by rational judgment. Men deliberate about what is to be done.* Draw the conclusion.)

16.9. **Because Babylon is vile, it does not follow that Jerusalem is vile.**

ERIC GILL

(The hidden minor is: *Jerusalem is not Babylon.* The conclusion is: *Jerusalem is not vile.* Find the major.)

16.10. **Man is the only animal that laughs and weeps, for he is the only animal that is struck by the difference between what things are and what things ought to be.**

WILLIAM HAZLITT

(The hidden major is: *The animal that is struck by the difference between what things are and what things ought to be is the only animal that laughs and weeps.*)

16.11. **The value of any commodity . . . to the person . . . who wants . . . to exchange it for other commodities is equal to the** quantity of labor which it enables him to purchase or command. Labor, therefore, is the real measure of the exchangeable value of all commodities.

ADAM SMITH

(The middle term is: *The value of any commodity to the person who wants to exchange it for other commodities.*)

16.12.   Hence, as God is supremely immutable, it belongs to Him to be eternal.

ST. THOMAS AQUINAS

(NOTE: The major premise can be put: *Whatever is supremely immutable is eternal.*)

16.13.   It is the party leaders who must be got rid of. For you see, a party leader is just like a wolf — like a starving wolf; if he is to exist at all he needs so many small beasts a year.

HENDRIK IBSEN

(NOTE: Dr. Stockmann, a character in Ibsen's *An Enemy of Society*, can be considered here to be proving either of two things or both: (a) The party leaders must be exterminated; (b) The party leader is like a wolf. State either argument.)

16.14.   And out again I curve and flow
　　　　To join the brimming river,
　　For men come and men may go,
　　　　But I go on forever.

ALFRED LORD TENNYSON

(To see the argument in this stanza from "The Song of the Brook," put as the major: *Whatever goes on forever curves and flows out again to join the brimming river.*)

16.15.   The power of gravity is of a different nature from the power of magnetism; for the magnetic attraction is not as the matter attracted. Some bodies are attracted more by the magnet; others less; most bodies not at all. The power of magnetism in one and the same body may be increased and diminished; and is sometimes far stronger for the quantity of matter than for the power of gravity. . .

ISAAC NEWTON

(NOTE: Put as the major premise: *Whatever things have distinct properties are different.* Show how the minor premise is established by induction.)

16.16. The medieval Catholic regarded all bodily creatures . . . as mirrors of their Creator and the world of spirit. Each therefore is a symbol of a spiritual, ultimately a Divine, Reality.

E. I. WATKIN

(The middle term is: *That which is a mirror of the Creator and the world of spirit.* The minor term is: *Each creature.*)

16.17. Indeed if I have dwelt at some length upon the character of our country, it has been to show that our stake in the struggle is not the same as theirs who have no such blessings to lose, and also that the panegyric of the men over whom I am now speaking might be by definite proofs established. That panegyric is now in a great measure complete; for the Athens that I have celebrated is only what the heroism of these and their like have made her.

THUCYDIDES

(NOTE: There are two syllogisms in the foregoing passage. Find one of them.)

16.18. An educated young man likes to think; he likes ideas for their own sake and likes to deal with them disinterestedly and objectively. He will find this taste an expensive one, much beyond his means, because the society around him is thoroughly indisposed toward anything of the kind. It is preëminently a society, as John Stuart Mill said, in which the test of a great mind is agreeing in the opinions of small minds. In any department of American life this is indeed the only final test; and this fact is in turn a fair measure of the extent to which our society is inimical to thought. The president of Columbia University is reported in the press as having said the other day that "thinking is one of the most unpopular amusements of the human race. Men hate it largely because they cannot do it. They hate it because if they enter upon it as a vocation or avocation it is likely to interfere with what they are doing." This is an interesting admission for the president of Columbia to make — interesting and striking. Circumstances have enabled our society to get along rather prosperously, though by no means creditably, without thought and without regard for thought, proceeding merely by a series of improvisations; hence it has always instinctively resented thought, as likely to interfere with what it was doing. Therefore, the young person who has cultivated the ability to think and the taste for thinking is at a decided disadvantage, for this resentment is now stronger and more heavily concentrated than it ever was. Any doubt on this point may be easily resolved by an examination of our current literature, especially our journalistic and periodical literature.

ALBERT JAY NOCK

(NOTE: There are several arguments in this passage. Find at least two.)

16.19.   No subject [other than heat] has more extensive relations with the progress of industry and the natural sciences; for the action of heat is always present, it penetrates all bodies and spaces, it influences the processes of the arts, and occurs in all the phenomena of the universe.

JOSEPH FOURIER

(NOTE: Despite the grammatical appearance, both premises in this argument are A propositions. The conclusion, in more simplified grammar, will read: Heat has of all subjects the most extensive relations with the progress of industry and the natural sciences.)

5. In the following passage, state the conclusion that Lewis is trying to reach and show how he establishes it by induction:

16.20.   Everyone has heard people quarrelling. Sometimes it sounds funny and sometimes it sounds merely unpleasant; but however it sounds, I believe we can learn something very important from listening to the kind of things they say. They say things like this: "How'd you like it if anyone did the same to you?" — "That's my seat, I was there first" — "Leave him alone, he isn't doing you any harm" — "Why should you shove in first?" — "Give me a bit of your orange, I gave you a bit of mine" — "Come on, you promised." People say things like that every day, educated people as well as uneducated, and children as well as grown-ups.

Now what interests me about all these remarks is that the man who makes them is not merely saying that the other man's behaviour does not happen to please him. He is appealing to some kind of standard of behaviour which he expects the other man to know about. And the other man very seldom replies: "To hell with your standard." Nearly always he tries to make out that what he has been doing does not really go against the standard, or that if it does there is some special excuse. He pretends there is some special reason in this particular case why the person who took the seat first should not keep it, or that things were quite different when he was given the bit of orange, or that something has turned up which lets him off keeping his promise. It looks, in fact, very much as if both parties had in mind some kind of Law or Rule of fair play or decent behaviour or morality or whatever you like to call it, about which they really agreed. And they have. If they had not, they might, of course, fight like animals, but they could not *quarrel* in the human sense of the word. Quarrelling means trying to show that the other man is in the wrong. And there would be no sense in trying to do that unless you and he had some sort of agreement as to what Right and Wrong are; just as there would be no sense in saying that a footballer had committed a foul unless there was some agreement about the rules of football.

C. S. LEWIS

Chapter 17: THE CATEGORICAL SYLLOGISM: ITS RULES

Like the proposition and the concept, the syllogism is a natural formal sign of an order that things possess when considered by the mind. Like those other two signs which it presupposes, the syllogism is a logical relation or logical form. As such, it has its own laws and principles. Just as the body of man has characteristics that are studied in biology, so the syllogism has a structure which is studied in logic. There are laws of logic, just as there are laws of nature. Where the laws of the syllogism are obeyed, the syllogism will perform its proper work, which is to put order into our thoughts about things.

There must be three terms. In the case of the categorical syllogism, there are five rules which must be obeyed in order that an argument be correct and valid. Consider the following case:

17.1. All gasoline is liquid.
All kerosene is inflammable.
Therefore, all gasoline is inflammable.

This is obviously not a valid syllogism. The reason is that it has four terms: gasoline, kerosene, inflammable, and liquid. By sheer accident, the conclusion happens to be true. But, when there are four terms in a syllogism, the conclusion cannot properly relate two terms to each other because the premises have failed to relate the two terms to a common third term. Gasoline is compared with liquid, and kerosene with inflammable. W is compared to X, and Y to Z. But we cannot compare W and Z in the conclusion since we have not compared them to a common third term in the premises.

To have four terms violates the very nature of a syllogism, and the result is simply no syllogism at all.

One of the more common ways of forming a syllogism with four terms is to use equivocal expressions, words having more than one meaning. The following is a very exaggerated example of an equivocal term in a syllogism.

> 17.2. All liberals are freethinkers.
> All educated men are liberal.
> Therefore, all educated men are freethinkers.

In this apparent syllogism, liberal is used in two distinct senses: Liberal as applied to education means education where the mind has for its end the mind's own good, namely knowledge. In its second meaning, liberal, because of certain historical circumstances, means freedom from all restraint; the liberal, in this sense, is the freethinker, divorced from all the conviction that flows from the pursuit of truth. "Liberal" is used, in each case, for quite opposite meanings. The apparent syllogism in 17.2 in reality has four terms because one of the terms is equivocal.

With the preliminary notion that by *impression* is meant sense impression or sensation, let us examine the following passage:

> 17.3. **Now since all ideas are derived from impressions, and are nothing but copies and representations of them, whatever is true of the one must be acknowledged concerning the other.**
> **DAVID HUME**

The meaning of this passage can be formulated as follows:

> 17.4. What is true of originals is true of copies.
> Ideas are copies of (sense) impressions.
> Therefore, whatever is true of (sense) impressions is true of ideas.

It is obvious that there are more than three terms in Hume's argument. For one thing his notion of truth is equivocal. Only in a qualified way can what is true of originals be true also of copies. In one sense, what is true of a person may be true also of a picture; for instance, the picture will look like the person. But in a much deeper sense, what is true of the one is not true of the other. The picture is merely canvas and pigment. The person is alive. Hume's notion of truth, here, is thus equivocal.

Even if we admitted that an idea is a copy or representation of a sense impression, it would not thereby follow that an idea is the same as the sense impression, nor that what is true of one is true fully of the other. A representation of arsenic is not arsenic, and what is true of arsenic, e.g., its poisonous character, is not true of the idea of arsenic. We may then affirm that Hume's conclusion does not follow.

What we have just discussed may be summarized as follows:

Rule I: *A syllogism must have three and only three terms.*

The distribution of terms. Next consider the following cases:

17.5.   All scientific knowledge is a work of reason.
        All scientific knowledge is true.
        Therefore, all that is true is a work of reason.

17.6.   All married people know about marriage problems.
        No priests are married people.
        Therefore, no priests know about marriage problems.

In analyzing the foregoing arguments let us recall, from Chapter 15, our rules concerning the quantity and quality of propositions.

(a) Universal propositions have universal or distributed subjects and particular propositions have particular or undistributed subjects.

(b) Affirmative propositions have particular or undistributed predicates, and negative propositions have universal or distributed predicates.

In **17.5,** the minor term (true) as predicate of an affirmative proposition is undistributed in the minor premise but distributed as subject of a universal proposition in the conclusion, and in **17.6,** the major term (know about marriage problems) as predicate of an affirmative proposition is undistributed in the major premise but distributed as predicate of a negative proposition in the conclusion. In each case, a term is used in a wider extension in the conclusion than in the premises. Where this occurs, the conclusion says more than the premises warrant. The conclusion, as the effect of the premises, cannot contain more than its causes. **17.5** and **17.6** are, therefore, invalid syllogisms. **17.5** has what is called an invalid minor term and **17.6** an invalid major term. The invalidity is caused by the use of each term in a wider extension in the conclusion than in the premises.

Let us look at one more case.

17.7. There are no public institutions for the education of women, and there is accordingly nothing useless, absurd, or fantastical in the common course of their education.

ADAM SMITH

The argument may be formulated in the following way:

17.8. All people educated in public institutions are persons whose education involves the useless, absurd, and fantastical.
No women are educated in public institutions.
Therefore, no women are persons whose education involves the useless, absurd, and fantastical.

The syllogism is invalid, because of an invalid major or minor term. The reader is left to determine which term is invalidly used.

As a result of the preceding analysis, we may now formulate the following:

Rule II: *No term may have a wider extension in the conclusion than it had in the premises.*

In the understanding of this rule, it should be noted that a term may have less extension in the conclusion than it had in the premises, and it may have the same extension in both cases. The rule says only that a term may not have a greater extension in the conclusion than it had in the premises.

The undistributed middle. Now consider this case:

17.9. All chickens are born from eggs.
All turkeys are born from eggs.
Therefore, all turkeys are chickens.

It is apparent at once that there is something wrong with this reasoning. The search to find the error will enable us to learn something more about the syllogism. Since it is clear that the major and minor terms satisfy Rule II, let us inspect the middle term. As predicate of affirmative propositions, the middle term in both premises is undistributed and particular. Does this make a difference in the function of the middle term?

To answer this question, recall that the middle term is the common term to which the major and minor terms are related in the premises. Any term in its function as a middle must be compared to both the major and minor terms by the very nature of the syllogism itself. However, where the middle term is particular or undistributed in extension, there is no common third term.

In our example 17.9, *chickens* are compared *to things born from chickens' eggs,* and *turkeys to things born from turkeys' eggs.* W is compared to X, and Y to Z, but W and Y are not compared to a common third term. This is equivalent to putting four terms in a syllogism.

A circle diagram can help to clarify our analysis. Let the large circle represent the whole extension of *animals formed from eggs,* and let the smaller circles represent particular extensions of *animals formed from various kinds of eggs.*

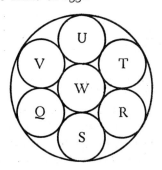

Thus, let Q represent animals formed from chickens' eggs, R animals formed from turkeys' eggs, S things formed from pigeons' eggs, etc. Our syllogism compares chickens with Q and turkeys with R. Hence, the extreme terms of the conclusion, not being compared with a common third term, cannot be compared with each other. Our syllogism involves the fallacy of an undistributed middle term.

Arthur Eddington has written the following:

> **17.10. My own practice would probably be covered by the definition that a thing may be said to be real if it is the goal of a type of unity to which I personally attach importance.**

It is clear that Eddington is intending to identify what is real by laying down the following major premise:

> **Whatever is real is the goal of a type of unity to which I attach importance.**

It would be almost impossible to complete this syllogism without committing the fallacy of an undistributed middle term. As subject of a minor premise, whose predicate "the goal . . ." would be that of the major, we could put men, animals, plants, Martians, the day after tomorrow, unicorns, etc. Eddington's definition of what is real thus provides a major premise for a syllogism that is almost sure to be invalid by having an undistributed middle term. All of this analysis leads to the following:

Rule III: *The middle term must be distributed at least once.*

This rule, it should be noted, does not require that the middle term always be distributed (universal) but only that the middle term be distributed once. The following syllogism, where the middle term is distributed only once, is valid:

> 17.11. All eggs are fragile.
> Some eggs are white.
> Therefore, some white things are fragile.

The reader can verify this by drawing a large circle representing all the fragile eggs which, according to the major premise, constitute all the eggs that there are. Those eggs that are white will be in it.

The case of two negative propositions. Let us analyze another argument.

> 17.12. Nothing easy is worthwhile.
> Nothing good is easy.
> Therefore, nothing good is worthwhile.

Once again there is an invalid syllogism and hence no syllogism at all. The reason lies in the two negative premises. Where both extremes differ from the third term, it is impossible to conclude whether they differ or not in relation to each other. To say, for instance, that Jack and Virginia are not related to Dorothy does not entitle us to conclude whether they are related to each other or not. Jack and Virginia may be brother and sister and Dorothy may be unrelated to either, or Jack and Virginia may be two neighbors while Dorothy may be a third neighbor. Our premises do not entitle us to say which of these two cases holds, if either. Things that are each unrelated to a third thing may or may not be related to each other. Hence:

Rule IV: *From two negative premises, no conclusion can be drawn.*

The conclusion and the weaker part. There are two final cases, leading to a fifth and final rule:

> 17.13. No dishonest person is trustworthy.
>   Some lawyers are dishonest.
>   Therefore, all trustworthy persons are lawyers.
> 17.14. No man is perfect.
>   Some men are presidents.
>   Therefore, some presidents are perfect.

It will be observed that in 17.13 one of the premises is particular while the conclusion is universal, and in 17.14 one of the premises is negative while the conclusion is affirmative. The relationship of the premises to the conclusion in each case violates the principle of causality. As the effect of the premises, the conclusion in each case would be greater than its cause. For the universal conclusion in 17.13 is certainly stronger than the particular proposition which forms the minor premise, and the affirmative conclusion in 17.14 is stronger than the negative proposition which forms the major. By the principle of causality the conclusion, as the effect of the premises, can say no more than the premises warrant. Hence the following:

Rule V: *The conclusion must follow the weaker part.*

A particular proposition is weaker than a universal one, and a negative proposition is weaker than an affirmative one. Expanded in light of these remarks, Rule V states that if a premise is particular the conclusion must be particular, and if a premise is negative the conclusion must be negative.

Problems

1. State the rules for the categorical syllogism.
2. Give a reason for each rule.
3. Explain how each rule is related to the nature of the syllogism.
4. Explain how a violation of Rule V might sometimes be also a violation of Rule II.
5. Criticize the following arguments in the light of the rules for the categorical syllogism. Should any of the syllogisms be valid, mark them as such:

   a) All who come from bad homes are victims of parental neglect.
   Some juvenile delinquents do not come from bad homes.

(1)

the concerto is sent to the members

M is P
S is M
S is P

Studying is done by students
students study their only.
easily are escilcaly freshman
freshman are students

Pio M
M is S
S is P

2) all trees have green leaves
all ... have green leaves
all oaks are trees

P is M
S is M?
S is ?

3) flowers have

Tulips have petals   M is P
Tulips are flowers   M is S
flowers have petals   S is P

1) Music is sweet to the ears.

Therefore, some juvenile delinquents are not the victims of parental neglect.

b) All matter obeys wave equations. *S is M*
All waves obey wave equations. *P is M (fig 2)*
Therefore, all matter is waves. *S is P*

c) All that is free from direction is for its own sake. *M is P*
No art is free from direction. *S is M (fig. 1)*
Therefore, all art is for its own sake. *S is P*

d) All books are printed. *M is P*
The book of nature is a book. *S is M (fig. 1)*
Therefore, the book of nature is printed. *S is P*

e) All that is good is pleasant. *P is M*
All eating is pleasant. *S is M (fig. 2)*
Therefore, all eating is good. *S is P*

f) All human action is conditioned by circumstances. *M is P*
All human action involves morality. *M is S (fig. 3)*
Therefore, all that involves morality is conditioned by circumstance. *S is P*

g) Some men are heavy. *M is P*
No man is descended from an ape. *M is S (fig. 3)*
Therefore, all descendants from an ape are heavy. *S is P*

h) All patriots are voters. *P is M*
Some citizens are not voters. *S is M (fig. 2)*
Therefore, some citizens are not patriots. *S is P*

i) Whatever is desirable is lovable. *M is P*
Nothing that causes pain is desirable. *S is M (fig. 1)*
Therefore, nothing that causes pain is lovable. *S is P*

j) No oak trees bear fruit. *S is M*
No maple trees bear fruit. *P is M (fig 2)*
Therefore, no oak trees are maples. *S is P*

k) All Communists favor more social legislation. *P is M*
Some Congressmen favor more social legislation. *S is M (fig. 2)*
Therefore, some Congressmen are Communists. *S is P*

l) All educated people have worked hard. *M is P*
Some students are not educated. *S is M (fig. 1)*
Therefore, some students have not worked hard. *S is P*

m) Mathematicians know what mathematics is. *M is P*
No philosopher is a mathematician. *S is M (fig. 1)*
Therefore, no philosopher knows what mathematics is. *S is P*

6. The following arguments violate the rules discussed in this chapter. Before criticizing the arguments, put each one in the

proper syllogistic form as in exercise 4 at the end of the preceding chapter:

> 17.15. . . . all living things again including ourselves work according to regular laws, in just the same way as do non-living things, except that living things are much more complicated . . . Looked at objectively and scientifically, a man is an exceedingly complex piece of chemical machinery.
>
> JULIAN HUXLEY

(NOTE: Put as the minor premise: Man works according to regular laws, i.e., those governing the physical world.)

> 17.16. Never in past geologic time can there have been so complex a vegetation as today, for never were there so many climates, such mountains, such deserts, such seas, such arctics, such island archipelagos, such insularity everywhere.
>
> DONALD CULROSS PEATTIE

(NOTE: Peattie is trying to conclude: Past geologic time did not permit complex vegetation like ours. He is using as a minor: A variety of climates, mountains, deserts, seas, arctics, islands, and other insularity permits complex vegetation like ours.)

> 17.17. A machine can handle information; it can calculate, conclude, and choose; it can perform reasonable operations with information. A machine, therefore, can think.
>
> EDMUND CALLIS BERKELEY

(NOTE: Berkeley is assuming as a major premise the well-known truth: One who can think can handle information, calculate, conclude, choose, and perform reasonable operations with information.)

> 17.18. To imagine a man perfectly free and not subject to the law of inevitability, we must imagine him all alone, *beyond space, beyond time, and free from dependence on causes.*
>
> LEO TOLSTOY

(NOTE: Tolstoy is trying to argue that no man is free because whatever is beyond space, time, and dependence on causes is free.)

> 17.19. A miracle is a violation of the laws of nature; and as a firm and unalterable experience has established these laws, the proof against a miracle, from the very nature of the fact, is as entire as any argument from experience can possibly be imagined.
>
> DAVID HUME

(NOTE: Hume is trying to argue that miracles are not possible because what is established by firm and unalterable experience is possible.)

17.20. Mathematicians . . . do not ascend into any inquiry concerning those transcendental maxims which influence all particular sciences . . . Mathematics . . . doth consequently participate of the errors involved in them.

GEORGE BERKELEY

(NOTE: Think of Berkeley's argument as an attempt to prove that since mathematics is not a study of the maxims which influence all the sciences it participates in the errors of these sciences.)

17.21. The importance of Man, which is the one indispensable dogma of the theologians, receives no support from a scientific view of the future of the solar system.

BERTRAND RUSSELL

(NOTE: Russell is arguing in this context that the cosmos has existed and will exist for long ages and that man's residence on earth has been very short; in other words, since whatever is long in duration is important, man is not important.)

17.22. What things may be in themselves, I know not, and need not know, because a thing is never presented to me otherwise than as a phenomenon.

IMMANUEL KANT

(NOTE: Would it be correct to formulate Kant's argument as follows: Whatever is presented as a phenomenon, i.e., appearance, is known; but what things are in themselves is not presented as a phenomenon; therefore, what things are in themselves is not known. After deciding whether our formulation is equivalent to Kant's, discover whether the syllogism is valid.)

17.23. Metaphysical propositions are neither true nor false because they assert nothing.

RUDOLF CARNAP

(The major can read: Whatever does not assert anything is neither true nor false.)

17.24. Solid bodies are related, with respect to their possible dispositions, as are bodies in Euclidian geometry of three dimensions. Then the propositions of Euclid contain affirmations as to the relations of practically rigid bodies.

ALBERT EINSTEIN

(Einstein's argument may be translated: Geometry and natural science study solid bodies; therefore, geometry is a natural science.)

17.25. But he [Hobie, a cat] cannot master words and language.

This is in some respects fortunate for Hobie, for he will not suffer from hallucinations provoked by bad language.

STUART CHASE

17.26.   Since evil occurs, God must be willing that it should occur.

WILLIAM PEPPERELL MONTAGUE

(Write as the minor: *God wills what occurs.*)

17.27.   Since no man has a natural authority over his fellow, and force creates no right, we must conclude that conventions form the basis of all legitimate authority among men.

JEAN-JACQUES ROUSSEAU

(Rousseau is arguing that since no man is a natural authority and all men are determined by convention, therefore determination by convention is an [natural] authority.)

Chapter 18: THE CATEGORICAL SYLLOGISM: ITS FIGURES

18.1. Anything composed of parts is destructible.
Everything physical is composed of parts.
Therefore, everything physical is destructible.

18.2. All laws protect freedom.
No evils protect freedom.
Therefore, no evils are laws.

18.3. All cows are herbivorous.
All cows give milk.
Therefore, some animals that give milk are herbivorous.

The three figures. The principle of the categorical syllogism is that two terms, identified in the premises with a third term, are identified in the conclusion with each other and that two terms, one of which in the premises is identified with a third while the other is not, are disjoined from each other in the conclusion.

The middle term, hereafter designated as M, is the key to the syllogism. It represents the cause or reason why the minor, S, and the major, P, are united or not in the conclusion. Without a middle term there is no syllogism, but only direct, noncausal knowledge, e.g., that the sun is shining.

The middle term may take various positions in a syllogism. In 18.1 it is the subject of the major premise and predicate of the minor. In 18.2 it is the predicate of both premises, and in 18.3 it is the subject of both premises. The position of the middle term in the premises determines what is called the figure of the syllogism, where figure is to be understood as the arrangement of terms in the premises. Figure is usually regarded as a property only of the categorical syllogism.

M is P	P is M	M is P
S is M	S is M	M is S
S is P	S is P	S is P

Thus, in 18.1, the syllogism is of the form: M is P, S is M, S is P. This is called the first figure, and in it the middle term is the subject of the major premise and predicate of the minor.

In 18.2, the syllogism is of the form: P is M, S is M, S is P. This is called the second figure, and in it the middle term is the predicate of both premises.

In 18.3, the syllogism has the form: M is P, M is S, S is P. This is called the third figure, and in it the middle term is the subject of both premises.

The two weak figures. Certain observations can be made about these figures in the way of showing their relative merits.

In the second figure, only a negative conclusion can be drawn, as an examination of the middle term shows. In order for it to be distributed at least once, one of the premises must be negative. If both were affirmative, the middle term as the predicate in each case would always have an undistributed extension. Once there is a negative premise, there must also be a negative conclusion according to the weaker-part rule of the preceding chapter.

As only a negative conclusion can be drawn in the second figure, only a particular conclusion can be drawn in the third. To show this, let us assume that the conclusion is universal and then show the assumption to be impossible.

If S is distributed to make the conclusion universal, it must also be distributed in the minor premise. The only way in which S could be distributed in the minor premise would be for the minor premise to be negative so that its predicate will be universal. But if the minor premise is negative, the conclusion must also be negative by the weaker-part rule, and that means that P in the conclusion will be distributed. The only way in which it could be validly distributed in the conclusion would be on the grounds of its being distributed in the major premise. The major premise, for its predicate to be distributed, would likewise have to be negative, and since, on our supposition that the conclusion is universal, the minor must also be negative, we now have a syllogism with two negative premises from which, of course, no conclusion can be drawn. Our supposition of a universal conclusion must, therefore, be impossible. Hence, in the third figure, only a particular conclusion can be drawn.

In the terminology of the last chapter, only a weak conclusion can be drawn in the second and third figures. The most perfect figure is the first. Both particular and negative conclusions can be drawn in it, but it is the only figure where universal, affirmative conclusions can be drawn. Since scientific knowledge is always universal and primarily affirmative in content, the first figure of the syllogism is the only one that is strictly scientific.

The fourth figure. On the basis of possible positions of M, it would seem that there can be still another figure: P is M, M is S, S is P. Such a figure, where the middle term is the predicate of major premise and the subject of the minor has been alleged in the history of logic as a so-called fourth figure of the syllogism.

But it is not a genuine figure.

In order to understand why this is so, it must be pointed out that the middle term does not function as a merely mechanical link between S and P. In a more proper sense, it is called a middle term because it is intermediate in its extension between S and P. In the perfect figure, S is in M and M is in P. In 18.1, *physical* has the least extension among the three terms; what is composed of parts has a wider extension, since it includes both physical and mathematical; and what is destructible is still wider since it includes everything outside of God. In the first figure, S is in M and M is in P. The second figure, where P is in M and S is in M, preserves one of these relations (the one underlined), and in the third figure, where M is in P and M is in S, the other relation is preserved. The second and third figures yield imperfect syllogisms. To the extent that they preserve one of the relations in the premises of a perfect syllogism, they are syllogisms, and to the extent that these relations are missing, they are imperfect.

But the alleged fourth figure preserves nothing of the relationship among the terms of the perfect syllogism and hence fails to provide a syllogism at all. It is possible, in grammar, to have a fourth figure, but logically such an expression does not constitute a syllogism.

The syllogism is not a mere mechanism. Its character depends upon the extension of terms and not upon their merely mechanical position according to possible algebraic combinations of M, S, and P.

Problems

1. What is meant by a figure of a syllogism?
2. Define the three figures.
3. Show why the second figure yields only a negative conclusion and the third only a particular conclusion.
4. Why is the fourth figure not a genuine figure of the syllogism?
5. Identify the figures of the following arguments:
   a) No mushrooms are toadstools.
      Some fungi are toadstools.
      Therefore some fungi are not mushrooms.
   b) All horses are quadrupeds.
      Some horses are fast.
      Therefore, some fast things are quadrupeds.
   c) Whoever learns everything too soon will never know anything.
      Some men learn everything too soon.
      Therefore, some men will never know anything.

6. The German philosopher, Hegel, denied the principle of contradiction: It is impossible for a thing to be and not be at the same time. Here is a summary of his argument:

> 18.4.   Being is abstract and general.
>   Non-being is abstract and general.
>   Therefore, non-being is being.
>
> GEORG HEGEL

(What is the figure of the argument? Is the argument valid?)

7. From the following propositions, construct an argument and identify the figure involved:

> 18.5.   Play . . . is a sign of imperfect adaptation. It is proper to childhood.
>
> GEORGE SANTAYANA

> 18.6.   . . . every body is in potentiality. It is therefore impossible that God should be a body.
>
> ST. THOMAS AQUINAS

(St. Thomas is drawing the conclusion: *God is not a body*, using the suppressed minor premise: *God is not in potentiality*. What figure is being used, if the syllogism is to avoid the fallacy of two negative premises?)

8. Construct an argument from the following propositions, and identify the figure involved:

18.7. Doctors can cure people by chemical and surgical interference, but they can only keep them well by teaching them.

GILBERT HIGHET

18.8. What distinguishes an historian of religions from an ordinary historian is that he is concerned with facts which, while they are historical facts, are manifestations of behavior far transcending the ordinary historical behavior of human beings.

MIRCEA ELIADE

(Write as the conclusion: *An historian of religions is not an historian of fact*, and arrange the premises so that the syllogism will be in the second figure.)

18.9. An electron [when studied] had an electric charge. It had mass. It had an angular momentum. It had a magnetic moment. It had position and velocity. And these things seemed to justify the designation of it by the term "particle."

W. V. HOUSTON

(If you take as the major premise: *All particles have charge, mass, angular momentum, position, and velocity,* can you draw a valid conclusion in the second figure? Explain.)

18.10. For, I ask, what is man in Nature? A cipher compared with the Infinite, an All compared with Nothing, a mean between zero and all.

BLAISE PASCAL

(Formulate an argument from this passage to draw the conclusion that: *Man is a mean between nothing and everything.* Use as the major premise: *Whoever is a Nothing in comparison with the Infinite and an All in comparison with Nothing is a mean between nothing and everything.* Identify the figure of the syllogism.)

18.11. To a good many students of contemporary literature, the late André Gide was coming to displace James Joyce as the representative man of letters of our generation, and Gide was no surrealist. . .

JOSEPH WOOD KRUTCH

(How can we show from a minor premise: *Gide was a representative man of letters of our generation,* that *some representative man of letters was not a surrealist.* In what figure will the syllogism be?)

18.12. He [modern man] finds himself surrounded by marvellous instruments, healing medicines, watchful governments, comfortable privileges. On the other hand, he is ignorant how difficult it is to invent those medicines and those instruments and to insure their production in the future.

ORTEGA Y GASSET

(If a conclusion is drawn from these two propositions, in what figure will the syllogism be?)

18.13.   For we can explain nothing but what we can reduce to laws whose object can be given in some possible experience. But freedom is a mere idea, the objective reality of which can in no way be shown according to natural laws or in any possible experience.

IMMANUEL KANT

(If Kant is drawing a conclusion from the following premises: *Whatever is an object of possible experience is explainable* and *Freedom is not an object of possible experience*, state the figure employed and evaluate the syllogism.)

Chapter 19:   THE HYPOTHETICAL SYLLOGISM

There is another type of syllogism besides the categorical one. It is called the hypothetical syllogism, and it in turn is subdivided into the conditional syllogism, the disjunctive syllogism, and the conjunctive syllogism. The latter will be discussed in Chapter 34. The present chapter will be concerned only with the conditional and the disjunctive syllogisms.

19.1. If federal public housing will be undertaken, taxes will rise.
Federal public housing will be undertaken.
Therefore, taxes will rise.
19.2. If federal public housing will be undertaken, taxes will rise.
Taxes will rise.
Therefore, federal public housing will be undertaken.

The way to affirm in a conditional syllogism. Both of these cases illustrate the conditional syllogism — a syllogism in which the major premise is a conditional proposition. The "if" clause in this premise is called the *antecedent*; the concluding clause is called the *consequent*.

19.1 is a valid argument. The major premise gives a condition upon which the consequent depends for its truth. The minor premise, by affirming the antecedent, states that this condition is fulfilled; and the conclusion then affirms the consequent which the truth of the antecedent requires.

19.2, however, is invalid. The minor premise affirms the consequent and the conclusion affirms the antecedent. But the truth of the consequent does not necessarily involve the truth of the antecedent. Taxes could rise because of numerous other circumstances besides public housing legislation. For instance, an outlay for defense, economic aid to foreign nations, federal subsidies for education, federal public housing — all could cause an increase in taxes, and to affirm that taxes will rise does not, in itself, enable us to conclude which of the possible causes have produced the increase. Hence, it is invalid in a conditional syllogism to affirm the consequent and then affirm the antecedent. This is called the fallacy of affirming the consequent.

Rule I: *Affirm the antecedent and affirm the consequent.*

A critical awareness of this rule is especially important in the evaluation of theories in physical and biological investigations. In such fields of knowledge, an hypothesis, like Dalton's atomic theory (16.6), is often proposed and consequences deduced from it that can be tested by observation. If the consequences drawn from a theory agree with results of experiment, the theory itself is supported. Such a procedure, however, runs the risk of affirming the consequent prior to affirming the antecedent, and many who are unacquainted with logical laws actually commit this fallacy by holding a theory to be true because of the true consequences to which it leads. Respectable scientists are, of course, aware that a theory is only tentative and that no matter how strong a theory may be, there may some day be another theory to account as well, or even better, for the facts.

Scientific method and affirming the consequent. This is not to say that procedures like Dalton's are to be rejected. Where we are dealing with a world too large or small to be experienced or too distant in space or time to be directly known, we can make only conjectures and then choose the theory whose consequences best agree with what we observe. There is simply no other way of proceeding in areas too remote to be experienced directly. But the logical limitations of such reasoning should always be remembered lest a theory, at most only probable, be taken as true. Moreover, it should be borne in mind that there are other valid means of obtaining knowledge besides that of hypothetical reasoning.

Chemistry, physics, and biology are each organized internally by a broad theory of some kind. In chemistry, the atomic theory, supported more firmly but still not fully proved by evidence acquired since Dalton's time, remains the leading idea organizing the whole field. The reasoning here proceeds:

If the atomic theory is valid, then chemistry can explain chemical compounds, etc., by means of it.
But by means of it, chemistry can explain chemical compounds, etc.
Therefore, the atomic theory is valid.

Biology is organized by the theory of evolution. The major premise reads:

If the evolutionary theory is accepted, then biology can explain the origins and structures of living things by means of it.

The minor premise and the conclusion are similar in their logical direction to the example above which is taken from chemistry. The Newtonian system of physics is organized by the theory of universal gravitation. The reasoning runs from the major premise:

If universal gravitation holds, then physics can account for observed cosmic motion, e.g., motions on the earth, motions in the heavens, the behavior of the tides, etc.

The minor premise and conclusion are similar in structure to those of the foregoing examples.

Where such explanations are taken as anything more than probable, there is the fallacy of affirming the consequent. Theories should be accepted as the best knowledge we can get in dealing with that part of the universe which is closed to our direct experience, but by the same token such theories should be accorded only a provisional acceptance, to be held until a better explanation is devised.

From another viewpoint, it may look as though the procedures in chemistry, biology, and physics have not been fairly presented. More specifically, it might seem possible to change the major premise in the example from chemistry so that it will say: If chemistry can explain chemical compounds, etc., by means of the atomic theory, then the atomic theory is valid. The same reversal of direction might seem possible in connection with the evolutionary theory of biology and with the theory of universal gravitation.

But our new grammatical expression does not reflect the logical movement of the mind in its approach to these three theories of modern science. Atoms are somehow regarded as the causes or reasons for the observed facts which they explain. They are taken as the conditions and the chemical compounds, etc., are regarded as their consequences. Our initial formulation of the reasoning to the atomic theory is in accordance with the logical direction which such reasoning embodies. The same is true of the theories of evolution and gravitation. It is quite generally admitted by the scientists themselves that theories are accepted because of the consequences to which they lead. The law against affirming the consequent of a conditional syllogism and then affirming the antecedent should lead us to follow the example of scientists themselves in being quite cautious about scientific theory.

The way to deny in a conditional syllogism. Let us now consider another conditional argument:

> 19.3.   If Russia is ready for atomic war, it has a stockpile of H bombs.
> Russia does not have a stockpile of H bombs.
> Therefore, Russia is not ready for atomic war.
>
> 19.4.   If Russia is ready for atomic war, it has a stockpile of H bombs.
> Russia is not ready for atomic war.
> Therefore, Russia does not have a stockpile of H bombs.

19.3 is a valid argument, but **19.4** is not. Let us see why.

As in the previous two cases, the major premises affirm that the consequent is true on condition that the antecedent is true. To deny the consequent, as in **19.3**, is to deny also a condition which would necessarily produce it. Hence, in a conditional syllogism, where the minor premise denies the consequent, the conclusion denies the antecedent.

But in **19.4**, where we deny the antecedent, we are simply denying one of the conditions which would produce the consequent, i.e., a large stockpile of H bombs. Russia could be unprepared for atomic war and yet possess a large stockpile of H bombs; for instance, she may not have the air force or the civilian defense to make her wholly ready for atomic war, although she could possess one of the elements of preparedness, namely the bombs in question. Hence, to deny that Russia is wholly ready for atomic war does not deny that she has at least one of the factors which would contribute to that readiness, namely, a stockpile of H bombs. In short, it is invalid to deny the antecedent of a conditional syllogism and then deny the consequent.

Rule II: *Deny the consequent and deny the antecedent.*

There are then two valid procedures and two invalid ones in resolving the conditional syllogism:

Valid procedures	Invalid procedures
Affirm antecedent and affirm consequent.	Affirm consequent and affirm antecedent.
Deny consequent and deny antecedent.	Deny antecedent and deny consequent.

The disjunctive syllogism. The disjunctive syllogism is a hypothetical syllogism in which the major premise is a disjunctive proposition.

> 19.5. Either liberal knowledge is for its own sake, or it is for the sake of something else.
> Liberal knowledge is not for the sake of something else.
> Therefore, it is for its own sake.
> 19.6. Either government is for the common good or it is for the good of only the few.
> Government is for the common good.
> Therefore, it is not for the good of only the few.

This is the simplest kind of disjunctive syllogism. In it there are just two alternatives.

Both of these syllogisms are valid, and it is easy to see that they involve simple rules. In **19.5** the disjunctive syllogism is resolved by the following:

Rule I: *Deny one of the alternatives and affirm the other.*

In **19.6**, the disjunctive syllogism is resolved by the following:

Rule II: *Affirm one of the alternatives and deny the other.*

If there are more than two alternatives, e.g., either a living thing is a plant or it is an animal or a man, these simple rules must be modified. But for the present, we need not worry about more complicated disjunctive arguments. It is also possible to have alternatives which do not exclude each other, as will be shown in Chapters 33–34. But this kind of disjunction will not be considered in this chapter.

What makes a disjunctive syllogism invalid is usually not a violation of one of the foregoing two rules but failure to construct a valid disjunctive premise. To be a valid major premise in a disjunctive syllogism, a disjunctive proposition must fulfill the following two requirements: First, the enumeration of alternatives must be complete; and second, the alternatives must exclude one another.

The following disjunctive proposition would contradict the first requirement: *Either the Red Sox or the Yankees will win the pennant.* The alternatives are incomplete since it is possible for any other team in the American League to win the pennant. The proposition, kept in the form of two alternatives, should be amended to read: *Either the Red Sox or some other American League team will win the pennant.* In this form, the proposition can be a valid premise in a simple disjunctive argument.

The following proposition would violate the second requirement: *The healthiest class of people are either Americans or farmers.* Here the alternatives do not exclude each other, because there are farmers who are Americans. The proposition should be amended to read in one of the following ways: *The healthiest class of people are either Americans or non-Americans. The healthiest class of people are either farmers or nonfarmers.* In either of these forms, a disjunctive proposition can be the premise of a simple disjunctive syllogism.

The priority of the categorical syllogism. The categorical syllogism, however, is the fundamental type of argumentation. It is here that it can be best seen that in a syllogism we compare two things with a common third thing and then compare the two things with each other.

The disjunctive syllogism can be reduced to the conditional form and the conditional syllogism can be reduced to categorical form. Let us show this in **19.6.** Changing 19.6 from disjunctive to conditional form, we have:

> **If government is for the common good, it is not for the good of only the few.**
> **Government is for the common good.**
> **Therefore, government is not for the good of only the few.**

Now let us change it from the conditional to the categorical syllogism:

Anything that is for the common good is not for the good of only the few.

Government is for the common good.

Therefore, government is not for the good of only the few.

To argue in syllogistic form is basically to use the categorical syllogism.

Problems

1. Define the hypothetical syllogism and identify its various types.

2. What is the reason for calling the disjunctive proposition hypothetical?

3. State the rules for the conditional syllogism.

4. Explain the relationship of scientific theory to "affirming the consequent."

5. State the rules for the disjunctive syllogism. What is the most common fallacy in connection with the disjunctive syllogism?

6. Show how the disjunctive syllogism is reducible to the conditional and the conditional to the categorical.

7. Reduce the disjunctive syllogism in 16.4 to a conditional syllogism.

8. Evaluate the following arguments:

   a) If life exists on Mars, then Mars has an atmosphere.
      Mars has an atmosphere.
      Therefore, life exists on Mars.

   b) Either the football team won or it lost.
      It did not win.
      Therefore, it lost.

   c) If life involves quantity, it is physical.
      Life does not involve quantity.
      Therefore, life is not physical.

   d) If atoms are ultimate particles, they are indivisible.
      Atoms are not indivisible.
      Therefore, they are not ultimate.

9. Evaluate the following arguments:

19.7. If the real nature of any creature leads him and is adopted to such and such purposes only, or more than to any other; this is reason to believe that the author of that nature intended it for those purposes. Thus, there is no doubt that the eye was intended for us to see with.

SAMUEL BUTLER

(Taking the last statement as evidence for the antecedent, what follows?)

19.8.   But if art passes from mind to mind, it would leave one mind and abide in another; in this case, nobody would teach an art except by losing it. . .

ST. AUGUSTINE

(The second proposition denies the consequent.)

19.9.   Let us weigh gain and loss in calling heads that God is. Reckon these two chances: if you win, you win all; if you lose, you lose naught. Then do not hesitate, wager that He is.

BLAISE PASCAL

(Show that this argument is disjunctive. What kind of proposition is employed to prove each alternative?)

19.10.   It is not enough to say that history is historical judgment, it is necessary to add that every judgment is an historical judgment or, quite simply, history. If judgment is a relation between a subject and a predicate, then the subject or the event, whatever it is that is being judged, is always an historical fact, a becoming, a process under way, for there are no immobile facts nor can such things be envisaged in the world of reality.

BENEDETTO CROCE

(Croce's initial proposition depends for its validity on the disjunctive proposition which the passage contains. Evaluate this proposition carefully.)

19.11.   If ideas, meanings, conceptions, notions, theories, systems are instrumental to an active reorganization of the given environment, to a removal of some specific trouble and perplexity, then the test of their validity and value lies in accomplishing this work. If they succeed in their office, they are reliable, sound, valid, good, true. If they fail to clear up confusion, to eliminate defects, if they increase confusion, uncertainty and evil when they are acted upon, then they are false. Confirmation, corroboration, verification lie in works, consequences. Handsome is that handsome does. By their fruits, ye *know* them.

JOHN DEWEY

(Evaluate this philosophy for finding what is true.)

19.12.   The refutation of realism will therefore be sufficiently accomplished if it can be shown that we do *not* know that any single entity exists unexperienced.

W. T. STACE

(Implicit in this argument is the following proposition: If we know that any single entity exists unexperienced, realism must be accepted. Would Stace's argument refute realism?)

10. Formulate the conditional syllogisms involved in the following arguments:

For the geocentric theory of astronomy:

19.13. Now with this done, if one should next take up the earth's position, the observed appearances with respect to it could be understood if we put it in the middle of the heavens . . . it is once for all clear from the very appearances that the earth is in the middle of the world. . .

PTOLEMY

For the heliocentric theory:

19.14. Now if precisely the same effect follows whether the earth is made to move and the rest of the universe stay still, or the earth alone remains fixed while the whole universe shares one motion, who is going to believe that nature (which by general agreement does not act by means of many things when it can do so by means of few) has chosen to make an immense number of extremely large bodies move with inconceivable velocities, to achieve what could have been done by a moderate movement of one single body around its own center?

GALILEO

(Galileo is arguing in effect that if the heliocentric theory is accepted, a mathematically simpler explanation can be obtained than under Ptolemy's system.)

11. Discuss the following argument:

19.15. A man cannot be the slave of two masters. He will either hate the one and love the other, or, at least, be attentive to the one and neglectful of the other.

ST. MATTHEW

12. How would you criticize a philosophy that filled the following requirement:

19.16. The whole function of philosophy ought to be to find out what definite difference it will make to you and me, at definite instants of our life, if this world-formula or that world-formula be the true one.

WILLIAM JAMES

Chapter 20: INDUCTION

20.1. The qualities of bodies which admit neither intensification nor remission of degrees, and which are found to belong to all bodies within the reach of our experiments, are to be esteemed the universal qualities of all bodies whatsoever.

ISAAC NEWTON

This is one of Newton's "four rules of reasoning." He provides examples to illustrate his rule. It will be of interest to compare his rule with the principle underlying the two kinds of syllogism we have just been examining.

All bodies found in our experience are extended, he would argue, and so we conclude that extension belongs to all bodies that exist. The same kind of generalization takes place, according to Newton, when hardness and impenetrability are predicated universally in our material world. Because such qualities are observed in all bodies within our experience, they are, Newton says, attributed to all bodies everywhere.

The process of reasoning which Newton describes here is called induction. Induction is the passage of the mind from particular cases of a given kind of thing to a general or universal notion concerning all cases of the same kind. It is a movement from knowledge of individuals to a generalization about a whole species and at times a movement from knowledge of several species to a conclusion about a whole genus.

The problem of induction. There is a serious problem in defense of the procedure just outlined. What is the basis for Newton's rule? If in induction the mind examines a relatively few cases of a certain kind, how can it make a conclusion regarding all the cases of a given kind? How can it know the unexamined cases without examining them? Newton admits that hardness or resistance is observed in only some bodies because there are many other bodies besides those we observe. By what right can he predicate hardness of all bodies, including those we do not observe? By what formula, in short, does induction move from *some* to *all?*

The problem of induction is all the more serious because of the relative frequency of inductive knowledge. Nearly all of our knowledge is inductive — a generalization about a whole kind of thing based upon experience of only a few cases of that kind. Here are some examples of propositions reached through induction:

20.2. All snow is white.
20.3. Man is rational.
20.4. All of the apostles were Jews.
20.5. Malaria is carried by mosquitoes.
20.6. All hydrogen is combustible.
20.7. Electric current is proportional to voltage divided by resistance.
20.8. Being cannot be non-being while it is being.
20.9. The majority party in Congress usually loses seats in the off-year election.
20.10. All members of the jury were women.
20.11. The whole is greater than any of its parts.
20.12. Penicillin cures pneumonia.
20.13. All dogs bark.

Not all of these examples are of equal certitude, nor do they all involve the same kinds of induction, as will be later seen. But they are all passages from the particular to the universal, from the experience of individual instances of a thing to a proposition stating a general truth.

Induction not syllogistic. Induction is not a syllogism. It does not connect two terms by means of a third. In the case of **20.13** above, men have undoubtedly heard dogs bark ever since man himself has existed on earth, and in the course of experience, the proposition could be formed: *All dogs bark.* But no one has heard every dog. Each has heard A bark, B bark, C bark, etc., and if not helped by his parents or others, he could still form on his own the proposition: *All dogs (A, B, C, and all the other dogs that there are) bark.* But nowhere have S and P, of the conclusion, been compared as in a syllogism to a common middle term. Induction, therefore, lacks a middle term. That is its chief difference from the syllogism.

Another important but less fundamental difference between the syllogism and induction is that in the syllogism the mind moves from the more universal to the less, whereas induction reverses this direction. On this basis, many logic books of the past have distinguished two kinds of reasoning, deductive syllogisms and inductive syllogisms. This is a misleading distinction, for induction itself is not a syllogism, and deduction is not the only opposite of induction. It is not necessary to enter further into this problem here, except to conclude that man has two ways of knowing: induction and syllogism, and that the one is not reducible to the other.

In relating induction to the syllogism, the following syllogism based upon a classic example in Aristotle may be helpful:

> 20.14. The cow, the goat, and the deer are ruminants.
> The cow, the goat and the deer are horned animals.
> Therefore, all horned animals are ruminants.

This is reasoning by induction, but as the argument stands the minor term in the conclusion has a wider extension than in the minor premise. Hence, this piece of reasoning cannot be a syllogism. The conclusion of this argument is reached not by a syllogism but by induction. But by what principle is induction justified?

In most of our inductions, and especially in the inductions that are used in science, we are unable to examine all the members of a species which a generalization concerns. Besides this, even if such an examination were actually made of all the members of a species here and now, the mind could never be sure that its search for new members of the same species was over for all times and places. Perhaps in some other part of the world or in some other age, past or future, there is evidence that could destroy our conclusion reached by complete induction. Induction, and certainly the kind ordinarily used by sciences, cannot be justified on principles that make the syllogism possible.

Abstractive induction. In order to justify the process of going from the less universal to the more universal, induction must be divided into its types. There are two major types of induction:

I. There is, to begin with, the kind of induction which is performed in the first act of the mind to reach universal essences.

This may be called abstractive induction, because the process by which the mind leaves aside the individual character of sensible reality to consider the universal essences or nature of things is called abstraction.

20.3 is certainly an example of this kind of induction. Other examples are **20.8** and **20.11**.

All knowledge comes to us through sense experience. The external senses gradually come to discriminate among the various colors and sounds in the world about us, and while still in the order of sensation, the rise from the particular to the universal is greatly assisted by the internal senses, such as memory. Finally, after the data of the physical world have been suitably organized by the senses, the intellect is able to reach an understanding of the universal. Essences are not given ready-made for a simple and effortless grasp by our knowing powers. Years of experience lie behind the universals we now know, in a distinct and reflective way, by abstractive induction.

Induction, in the sense of abstraction, is the most fundamental operation of the mind. All our knowledge is inductive in origin, and abstractive induction is necessary, as will be seen, even for the other kinds of induction to operate. The propositions that go to form our syllogisms are usually dependent on induction and, when the premises in themselves express certain truths, on abstractive induction.

Not all knowledge can be acquired through a middle term and this middle term through another middle term, and so on indefinitely. In this way, an infinite series would be opened, and knowledge, without a starting point in the series, could never begin. Although it is true that the premises of syllogisms may be obtained as the conclusions of other syllogisms, this process cannot go on forever. Knowledge obtained indirectly and by means of a syllogistic middle term must eventually be based on a knowledge that is direct and without a middle term. The most fundamental form of such knowledge is abstractive induction. Without it, there could never be a proposition like *All dogs bark*, because in order to know even that the various dogs of our experience are barking creatures it is necessary first to have the vague knowledge of a dog as quadruped or at least as an animal, and such knowledge rests finally upon our power to abstract universal essences. It is a sufficient defense of abstractive induction to argue that without it there could be no other knowledge; without the abstraction of the universal, as discussed in Chapter 5, nothing could be related to anything else. Surely this is an argument that abstractive induction is justified.

Induction by complete enumeration. II. The second kind of induction may be called for the sake of simplicity enumerative induction. In turn it may be subdivided into: (a) induction by complete enumeration, where all cases of a certain kind are examined; and (b) induction by incomplete enumeration, where there is an examination of only some cases of a given kind to reach a universal proposition.

Examples 20.4 and 20.10 require a complete enumeration of all cases of the subjects involved in the proposition if the proposition itself is to be of universal quantity. There is simply no other way of forming such propositions short of the complete enumeration of all instances of the subjects concerned. But where the complete enumeration is possible for all instances of a subject, the induction is often unimportant, at least from a scientific point of view.

Abstractive induction underlies induction by complete enumeration. In order to form the various individual propositions, *Peter was a Jew, John was a Jew, Andrew was a Jew, etc.,* the mind must make an abstraction in order to put the particular subjects within the universal type, i.e., the mind must form the universal concept of Jews.

It will be useful for later purposes to make a subdivision within induction by complete enumeration. It need not cover every instance of the subject, but only sufficient instances to conform to the quantity of the proposition which induction reaches. In 20.4 and 20.10, the subject is universal, and all of its possible cases must consequently be examined in order to make the proposition in question. But consider the following induction: *Many forms of government exist: democracy is one; dictatorship is another; limited monarchy is still another.* Our conclusion here depends upon a count sufficient to cover the extension of the subject, but not all possible cases of the subject need be listed. To the examples brought forward, other forms of government, e.g., oligarchy, could be added; but the original proposition can be supported without such addition. It might be useful then to divide inductions by complete enumeration into those requiring an examination of all possible cases of the subject if the proposition is universal and those requiring an examination only of enough cases to coincide with the extension of the subject if the proposition is not universal.

There is no problem in justifying induction by complete enumeration in either of its forms. Since each case of the subject has been examined singly, the proposition reached by induction through complete enumeration is merely a summary of what is already known rather than an extension to new and unexamined cases of the subject.

But in induction by incomplete enumeration, the mind proceeds, without being confined to any more or less definite number, from some of the cases of the subject to a generalization about all cases. Consider examples 20.2, 20.5, 20.6, 20.7, 20.8, 20.12, and 20.13.

Induction by incomplete enumeration is so important that it will be given separate treatment in the next chapter.

Problems

1. What is the problem raised by induction? Explain this in terms of examples.

2. Contrast induction and the syllogism. Is there an inductive syllogism?

3. What are the types of induction?

4. Explain abstractive induction and show how it underlies all scientific knowledge. What is the justification for abstractive induction?

5. Explain the divisions of enumerative induction. What is the value of completely enumerative induction? Show how induction by complete enumeration presupposes abstractive induction.

6. Which of the following questions would be answered by induction alone, without the use of syllogisms:

a) Do men have souls?
b) Do most college graduates succeed in business?
c) Did the world have a beginning?
d) Does water boil at 210° F?
e) Is sterilization of the unfit morally wrong?
f) Do warm-blooded animals have lungs?
g) Is the human soul immortal?

h) Do elephants have tusks?
i) Must the blood circulate?
j) Is there a First Mover of the universe?
k) Have all of the United States Presidents been native-born?
l) Is the universe finite in size?
m) Do viruses take in food?

Chapter 21: INDUCTION BY INCOMPLETE ENUMERATION

Logic applied. Induction by incomplete enumeration is used widely in many fields, especially in the study of nature by the experimental methods of physics, chemistry, and biology. It is a much more complicated process to perform and to justify than the inductions so far discussed — abstractive induction and that kind of enumerative induction which proceeds by complete enumeration of instances.

In 20.6, for instance, there is obviously an example of induction by incomplete enumeration: *All hydrogen is combustible.* This proposition was formed, and rightly so, after only a tiny fraction of all the hydrogen in the world had been observed. How can we justify extending our knowledge of *some* hydrogen to a proposition about *all* of it?

The answer to this question depends upon considerations which take us beyond abstract logic and into the concrete world of experience and experiment where logic is applied. Such applications require that the mind, using logic, take into account the special kind of subject matter to which it is applied. It is true that the same general laws of logic are at the root of all good reasoning; yet it is also true that each of the different branches of knowledge, because of the nature of its subject matter, will in different ways determine the general laws of logic and add to them special and supplementary considerations. To expect logic to be applied in the same way in mathematical and moral science would be to overlook the way in which general logic is differently conditioned and complimented by attention to the differences in the concrete subject matter to which general logic is applied.

Order in the field of application. In our approach to the material world, it is impossible to be unaware that nature as a whole is ordered. Such an order does not mean absolute permanence or fixity; in fact there is motion rather than rest prevailing through the whole universe. Yet in the very motions of material things, there is some kind of uniformity that cannot escape attention. Physical realities cannot do what they please. The stars do not wander at random through the heavens. The cycle of the seasons is, for the most part, quite regular. Heavy bodies fall to the ground, and smoke tends upward. In the living world the order is still more evident. Like gives birth to like; the same structures have the same functions; plants and animals are somehow taken care of in nature and usually reach at least some measure of perfection. All this adds up to the fact that there is a high degree of order prevailing in our cosmos, and it is this common knowledge of the order in nature which permits the use, as proper to each area in natural studies, of induction by incomplete enumeration. Such induction is a matter of finding the proper details of this general order that is commonly perceived.

Looking at the universe, not in all of its distinct parts, but in general and as a whole, it is evident that our cosmos shows an order, and if there is order in the whole there must also be a kind of order in the parts themselves. To come back to our generalization about hydrogen, it could certainly be argued that hydrogen is not free to be combustible today and to be noncombustible tomorrow under the same circumstances and conditions. If anything could do anything, the cosmos would become a chaos. But as experience and observation disclose, the universe is certainly no chaos. It is regulated and determined as a whole and hence is ordered in its parts as well. It is this order within the various parts of the universe that enables us to make that kind of induction which proceeds by incomplete enumeration.

The principle of induction. The principle underlying induction by incomplete enumeration may be formulated as follows: *Under the same causes and conditions, a material thing, because of the order as reflected by the universe as a whole, will tend to act in the same way.* If each individual thing could vary its actions, the over-all order would perish. It is the order in the universe as a whole, evident even to common experience, which leads us to expect an order in the parts, as we analyze each of them separately.

The problem of chance is too complicated to discuss here. Though playing its part in the activities of material things, chance events like monstrosities in the animal world and tidal waves and earthquakes in the world of inanimate nature are exceptions to the ordinary. For the most part, nature is ordered, and even if our best inductions about nature must always be qualified by the possibility that chance may interfere with our expectations, such inductions are true for the most part just as nature is ordered for the most part. As such, our inductions concerning nature can have a type of universality about them. They are true *in general*.

It is the order in nature which allows us to conclude: *All hydrogen is combustible* after examining only *some* of it. By such an order we argue, as in **20.5**: *Malaria is carried by mosquitoes* or, as in **20.7**: *Electric current is proportional to voltage divided by resistance.* In each case only a part of the possible extension of the subject has been observed.

Under the same causes and conditions, a material being, because of the order as reflected in the universe as a whole, will tend to act in the same way.

But the principle of nature's order does not authorize any easy generalizations based upon a few random observations of phenomena in nature. An adequate number of cases, depending once more on the nature of the subject matter, must be examined and examined indeed under conditions sufficient to test the generalization that is to be made. Such conditions are again to be determined not in general but according to the various requirements of the various fields of human knowledge.

For instance, to determine whether hydrogen is combustible, it would be necessary to experiment a number of times in different circumstances until the possibility can be ruled out that the initial experimental result was a freak. In a field like experimental medicine, when the effects of a new chemical are to be determined, the experimenter does not confine his experiments to a single animal, like a mouse. The mouse in question may have peculiar immunities or other peculiar experimental conditions might exist in its case which would not reveal the typical effects of the chemical on mice.

So the experimenter tests his drug on a great number of mice. Furthermore, mice may have a peculiar characteristic with respect to the chemical concerned, and so rats are tested and then guinea pigs and a number of other higher animals. Finally, when judged safe, tests are made on men and women of all ages, different blood types, etc. Only then is it logical to make anything like a generalization concerning the effects of the chemical on animal, and especially on human, life.

Such an inductive generalization is grounded, once more, on the principle that nature is ordered and that like causes and conditions will always tend to the same results. Hence, once the drug has been adequately tested on some men, doctors feel safe in predicting its results on the generality of men.

Thus far we have seen two kinds of induction: abstractive induction and enumerative induction. The first type was treated in the preceding chapter and induction by complete enumeration was also treated there. In the present chapter, induction by incomplete enumeration was briefly examined with a view, mainly, to discover the basis on which it rests.

Induction by abstraction and by incomplete enumeration. But there is one more problem that remains to be treated. It is not so much a new problem as a difficulty that might lead to a confusing of the inductions so far discussed. Abstractive induction, which leads to a distinct and explicit knowledge of general propositions, does not arise easily and quickly; it depends sometimes on years of experience and on a considerable degree of maturity before a reflective possession is reached of the generalizations involved. How then does abstractive induction differ from induction by incomplete enumeration? Are they essentially different actions? Or do they differ only because abstractive induction, in order to generalize, needs less cases than induction by incomplete enumeration? If the last question is answered in the affirmative, then it would seem that abstractive induction and induction by incomplete enumeration differ only in degree.

There is no doubt more similarity, at least from one angle, between abstractive induction and induction by incomplete enumeration, than there is a similarity between the two kinds of enumerative induction themselves. For induction by complete enumeration is a summary of what is already known, while abstractive induction and induction by incomplete enumeration both extend beyond the cases actually examined to a knowledge of what similar cases will be.

But abstractive induction and induction by incomplete enumeration differ considerably from each other.

There are certainly cases that can be identified as abstractive induction, e.g., the whole is greater than its parts. The strength of the conclusion does not depend intrinsically on the number of cases examined, but is evident from the very nature of the subject and predicate. We are dependent on experience for a knowledge of both terms, but as soon as the mind understands what the subject and predicate mean, it understands that the proposition in question is necessarily true. It is not necessary to appeal here to the order of nature to make the proposition universal.

There are other cases where the connection between subject and predicate is not evident from the very nature of the terms but depends upon the number of cases examined. There is nothing in the nature of hydrogen or of combustibility to compel the mind to put them together when once they are understood. That they belong together must be determined by a sufficient number of experiences, and the order of nature plays a central role.

There is, then, a distinction in principle between abstractive induction and induction by incomplete enumeration. One depends on experiences only to get the meaning of the subject and the predicate of the universal proposition. The other is dependent on experience to supply samples of a proposition and, unlike the first case, the generalization is made on the basis of the order of nature.

The distinction between the two inductions exists, but as often happens there are borderland cases where the mind cannot find how and where a distinction applies. There is, for instance, a distinction between art and nature. Cases can clearly be cited that there are certain things which are by nature, iron, copper, and lead; and there are other things that are by art, for example an ash tray. But suppose a rock is found that is shaped like an arrow. Was this shape formed naturally, or is it perhaps a work of art, the work of Indian warriors, that was long buried but somehow came again to the surface of the earth? One or the other alternative may be true without our knowing which is the case. In other words, our lack of knowledge of distinctions does not destroy distinctions in the nature of things outside of knowledge. In our present case, while extremes can be distinguished so that certain propositions can be called the fruit of abstractive induction and others the work of incomplete enumeration, there may be borderland cases which we cannot put in one or the other class. But this does not mean that such propositions belong to both classes or that our distinction in principle must be abolished. It merely means that we do not have enough knowledge to decide to which class a proposition belongs.

Problems

1. Show that nature is ordered, either by analyzing a part of nature, e.g., iron, or by an examination of the cosmos on a larger scale.

2. What is the relation between the order of nature and induction by incomplete enumeration?

3. Does the order of nature make for quick and easy generalizations? Explain.

4. Compare abstractive induction and induction by incomplete enumeration. Then contrast the two operations.

5. Explain why the following arguments, either in whole or in part, are or are not inductions and in each case where there is induction, identify its kind and give the basis for the generalization. Criticize any logical faults in the passages:

> 21.1. The man of the machine age is a calculating animal. We live in a welter of figures, cookery recipes, railway timetables, unemployment aggregates, fines, taxes, war-debts, overtime schedules, speed limits, bowling averages, betting odds, billiard scores, calories, babies' weights, clinical temperatures, rainfall, hours of sunshine, motoring records, power indices, gas-meter readings, bank rates, freight rates, death rates, discount, interest, lotteries, wave-lengths, and tire pressures.
>
> LANCELOT HOGBEN

(NOTE: Ask what Hogben is trying to show and then how he tries to show it.)

> 21.2. There is a certain moral failure, too, on the part of an educational institution that does not allow the student to make his own the treasure of the accumulated thoughts of the race. So the

failure of the elective system was a moral failure. The official historian of Harvard said of President Eliot that he had defrauded the Harvard students of their cultural heritage.

ROBERT M. HUTCHINS

21.3. Thanks to a vast number of observations, we know that anyone transported from sea level to a high altitude shows symptoms of mountain sickness. After a few weeks these symptoms disappear; the person has become acclimatized. The examination of the blood then shows that the red corpuscles have greatly multiplied. It is thus legitimate to deduce that the organism adjusts itself to the rarefaction of oxygen in the atmosphere by increasing the quantity of hemoglobin capable of stabilizing this gas. This brings to light many aspects of the law of adaptation.

ALEXIS CARREL

21.4. All birds of the same species in every age and country, build their nests alike: In this we see the force of instinct. Men, in different times and places, frame their houses differently: Here we perceive the influence of reason and custom.

DAVID HUME

21.5. Despite our tensions, the United States remains a happy land, the land of good cheer, God's country. It produces the Optimists' Club, the glad books, the Boosters' society, manuals on how to attain peace of mind, songs to the effect that though I want to be happy, I can't be happy unless you are happy too, and office posters saying: If you can't boost, don't knock.

HOWARD MUMFORD JONES

21.6. The chromosomes in our germ cells are not affected by any change that takes place within our body cells.
What this means is that no change . . . made in us in our lifetimes . . . can be passed on to our children through the process of biological heredity.

AMRAM SCHEINFELD

21.7. There are many democracies: ancient democracy and modern democracy; Eighteenth Century democracy and Nineteenth Century democracy; Jeffersonian democracy and Jacksonian democracy; Eastern democracy and Western democracy; political democracy and social democracy; democracy in theory and democracy in practice.

RALPH BARTON PERRY

21.8. Things which are equal to the same thing are equal to one another.

EUCLID

21.9. As the species of the same genus usually have, though by no means invariably, much similarity in habits and constitution, and always in structure, the struggle will generally be more severe between them, if they come into competition with each other, than between the species of distinct genera. We see this in the recent extension over parts of the United States of one species of swallow, having caused the decrease of another species. The recent increase of the missel-thrush in parts of Scotland has caused the decrease of the song-thrush. How frequently we hear of one species of rat taking the place of another species under the most different climates!

CHARLES DARWIN

21.10. Gases, on the contrary, in whatever proportions they may combine, always give rise to compounds whose elements by volume are multiples of each other.

JOSEPH GAY-LUSSAC

21.11. It may safely be pronounced, therefore, that population, when unchecked, goes on doubling itself every twenty-five years, or increases in a geometrical ratio.

The rate according to which the productions of the earth may be supposed to increase, will not be so easy to determine. Of this, however, we may be perfectly certain, that the ratio of their increase in a limited territory must be of a totally different nature from the ratio of the increase of population. A thousand millions are just as easily doubled every twenty-five years by the power of population as a thousand. But the food to support the increase from the greater number will by no means be obtained with the same facility. Man is necessarily confined in room. When acre has been added to acre till all the fertile land is occupied, the yearly increase of food must depend upon the melioration of the land already in possession. This is a fund, which from the nature of all soils, instead of increasing, must be gradually diminishing. But population, could it be supplied with food, would go on with unexhausted vigour; and the increase of one period would furnish the power of a greater increase the next, and this without any limit. . .

THOMAS ROBERT MALTHUS

21.12. Sane peasants, healthy hunters, are all superstitious; they are superstitious because they are healthy and sane. They have a reasonable fear of the unknown; for superstition is only the creative side of agnosticism. The superstitious man sees quite plainly that the universe is a thing to be feared. The religious man maintains paradoxically that the universe is a thing to be trusted.

G. K. CHESTERTON

6. Which of the following samples of induction would require induction by complete enumeration? Explain.

a) All green plants give off carbon dioxide.

b) All of the sun's planets are smaller than the sun.

c) All water is composed of hydrogen and oxygen.

d) All of the plays of Shakespeare are good literature.

e) All the members of the class passed the test.

f) All wood burns.

g) There are four fundamental particles in the nucleus of atoms.

h) All cows are susceptible to cowpox.

i) The Himalayas have the highest peaks in the world.

j) Greece had the greatest civilization of all the nations in antiquity.

k) All mahogany is hardwood.

l) All who ate the potato salad got food poisoning.

m) All electricity is either positive or negative.

PART V: THE KINDS OF ARGUMENT

Chapter 22: THE DEMONSTRATIVE SYLLOGISM

22.1. Whatever is composed of parts is destructible.
All matter is composed of parts.
Therefore, all matter is destructible.

This is a classical argument in a form that can now be recognized as a syllogism. It is of interest here not because of its content but because of its peculiar logical qualities. It is a kind of syllogism that is called demonstration.

Demonstration is contrasted with the dialectical, the rhetorical, and the poetic syllogisms. Like the three other kinds, the demonstrative syllogism is a syllogism because it connects a subject and a predicate by means of a middle term. But what is it that makes it demonstrative and thus sets it apart from the dialectical, rhetorical, and literary syllogisms?

The middle term and certitude. The answer to this question introduces us to another phase of logic and a new part of this book. Up to the present time, arguments have been considered from only one aspect of their form. Syllogisms that simply unite two terms by means of a third turned out, for instance, to be categorical. But the middle term has certain properties which introduce us to another principle for dividing the syllogism. The middle term may be known as certain or in some measure less than certain, and the breakdown of the syllogism into the demonstrative, dialectical, rhetorical, and literary kinds is at bottom a division of argument in terms of its certitude. A demonstration is distinguished from its three opposites by the possession of a certain middle term.

Scientific knowledge may be best defined as certain knowledge in terms of causes or principles or reasons, and in this light demonstration may itself be defined as a syllogism which produces scientific knowledge. Other kinds of syllogism lead not to science but to something less, for example opinion.

It may seem beyond the scope of logic to divide syllogisms according to the certitude of their middle term or according to their end as, for example, science or opinion. But it should also be observed that even in discussing such divisions, logic is still concerned with the logical relations or logical forms by which it was identified in Chapter 1. Logic is not entitled to say, for instance, whether the middle term in 22.1 is certain or not or whether the conclusion is actually scientific knowledge. Logic is concerned with naming the conditions that make a syllogism scientific and with studying the qualities which make a syllogism demonstrative. In this respect, even our present task in Part V does not change logic from a study of logical relations to a concern with the physical world. Whether things composed of parts are destructible and whether all matter is composed of parts must be decided by a science other than logic. Logic does not define things like matter or parts; but it does define logical relations like demonstration and science. Hence, Part V is quite relevant to a study of logic; in this Part, the syllogism is still under logical consideration, but now divided according to a new principle of division, the certainty of its middle term.

The middle term has already been identified as the logical relation or logical form by which a subject and a predicate are connected. The middle term expresses the principle or cause or reason why the conclusion follows from the premises. Thus, the reason or cause why matter is destructible is that matter is composed of parts.

In any syllogism, the key concept is expressed by the word "because" or some similar term, e.g., Man is able to laugh because he is rational. The essence of a demonstrative syllogism, by contrast to the three others to be studied in ensuing chapters, is that the middle term represents a cause or reason or principle that is known with certainty to bring about the connection expressed in the conclusion. Science, the issue of demonstration, is, let us repeat, certain knowledge in terms of causes — which is another way of saying that the scientific or demonstrative syllogism is one that has a certain middle term.

The secret to the making of a syllogism, demonstrative or otherwise, is the discovery of a middle term, and the expert in finding such middle terms will be successful in argumentation. In a dispute, for instance, over the destructibility of matter, it need only be brought forward that matter is composed of parts in order to be firmly on the way to proving the proposition: *All matter is destructible.* Its composition by parts is the cause or reason or principle from which matter's destructibility necessarily flows as an effect.

If there is a dispute about man's being free, the proposition: *Man is free*, can be established by finding a middle term connecting the subject and predicate of the intended conclusion. This means finding the cause or principle from which man's freedom flows. In a dispute over the proposition: *No dog is free*, the demonstrator must find a middle term representing the cause or reason why the subject and predicate are divided.

In demonstration, the cause or middle term is certain.

The two kinds of demonstrations. There are two kinds of demonstration. In one of them, the conclusion predicates an attribute of the subject by a middle term that, in whole or in part, is the real definition of the subject and, as such, provides the real reason why the attribute belongs to the subject in question. Thus, freedom, an attribute, is predicated of man because man is rational. Rational is part of man's real definition. In 22.1 the very definition of matter, as known through abstractive induction, is that which is composed of parts, and hence the middle term expresses the cause or reason why, in the very nature of things, the attribute destructibility is predicated of matter.

In this kind of demonstration, the mind moves from real causes to real effects, and such a syllogism may be called a causal demonstration (*demonstratio propter quid*).

But there is another kind of demonstration, less perfect than the first type, but much more common in the life of reason. Let us consider a sample of this second kind of proof.

22.2. **Whatever operates in some of its acts without intrinsic dependence on the body is spiritual.**

The human soul operates in some of its acts without intrinsic dependence on the body.
Therefore, the human soul is spiritual.

The difference between this kind of demonstration and the ones involving human freedom or matter's perishability can be found in the kind of cause which each employs and the kind of definition, in whole or in part, which the middle term expresses.

In the argument about human freedom, the proof of the proposition: *Man is free*, flows from man's real definition as rational and depends on the real cause why the connection expressed in the conclusion is valid.

But 22.2 does not proceed through real causes. The middle term, *what operates in some of its acts without intrinsic dependence on the body*, is not the real cause of the soul's spirituality. On the contrary, the fact that the soul is spiritual causes it to act without intrinsic dependence on matter.

In a more positive vein, the soul's operation without intrinsic dependence on matter is the reason or cause why we know it to be spiritual. Such operations are the causes of our knowledge of the nature of the soul, and a demonstration which proceeds through causes of our knowledge may be called a factual demonstration or demonstration of fact (*demonstratio quia*).

There are then two kinds of demonstration: one which proceeds through a middle term which represents a cause of our knowledge of what is expressed by the conclusion and the other which proceeds through a middle term expressing the cause of the reality expressed by the conclusion.

Sunlight is not the cause of the sun, but rather the cause of our knowledge of the sun. Motion and order are not the causes of God, but rather causes of our knowledge of God as we discover Him through creatures.

As the mind uses real definition, either in whole or in part, as the middle term for the causal demonstration, so in the factual demonstration a nominal definition is employed. In our proof of God's existence, for example, He is nominally defined as the First Mover or Supreme Intelligence. Such expressions, as middle terms in our demonstration, say what we mean by the term, *God*.

The middle term, in a scientific or demonstrative syllogism of either type must be certain. From the viewpoint of logic, there is one important condition for the certitude of our causal knowledge and, at least for present purposes, one important characteristic of any science as a knowledge organized by its reference to certain causes or principles. Let us listen to Aristotle on the nature of scientific knowledge:

> When the objects of an inquiry, in any department, have principles, causes, or elements, it is through acquaintance with these that knowledge, that is to say scientific knowledge, is attained. For we do not think that we know a thing until we are acquainted with its primary causes, or first principles, and have carried our analysis as far as its simplest elements.*

Science and first principles. Why is it that scientific knowledge requires first principles? Why could it be argued from Aristotle's analysis that a science must begin with first principles in order to achieve certitude?

Demonstrations in a science may take their premises from the conclusions of other demonstrations; but somewhere there must be a beginning point which cannot be demonstrated by the science in question. If all demonstrations within the science depend upon such a starting point, then any attempt to demonstrate the starting point would already have to presume it. Such beginning points in a science are in one sense the presuppositions of the demonstrations within the science.

The starting point of a science is what we mean by a principle within it. A principle in general is a source from which anything flows in any manner whatsoever. To say first principle is to say something stronger. A first principle is a principle which is an ultimate source or beginning point within any order, say the order of arithmetic or geometry or the science of nature. From the first principles of geometry, the point and the line, everything in geometry is derived; but the point and the line are underived from anything in the geometrical order.

In a similar way, the unit, the source of all number, is the first principle of the arithmetical order. From it everything in arithmetic is derived; but the unit itself is not derived within the arithmetical order. Any complicated equation, say $16^2 = 256$, can be under-

---

* Aristotle, *Physics*, I, 1; 184 a 9.

stood and checked for correctness only by reference to the unit which must be first understood. But the unit cannot be understood in terms of arithmetic. It makes sense to ask, "How many fingers are there on one hand?" and to get a reply like "Five!" But it makes no sense to ask in arithmetic: "How many fingers are one finger?" The unit is thus a first principle in arithmetic, a starting point from which everything else is understood. By reference to it, everything in arithmetic is derived while it itself is underived in the arithmetical order. Without knowing it and using it, nothing in arithmetic could ever be certain.

In the attempt to illustrate what is meant by a first principle, our example from arithmetic has already given evidence why any science, because of its certitude, must begin with its own first principles. A science must have *principles* because it is causal knowledge; it must have *first* principles because, unlike mere opinion, science is certain knowledge. If arithmetic started without considering its first principle, it would have no means of checking its conclusions, and they would all lack certitude. Where a science does not begin at the beginning of its subject matter, it starts with principles that are not first but derived, and what lies behind them may upset the certitude of the conclusions drawn from our actual principles that were secondary and derived. First principles are a guarantee that a science will not begin with what is arbitrary, and in this respect, they give an order to the science in question. In accordance with our definition of logic in Chapter 2, to proceed in an orderly and correct manner, every science must begin with principles that are first and hence ultimate in the region of the real which is being considered.

Since a science is unable to perform demonstration until it has reached first principles, such principles cannot be demonstrated in the science which uses them. They are reached by induction.

The first principle of arithmetic is the unit. Geometry has two underived principles, the point and the line; logic also two, the subject and predicate. Theology is a science having as its first principles the articles of faith which it explains, defends, and uses as a basis for drawing conclusions. What the first principles of other sciences are presumes acquaintance with these sciences and remains to be discussed in the sciences themselves.

In this chapter, demonstration, by contrast to the dialectical, rhetorical, and literary syllogism, has been identified as a syllogism with a certain middle term or as a syllogism producing scientific knowledge as opposed to opinion.

Demonstration may proceed through causes of things and real definitions or causes of our knowledge of things and nominal definitions.

Demonstration has two characteristics of note here. Like any syllogism, it proceeds through principles because it gives causal knowledge and indeed through first principles because it gives certain knowledge. It is the first principles of a science that give it a certain beginning point and establish its orderly direction.

The three other kinds of syllogism (dialectical, rhetorical, and literary) will be discussed in the ensuing three chapters.

Problems

1. Name the four kinds of syllogism and show the basis for the division. What is the chief characteristic of demonstration?

2. What does the middle term in any syllogism represent?

3. Differentiate between causal and factual demonstration.

4. What is a principle? What is a first principle? Why is it necessary that a demonstration be based ultimately on first principles?

5. Compare Aristotle's notions, one of science and the other of demonstrated knowledge, to show that they are related.

6. Explain whether or not the following are demonstrations:

    a) Euclid's theorem in **1.2**
    b) Galileo's argument in **1.1**
    c) Dalton's argument in **16.6**
    d) Ptolemy's argument in **19.13**
    e) St. Thomas' argument in **1.3**

7. In 1628, William Harvey gave the following proof for the circulation of the blood through the body: He determined first of all that with each beat blood flows in and out of the heart; and, knowing that the quantity of the blood in the body is finite, he reasoned:*

---

*The syllogism here is taken from *Science in Synthesis* by W. Kane *et al.* (River Forest, Ill., 1953), p. 105.

22.3.   A finite quantity of matter perpetually flowing past a fixed point must circulate.

The blood is a finite quantity of matter perpetually flowing past a fixed point.

Therefore, the blood must circulate.

Did Harvey demonstrate the circulation of the blood? Would it have been a better proof simply to watch under a microscope the movement of the blood in the smaller blood vessels and to conclude, by induction, that the blood circulates? If Harvey did give a demonstration, is his proof causal or factual?

Chapter 23: THE DIALECTICAL SYLLOGISM

23.1. The principles [of nature] in question must be either (a) one or (b) more than one.

If (a) one, it must be either (i) motionless, as Parmenides and Melissus assert, or (ii) in motion, as the physicists hold, some declaring air to be the first principle, others water.

If (b) more than one, then either (i) a finite or (ii) an infinite plurality. If (i) finite (but more than one), then either two or three or four or some other number. If (ii) infinite, then either as Democritus believed one in kind, but differing in shape or form; or different in kind and even contrary.

ARISTOTLE

Examples of dialectic. Aristotle is here setting out to find the first principles of nature, analogous to the unit in the arithmetical order and to the point and line of geometry. If there is to be knowledge of nature that is strictly scientific in the sense of the last chapter, such principles must be found; and, as indemonstrable within the science of nature, such principles can be reached only by induction.

But induction is not a wild and haphazard affair. To make an induction the mind needs a plan of inquiry. It must first raise questions and then reason out the consequences of the questions until the answer can be checked by experience. Demonstration reaches propositions that are certain and true without fear that the contradictory proposition will hold; such is the conclusion of our syllogism, 22.1. In the dialectical syllogism, on the other hand, there is always a question that may be answered yes or no; in syllogistic form, the consequences of each of the two possible answers is developed so that, after the dialectical arguments are each complete, the mind can then make an induction to find which of the two answers corresponds to experience. Prior to such an induction and in its purely dialectical arguments, the mind is not fixed upon one conclusion to the exclusion of the other, but is open to both of them.

Dialectic may be regarded as a logic of questioning, and the dialectical syllogism, far from containing a certain middle term, is based on questions. It provides the mind with a plan of inquiry so that deliberate inductions can be made. Let us watch Aristotle using the dialectical syllogism. Accepting alternative (a, i), that the principles of motion are one, Aristotle could construct the following dialectical syllogism:

> 23.2.   If nature contains only one motionless principle, there can be no change.
> But, by alternative (a, i) nature contains only one motionless principle.
> Therefore, there can be no change.

The major premise is established by considering that change, if it exists, always involves at least two principles, the *old* that existed before the change and the *new* that exists after it. If either of these were missing, i.e., if anything in nature contained only one principle, it could not change. After his dialectical conclusion which denies change, Aristotle could look inductively at the real world and find that change does take place. Hence, the initial assumption leading to a denial of change must be ruled out. In a similar fashion, Aristotle sifted through the other questions until he came to one whose answer enabled him to make an induction to the principles of nature or change and to defend his induction by the dialectical syllogism used in making it.

As providing a plan of inquiry through the raising of questions, dialectic is a way of discovering principles by induction and defending them when they are questioned by an adversary. Anyone insisting, for instance, that nature has only one principle could be confronted by a syllogism like that in 23.2.

To use an example less abstract than Aristotle's, let us suppose that a research worker were trying to determine the effect of frequent hair washing on human bald-headedness. Should he examine people at random, he would no doubt never find the correlation he was after, except possibly by accident. To proceed in an orderly manner, he needs some kind of plan. He can raise certain questions and rule out their answers at once, thus making his whole project more manageable. Is baldness universal? If it is, then women should be bald-headed; but, since experience shows that they are not, they can be ruled out of the investigation. Have all bald-headed men washed their hair frequently prior to being bald? This question also, when answered, leads to consequences that can be checked by experience. Skipping quickly over intermediate questions, the investigator would no doubt consider the class of men who have most frequently taken showers, for example professional athletes. Whether he finds the answer to his problem in this class or not, he will keep raising questions and drawing out their consequences until he at last finds the right question which gives an answer leading to the correct induction. Dialectic enables him also to defend his induction when it is questioned in dispute.

Dialectic and opinion. Dialectic, in the two cases so far discussed, is not induction. It is a preliminary to induction, clearing the ground so that certain questions can be eliminated and the remaining question prepared for checking in experience. Dialectic determines what is relevant to the solution of a problem without actually solving it. The solution is the work of another operation, usually induction.

Unlike genuine propositions, questions do not represent a real state of affairs outside the mind. What they stand for has, to the extent that we are dealing with questions, only a logical existence. Questions should lead to the securing of scientific propositions, but as pre-scientific, dialectic is a way of putting an initial and purely logical organization into our knowledge, thus preparing it to assume a later scientific status where things are represented no longer in a merely logical system but as they truly are in reality itself.

The scientific organization of knowledge is always preceded by foreknowledge. It does not originate suddenly and from a vacuum. Pre-scientific knowledge acquired by reason is called opinion; and by contrast with the certain character of science, opinion is only probable knowledge. Indeed, in most cases, the point of departure for a dialectical argument is the opinion received from others. By drawing out the consequences of the questions raised by such received opinion, the true and false can be sifted and ways can be suggested for obtaining experiential check of the conclusion.

Dialectic, as organizing our knowledge in a pre-scientific way, is the logic of the probable. Probable, in its strict etymological mean-ing which it had when used to define dialectic, means provable but not yet proved. So, at any rate, says St. Albert the Great, one of the eminent logicians of the middle ages.

In dialectic, we have not yet strictly proved anything, but we are on the way to proof. In the case of the project to determine the correlation between bald-headedness and frequent hair washing, the dialectician may narrow down the field of investigation and take one opinion in preference to another. But until he makes an induc-tion, he is not properly in the order of strict proof. In dialectic alone, we do not reach principles proper to any particular science.

Demonstration closes on truth. There is no fear that the contra-dictory of its conclusion is true. But dialectic, as such, is always open. In raising any question, the good dialectician will take the two contradictory answers to it and evolve the consequences of each until conclusions are found that can, presuming we are dealing with the sense world, be checked in experience. If no conclusive induction can be made through the appeal to experience, the mind must remain in a state of opinion, fearing to a greater or less extent that the contradictory of the opinion may be true.

These remarks may serve as a general introduction to what dialec-tic is. It is a logic of questioning which provides a plan of inquiry. It is a logic of the provable, and as preliminary to the scientific order, it can give the mind, in its own name, nothing more than opinion. Unlike demonstration which is certain and closed, dialectic, as such, is always open and fearful that its contradictory may be true. Dialectic can at most determine the relevance of propositions to the solution of a problem. It cannot solve the problem in its own right. When used by any science, dialectic never proceeds through principles proper to the science itself.

The dialectical syllogism. But it has not yet been shown why dialectic is syllogistic and how, more precisely, it differs from the demonstration.

In view of the fact that dialectic requires the drawing of con-sequences from questions, it always involves a discourse, the pro-cession from one thing to another. In the case of **23.2,** the argu-ment can be transformed from the hypothetical to the categorical syllogism, even though the new argument may not indicate, as well as the old did, that the original major premise has arisen from a question:

> **23.2a.** Whatever contains only one principle does not permit change.
>
> Any material thing contains only one principle.
>
> Therefore, any material thing does not permit change.

It is apparent that there is a syllogism here, similar to the demonstrations in the last chapter.

But there is one major difference.

In the dialectical syllogism, the middle term represents only a probable or provable cause. The cause remains only provable until our induction proves otherwise, either by showing that it is not a cause at all or by leaving our knowledge of it in greater or lesser provability. This is the central difference between the demonstrative and dialectical syllogisms.

Dialectic as tentative. Dialectic is a kind of scaffold that the mind builds in order to attain truth. After the truth has been reached, dialectic that helped to attain it should like any scaffolding be torn down and disregarded. That man is a rational animal or that matter is composed of parts we know to be true without continuing support from the dialectical apparatus we used to reach them. Such propositions are true unconditionally.

But for the most part, in the pursuit of truth, we are unable to dismiss the dialectical tools we have enlisted to our aid. In such cases, we do not reach absolute truth. Our truth is conditional. It is conditioned indeed by the dialectical framework we used to attain it. Our induction resulting from dialectic remains so colored by the dialectical conditions of reaching it that the induction may be called a dialectical induction.

In order to bring out the meaning of this rather abstract analysis, let us take an example:

Since the time of Copernicus, learned minds have assented to the proposition that our planetary system is heliocentric. Yet the only strong evidence to support this proposition is that the heliocentric theory of the heavens is mathematically simpler than the earlier geocentric view of Ptolemy.

Now a simpler explanation may be the best when there is no other evidence, but simplicity itself is no guarantee of truth. The complex explanation may still be closer to actual fact, or there may even be theories, not yet projected, which would explain the appearances of the heavens better than any hypothesis yet known. At any rate, there is no warrant, at present, to conclude that heliocentrism has been established as absolutely true. Such a conclusion is not in the same class with propositions like: *man is rational, matter is extended*. The evidence of mathematical simplicity is in favor of Copernicus; but there is a natural tendency of the mind, based upon a physical analysis of the appearances, to a geocentric position.

The two rival theories of astronomy afford a good illustration of the kind of argument in which the dialectical scaffolding is never dismantled. If you ask the question in one way, you will get a heliocentric answer; if you ask it in another way, you will get a geocentric answer. In each case, logic should compel us to state the question we are answering; this question is still intrinsically involved in our answers; neither of our answers is, in the literal sense of the word, unquestionable.

Hence any proposition which is true only from this or that viewpoint or with respect to this or that frame of reference can be at most relatively or dialectically true and never true in absolute sense. Such a judgment holds even of modern theories of postulational mathematics where true conclusions may be drawn with respect to the postulates with no guarantee that, apart from the postulates, the conclusions are, absolutely speaking, true.

The proposition that man is a rational animal, on the other hand, does not have any dialectical qualification. It is unquestionably true. The proposition that the world is heliocentric, however, is more or less provable. We are unable to think away the dialectical framework through which it was reached and to see the truth absolutely and through its own compelling internal evidence. We see it only through our dialectic. There is a constant danger in the life of reason to regard as scientific and certain what is only dialectically true, hence possibly wrong.

Aristotle, in his discovery of the first principles of motion, was able to throw away his dialectic because in this part of his study of nature he reached truth that is unqualified and unquestioned. For the most part, modern fields like physics, chemistry, and biology, do not allow knowledge of this type. By the definitions adopted in this chapter and the last, such studies in their present form are in general not scientific but dialectical. It would be trivial to quarrel over terminology, but under any name, it is extremely important to distinguish as types of knowledge between science, as taken in the preceding chapter, and dialectic, as described in this.

Questions and the questionable. Since dialectic deals with questions more than with certain answers that conform to reality, it would be appropriate to make a list of the four fundamental questions that the mind can ask about anything: (a) whether this is so, e.g., whether the sun is a source of heat; (b) why a thing is so, e.g., why the sun is a source of heat; (c) whether a thing is, e.g., whether oxygen exists; and (d) what a thing is, e.g., what oxygen is. Every question aimed at securing a scientific proposition can be reduced to one of these four.

The saying that a question well put is a question half answered goes back as far as Francis Bacon. Aristotle himself insisted that the discovery of truth is the solution of a doubt or a question, and Plato's dialogues are filled with questioning. To question well is to be a good dialectician.

The dialectical syllogism is a syllogism in which the middle term is uncertain. It is based on questions rather than on propositions already established as true. Dialectic, as a preliminary to induction, can prepare for science but in itself cannot reach farther than opinion. Sometimes the dialectic used to attain a truth can be disregarded when the truth is attained, and the truth is absolute and certain. For the most part, however, human knowledge, no matter how refined, always remains a qualified knowledge, where the kind of question asked remains an essential part of the answer given; and where an opposite answer, qualified in turn by an opposite question, remains more or less possible.

Problems

1. Define dialectic and give examples of its uses.

2. Compare dialectic to the demonstrative syllogism and to induction.

3. What is the state of mind at the end of a purely dialectical argument? What is meant by saying that dialectic is a logic of the probable and in this sense is pre-scientific?

4. Why is a dialectical argument syllogistic?

5. What is meant by saying that sometimes, after truth is attained, the dialectical tool for reaching it can be thrown away, while at other times the kind of question asked intrinsically qualifies the answer given? What is dialectical induction?

6. Show the relevance of dialectic to the Aristotelian interpretation of modern "science." Is modern science scientific in Aristotle's sense? Explain.

7. Identify dialectical elements in each of the following passages and find in each passage reference to one of the four dialectical questions. Note any transitions from the dialectical order to inductions.

23.3. Their world [that of the Mayas], once so certain, stable, dependable, and definite is gone. And why?

Here of course, is a first-rate mystery for modern skill and knowledge to unravel. The people were not exterminated, nor their cities taken over by an enemy. Plagues may cause temporary migrations, but not the permanent abandonment of established and prosperous centers. The present population to the north has its share of debilitating infections, but its ancestors were not too weak or wasted to establish the Second Empire after they left the First. Did the climate in the abandoned cities become so much more humid that the invasion of dense tropical vegetation could not be arrested, while fungous pests, insects, and diseases took increasing toll? This is hard to prove. Were the inhabitants starved out because they had no steel tools or draft animals to break the heavy sod which formed over their resting fields? Many experts think so.

PAUL B. SEARS

23.4. A more promising line of approach to our problem is to examine which, if any, of the planets is physically suitable for life. But we are at once confronted with the difficulty that we do not know what precise conditions are necessary for life. A human being transferred to the surface of any one of the planets or of their satellites would die at once, and this for several different reasons on each. On Jupiter he would be simultaneously frozen, asphyxiated, and poisoned, as well as doubly pressed to death by his own weight and by an atmospheric pressure of about a million terrestial atmospheres. On Mercury he would be burned to death by the sun's heat, killed by its ultra-violet radiation, asphyxiated from want of oxygen and dessicated from want of water. But this does not touch the question of whether other planets may not have developed species of life suited to their own physical conditions. . . . as the physical states of other planets are so different from that of our

own, it seems safe to say that any life there may be on any of
them must be very different from the life on earth.

JAMES JEANS

23.5. In order to begin exploration of an uncharted scientific field,
in which there is a lack even of the bare elements for posing clear-cut
questions, a unique type of imaginative power seems necessary.
This can be designated as the building of mental bridges. It consists of the visualization of the main elements of the design based
solely upon a few dimly lit building stones. Out of these elements
the imaginative scientist makes the first draft of the building plan.
He arrives at it not so much out of logical necessity, as out of an
artistic feeling of esthetic harmony. Further study of such a plan
of a whole field, however dim the outlines may be, will clearly
indicate at what point the actual work should begin. The drive to
think in such a fashion and the ability to do so may often be
found in individuals of otherwise mediocre attainments. In them
it may easily lead to delusion, when they do not appreciate that
this first sketch is only the preliminary step to an exact understanding
and that it should be erased once its purpose as a guide has been
accomplished. It is, in my opinion, a malady of present physiology
that the method of preliminary synthetic thinking is coming into
disrepute and that its application by the rising generation is in-
tentionally suppressed.

FRIEDRICH MIESCHER

23.6. For instance, there can hardly be a doubt that the animals
which fight with their teeth, have acquired the habit of drawing back
their ears closely to their heads, when feeling savage, from their
progenitors having voluntarily acted in this manner in order to
protect their ears from being torn by antagonists; for those animals
which do not fight with their teeth do not thus express a savage
state of mind. We may infer as highly probable that we ourselves
have acquired the habit of contracting the muscles round the eyes,
whilst crying gently, that is, without the utterance of any loud
sound, from our progenitors, especially during infancy, having experienced during the act of screaming, an uncomfortable sensation
in their eyeballs.

CHARLES DARWIN

23.7. How can it be that the only nation in the world with a
tradition of popular education produces 98 million movie-goers a
week who happily keep on paying their two bits, four bits, six bits
(and sometimes three times that much) to see and hear chopsticks
year in and year out? Or a symphonic arrangement of chopsticks
(scored by a great European producer making more money in a

month than in his entire previous career) in a spectacular production number that involves hundreds of identical pianos?

Is it because, for all our compulsory education, we're numbed to anything more challenging? Or do we keep coming back week after week simply for the want of something better to do? Is it that Hollywood can't play anything that requires more than two fingers and a kindergarten rhythm?

BUDD SCHULBERG

23.8. Are not the rays of light very small bodies emitted from shining substances? For such bodies will pass through uniform mediums in right [straight] lines without bending into the shadow, which is the nature of the rays of light. They will also be capable of several properties and be able to conserve their properties unchanged in passing through several mediums, which is another condition of the rays of light.

ISAAC NEWTON

Chapter 24:   THE RHETORICAL SYLLOGISM

24.1.   Fourscore and seven years ago our fathers brought forth upon this continent a new nation, conceived in liberty and dedicated to the proposition that all men are created equal. Now we are engaged in a great civil war, testing whether that nation, or any nation so conceived and so dedicated can long endure. We are met on a battlefield of that war. We have come to dedicate a portion of that field as a final resting place for those who here gave their lives that that nation might live. It is altogether fitting and proper that we should do this. But in a larger sense we cannot dedicate, we cannot consecrate, we cannot hallow this ground. The brave men living and dead who fought here have consecrated it far above our poor power to add or detract. The world will little note nor long remember what we say here, but it can never forget what they did here. It is for us, the living, rather to be dedicated here to the unfinished work which they who fought here have thus far nobly advanced. It is rather for us to be here dedicated to the great task remaining before us, that from these honored dead we take increased devotion to that cause for which they gave the last full measure of devotion; that we here highly resolve that these dead shall not have died in vain; that this nation, under God, shall have a new birth of freedom, and that government of the people, by the people, and for the people shall not perish from the earth.

ABRAHAM LINCOLN

Rhetoric and discourse.   Considering its length, the Gettysburg Address of Abraham Lincoln is one of the great speeches in our language. It is an excellent example of rhetorical argumentation. As in dialectic and demonstration, it is a form of syllogism in which from propositions, established and accepted, another proposition follows.

In order to locate the rhetorical syllogism within the context of

the two preceding chapters, it should be observed that in dialectic
— and even more so in demonstration — there is an appeal to the
intellect through rational evidence. In demonstration, there is
adequate evidence to convince the mind that the conclusion is
certain. In dialectic, the evidence is much weaker and the mind,
no longer convinced and certain of its premises, accepts the conclusion as only provable. In the rhetorical syllogism, however, the
evidence presented to the mind alone is weaker still, so much so
that reason, no longer open to purely rational argument, is finally
swayed by the will to accept or reject a given proposition. Unlike
the dialectician, the rhetorician presents his conclusion not merely
as true and hence appealing to the intellect but, in a special way,
as good and hence appealing to the will.

To return to the Gettysburg Address, Lincoln has presented a
discourse in which a conclusion follows not merely after a number
of "premises" but because of them. To reduce his argument to
the form of a syllogism may seem to drain it of the moving power
which it enjoys from, for instance, the very structure of its
sentences and the choice of its words. And yet words and syntax
are themselves subordinated to the rhetorical syllogism which uses
them in order to achieve the conclusion desired by the speaker or
writer. There is, in Lincoln's address, the following syllogism:

> 24.1a. If the Civil War soldiers died for a great ideal in
> government, we ought to be dedicated to their ideal.
> But Civil War soldiers did die for a great ideal in government.
> Therefore, we ought to be dedicated to their ideal.

To bring his audience to accept such a conclusion, Lincoln used
a kind of logic, as shown by the formal structure of the preceding
syllogism. But in order to be accepted, at least the major premise
depends on the emotional response of the audience, and it could be
shown also that even the minor premise has similar support from
the appeal to the good. The various devices used by Lincoln to
establish his premises — his reference to the glorious past, his tribute
to the valiant dead, and his struggle to achieve an identification of
interest between the fallen soldiers and their surviving countrymen — would all bear richer analysis than space here allows. For
our purposes, however, it is enough to observe that Lincoln employed

argument, a discourse, a syllogism and that the premises on which the conclusion rests depend, in part at least, on something less than merely rational evidence. The rhetorical syllogism addresses itself not to reason alone but also to the will and emotions.

The means of persuasion. The purpose of rhetoric is not to convince — because the only kind of evidence that brings conviction is not at hand; unlike demonstration and dialectic, rhetoric has for its purpose to persuade. Rhetoric is the art of the means of persuasion.

A universal art of the mind, rhetoric is employed by doctor and lawyer and merchant and chief. Politicians in and out of office use rhetoric in order to "sell" their programs to the people. Editorial writers and columnists of the daily press must, in a conscious or unconscious way, be good rhetoricians to be successful. Salesmen use rhetoric constantly, and nowhere is it more important than in modern advertising.

An advertisement for ladies' hair shampoo, to take an example, may carry the picture of a famous actress with her appropriate endorsement of the product; the *implication* is — note the presence of an implicit *argument* in the advertisement — that the hair shampoo should be purchased by ladies because they will *want* to be beautiful like the actress. Surely this is an appeal to *want* or appetite.

Or take the man with a patch over his eye as an advertisement for shirts. He stands out as a person of distinction, and the implication is that men who *want* to look distinctive will also buy the kind of shirt in question. Here is another appeal to the will.

Other advertisements play on the desire for health or for utility. Such and such a pill will make you feel *good*, or the new kind of house paint will prevent blistering and hence, in accordance with the *desire* of the homeowner, save work and expense.

Most advertising today appeals to the appearance of a prospective buyer or his possessions, to health or wealth, or to the utility of a product for personal or business use. Such advertising usually offers examples of rhetoric in its purest mode.

Aristotle lists three means for persuasion: "(1) to reason logically; (2) to understand human character and goodness in their various forms; and (3) to understand the emotions — that is, to name them and describe them, to know their causes and the way in which they are excited."*

The rhetorician must reason. This can be seen clearly in Lincoln's address where propositions are put together in order to build up to a conclusion. Reasoning is apparent even in the rhetoric of the advertiser. Without a content of reasoning, written or spoken language cannot appeal to a rational animal. Moreover, the reasoning must be logical: the conclusion must in some degree follow from the "premise" and not be disconnected or even contradictory with respect to what each "premise" says.

The second requirement of the rhetorician is the understanding of character in order to exploit the motives for good and evil in a listener or reader. Moreover, one of the tools of rhetoric is the reliance of an audience upon the goodness of the rhetorician's own personal character. Men believe a good man before a bad one.

That is why businesses, in their advertising, like to emphasize their reputation and why also campaign oratory often centers on the private life of an opponent. Quintillian defined a rhetorician as "a good man skilled in speaking."

The third means of persuasion is the understanding of the emotions of men. Knowing the likes and dislikes of his readers or listeners, and how such sentiments are controlled by thoughts and words and other signs, the rhetorician can the more effectively move his audience to the conclusion he intends. Lincoln appealed, among other things, to the patriotism of his audience and to their respect for the dead. Communism plays upon the hatred of the have-not nations for the haves.

The importance of rhetoric. It is obvious that rhetoric involves more than merely logical considerations and something besides the kind of evidence which convinces human reason when taken alone. Unlike demonstration and even dialectic, rhetoric always involves the ethical order, right and wrong, good and evil. A clever rhetorician can arouse men toward ends that are evil. The propaganda of the Communists and of the Nazis furnish cases of using rhetorical devices to influence whole nations, or at least great parts of them, to evil ends. That is why rhetoric so often has a bad meaning and why to call a piece of writing or speaking rhetorical is usually a way of condemning it.

---

* *Rhetoric*, I, 2; 1356 a 21.

But in any human communication on no matter what level the choice is never between being or not being rhetorical but between being rhetorical to good or bad moral purposes. Even to get others interested in a subject requires a respect for the rhetorical techniques which capture and sustain attention. Such an apparently abstract document as a book on theoretical physics cannot escape a style, and wherever there is style, there is rhetoric.

It is often said today that rhetoric is a lost art. This is not really the case. Rhetoric has changed in practice since the days of Demosthenes and Cicero, Newman and Macaulay, and even Chesterton and Belloc, but rhetoric, like character good or bad, is always with us. The importance of rhetoric today is made all the greater by the fact that so few are conscious of its presence and its power and hence remain uncritical of the rhetorical strategies and tactics used in the various media of communication. Rhetoric is always necessary, but rhetoric, alone and without rational control, is a dangerous explosive.

Divisions of rhetorical argument. Paralleling the distinction between syllogism and induction, rhetoric is divided into enthymeme and example.

An enthymeme is a truncated syllogism, a syllogism in which any or all of the three propositions are not fully stated; and sometimes one of them is not stated at all. In our study of the categorical syllogism, Chapter 16, we encountered numerous examples of enthymeme where the syllogisms were implied rather than stated. All syllogisms where a premise is suppressed or where one or more of the propositions is not explicitly stated are enthymemes. They are rhetorical because the writer or speaker leaves it to the good will of the reader or listener to complete the argument in question or to set it in its correct logical form. Rarely, even in philosophy books, are syllogisms encountered in their full and formal logical expression. This is but another argument as to the omnipresence of rhetoric in human expression.

As an enthymeme is a truncated or abridged syllogism, example is a truncated induction. In reasoning by example, one or several cases are given to illustrate a universal proposition, and the reader or hearer is invited to supply others so that the general principle will be accepted. Consider this example:

24.2. Taste, when it is spontaneous, always begins with the senses. Children and savages, we are often told, delight in bright and variegated colors; the simplest people appreciate the neatness of muslin curtains, shining varnish, and burnished pots.

GEORGE SANTAYANA

Santayana is using several examples of artistic taste as found in simple-minded human beings in order to establish the apparently universal proposition that taste always begins with the senses. If the inductive conclusion is to be accepted, the listed examples do not justify it by themselves. It is up to the hearer or reader to supply for himself the remaining examples necessary to justify the induction or else to concede, because of Santayana's reputation, that he could, if he cared, go on to list an adequate number of cases to prove his universal affirmative proposition beyond doubt.

Three kinds of syllogism, with their corresponding inductions, have been seen so far. The originality of a rhetorical, as opposed to scientific and dialectical argument, is that it seeks to persuade. In rhetoric, the mind, no longer capable of reaching purely rational support for its conclusion, makes appeal to will and emotion.

Problems

1. Define rhetoric and contrast it with demonstration and dialectic.
2. Show how rhetoric is a universal art.
3. What are the means of persuasion?
4. Explain the meaning of the term *enthymeme*.
5. Compare and contrast scientific induction, dialectical induction, and example.
6. Show why the following passages are rhetorical and name any rhetorical devices used to make a point:

24.3. Our papers have been making a great deal of American "know-how" ever since we had the misfortune to discover the atomic bomb. There is one quality more important than "know-how," and we cannot accuse the United States of any undue amount of it. This is "know-what" by which we determine not only how to accomplish our purposes, but what our purposes are to be. I can distinguish between the two by an example. Some years ago, a prominent American engineer bought an expensive player-piano. It became clear after a week or two that this purchase did not correspond to any particular interest in the music played by the piano but rather to an overwhelming interest in the piano mechanism.

For this gentleman, the player-piano was not a means of producing music, but a means of giving some inventor the chance of showing how skillful he was at overcoming certain difficulties in the production of music. This is an estimable attitude in a second-year high-school student. How estimable it is in one of those on whom the whole cultural future of the country depends, I leave to the reader.

NORBERT WIENER

24.4. After all this, it is surely superfluous to answer the question that has once been asked, Whether Pope was a poet? otherwise than by asking in return, If Pope be not a poet, where is poetry to be found? To circumscribe poetry by a definition will only show the narrowness of the definer, though a definition which shall exclude Pope will not easily be made. Let us look around upon the present time, and back upon the past; let us inquire to whom the voice of mankind has decreed the wreath of poetry, let their productions be examined, and their claim stated, and the pretensions of Pope will be no more disputed. Had he given the world only his version, the name of poet must have been allowed him: if the writer of the *Iliad* were to class his successors, he would assign a very high place to his translator, without requiring any other evidence of Genius.

SAMUEL JOHNSON

24.5. Its results [those of growth] are extraordinary achievements, which would be astounding if they were not so familiar. From a microscopic egg-cell there develops an embryo-plant which may grow, say, into a California "Big-Tree" — perhaps three hundred feet in height and over three thousand years ago. A frog is about three or four inches in length; its egg-cell is under a tenth of an inch in diameter; "the mass of the human adult is fifteen billion times that of the human ovum."

J. ARTHUR THOMPSON AND PATRICK GEDDES

24.6. There is not and there never was on this earth an Institution so well deserving of examination as the Roman Catholic Church. The history of that Church joins together the two great ages of human civilization. No other institution is left standing which carries the mind back to the times when the smoke of sacrifice rose from the Pantheon, and when camelopards and tigers bounded in the Flavian amphitheatre. The proudest royal houses are but of yesterday, when compared with the line of the Supreme Pontiffs. That line we trace back in an unbroken series, from the Pope who crowned Napoleon in the nineteenth century to the Pope who crowned Pepin in the eighth; and far beyond the line of Pepin the august dynasty extends till it is lost in the twilight of fable.

The republic of Venice came next in antiquity. But the republic of Venice was modern when compared with the Papacy; and the republic of Venice is gone, but the Papacy remains. The Papacy remains, not in decay, not a mere antique, but full of life and youthful vigor. The Catholic Church is still sending forth to the farthest ends of the world missionaries as zealous as those who landed in Kent with Augustine, and still confronting hostile kinds with the same spirit with which she confronted Attila. The number of her children is greater than in any former age. Her acquisitions in the New World have more than compensated for what she lost in the Old. Her spiritual ascendancy extends over the vast countries which lie between the plains of the Missouri and Cape Horn, a population as large as that which now inhabits Europe. The members of her communion are certainly not fewer than a hundred and fifty millions; and it will be difficult to show that all other Christian sects united amount to a hundred and twenty millions. Nor do we see any sign which indicates that the term of her long dominion is approaching. She saw the commencement of all the Government and of the ecclestiastical establishments that now exist in the world; and we feel no assurance that she is not destined to see the end of them all. She was great and respected before the Saxon had set foot in Britain, before the Frank had passed the Rhine, when Grecian eloquence still flourished in Antioch, when idols were still worshipped in the temple of Mecca. And she may still exist in undiminished vigor when some traveller from New Zealand shall, in the midst of a vast solitude, take his stand on a broken arch of London Bridge to sketch the ruins of St. Paul's.

THOMAS BABINGTON MACAULAY

24.7. Beethoven played a more decisive role in the evolution of music than any other single figure, not excepting Bach. It is only necessary to compare his earliest works with his last ones to recognize what progress the art of music made in his time — and largely owing to him.

DAVID EWEN

Mark Anthony's "Funeral Oration"

24.8.   Friends, Romans, countrymen, lend me your ears;
        I come to bury Caesar, not to praise him.
        The evil that men do lives after them;
        The good is oft interred with their bones;
        So let it be with Caesar. The noble Brutus
        Hath told you Caesar was ambitious;
        If it were so, it was a grievous fault,
        And grievously hath Caesar answer'd it.
        Here, under leave of Brutus and the rest, —
        For Brutus is an honorable man;

So are they all, all honorable men, —
Come I to speak in Caesar's funeral.
He was my friend, faithful and just to me:
But Brutus says he was ambitious;
And Brutus is an honorable man.
He hath brought many captives home to Rome,
Whose ransoms did the general coffers fill:
Did this in Caesar seem ambitious?
When that the poor have cried, Caesar hath wept:
Ambition should be made of sterner stuff:
Yet Brutus says he was ambitious;
And Brutus is an honorable man.
You all did see that on the Lupercal
I thrice presented him a kingly crown,
Which he did thrice refuse: was this ambitious?
Yet Brutus says he was ambitious;
And, sure, he is an honorable man.
I speak not to disprove what Brutus spoke,
But here I am to speak what I do know.
You all did love him once, not without cause:
What cause withholds you then to mourn for him?
O judgment! thou art fled to brutish beasts,
And men have lost their reason. Bear with me;
My heart is in the coffin there with Caesar,
And I must pause till it come back to me.

WILLIAM SHAKESPEARE

Chapter 25: THE LITERARY SYLLOGISM

25.1.   Much have I travelled in the realms of gold,
And many goodly states and kingdoms seen;
Round many western islands have I been
Which bards in fealty to Apollo hold.
Oft of one wide expanse had I been told
That deep-brow'd Homer rules as his demesne;
Yet never did I breathe its pure serene
Till I heard Chapman speak out loud and bold;
Then felt I like some watcher of the skies
When a new planet swims into his ken;
Or like stout Cortez when with eagle eyes
He star'd at the Pacific — and all his men
Look'd at each other with a wild surmise —
Silent as on a peak in Darien.

JOHN KEATS

Literature as discourse. The two extremes of literary pretension have always tended to be internally meaningless on the one hand or to be a mere servant of ends extrinsic to literature itself. By contrast to the first extreme, the genuine literary man always has something to say, and he escapes being a mere propagandist because the pooled resources intrinsic to the work can say it.

Indeed, every truly literary work will be found to be a syllogism of a very special type. If the poem of Keats is analyzed, it will be evident that even a romantic poet is, as a poet, engaged in discourse. Keats is challenging the mind with some sort of "proposition," namely that it is a worthwhile adventure to read Chapman's translation of Homer. Moreover, the proposition "follows" from certain "premises":

25.2.   Whatever is better than travelling through realms of gold, etc., is a delightful experience.

200

> Reading Chapman's *Homer* is better than travelling through realms of gold, etc.
>
> Therefore, . . .

As in poetry, so in other forms of literature like the novel, there is, in one way or another, a sequence of interconnected themes sweeping to a proper climax. In every genuine piece of literature containing all the literary elements, there is a logic to the plot, a plausibility to the character, and a connection between the various situations where the plot unfolds and the characters are engaged. In short, literature is always a discourse. It is a kind of syllogism.

Literature and language. But literature is argument of a very special type. By the very representation, pleasant or unpleasant, of the object under consideration, a literary work compels our commitment. In its appeal to the mind, no other form of syllogism can be content with merely representing its object in a beautiful or ugly way. Other arguments must bring up evidence extrinsic to each premise to establish both of them, while in literature such evidence emerges in some way from merely being properly expressed.

Moreover, in a scientific argument, to take an example, it would usually make no difference in the proof if a synonym were employed for a certain word, say *costly* for *expensive*. In poetry, on the other hand, even the sound of words becomes a means within the argument. Suppose that Keats had said not "stout Cortez" but "fat Balboa." Historically, he would have been correct, but if the new expression is inserted, part of the beauty in the poem will certainly be lost. This point might be illustrated better by reference to another work of Keats himself. It is said that in the first draft of his *Endymion* he wrote: "A thing of beauty is a constant joy," but later changed the line to its classic form: "A thing of beauty is a joy forever." The strictly intellectual content of both lines is the same, but the difference in poetic charm is immeasurable. The second line, with its short trochaic ending that trails off as though there were more to come, puts the sound into a much more genial harmony with the meaning intended. The first reading is closed, but the second is open, like the meaning of "forever" itself.

Sounds in literature evoke an emotional response to an object, coloring it for the right grasp of it by human reason.

In short, where there is poetry and indeed where there is any literature at all, the very medium of language is an essential part of the total effect of the composition. This is another way of saying that in literature what is represented and how it is represented cannot be separated as in science but coalesce into a single human expression. Science can always be paraphrased, but in literature the paraphrase always loses something essential to the original work. And so indeed, in greater or less degree, does even the best translation of the greatest classic. To use the language of logic, the scientist uses signs as a means of knowing other things; in literature, signs are an intrinsic part of what is known and communicated.

This may be a convenient place to compare the literary syllogism with demonstration, dialectic, and rhetoric. In any demonstration, there is a necessity about the evidence involved so that the mind is compelled to accept the conclusion of the argument and thus acquire scientific knowledge. In dialectic, there is less necessity, so that reason can reach no more than a probable conclusion and must settle, not for science, but for opinion. In the rhetorical syllogism, the evidence is so weak that reason, in reaching truth, needs the assistance of the will with its tendency to the good. Finally, in the literary syllogism, the mind has almost run out of discourse. In literature, there is so little appeal to rational evidence usual in proof that the mind is led to accept a conclusion by the delightful or loathesome way in which an object is represented to it. With reason then literature has been called the lowest kind of discourse (*infima doctrina*).

Thus far, scientific discourse has been contrasted to the literary argument in terms of their relation to language which is their medium of expression and to the necessity which accrues to their conclusions. Another sample of their differences can be found in their concern with the abstract and universal.

Image and idea. The scientist abstracts his ideas from individual things, but the poet refuses to take them away from the concrete circumstances in which they are embodied. Science, in other words, is purely intellectual, whereas literature, to communicate with an audience, uses sense images to express the universal in its concrete clothing. Let us watch this principle at work in Keats.

In conveying to his hearers that it is worthwhile to read the translation of Homer, he compares his own experience with what every experienced person would concede to be a rich adventure . . . traveling through the realms of gold, being on fabulous islands of the west. Homer did not seem very significant. Keats had heard Homer mentioned, but he never knew the grandeur of Homer until he chanced upon Chapman's translation. Then he felt like a man experiencing the three great things that most excite our emotions of awe, namely the stars, the sea, and the mountains. Much more could be added to such a paraphrase by way of detail, but the point really worth noting here is the images of great things directed to express a great experience, the universal objects of human wonder marshaled to help reveal the experience of a universal poet. The images like the sounds conspire with the thought as integral parts of the poem, and all of these elements are necessary to convey the impression which Keats wants to come through to us. The rhetorician, for example the advertiser, uses language and usually imagery to sell a product separate from both of them; but the literary artist produces a unity in which his means are part of the product itself.

Sound and image are at the core of literature, but great literary artists — to return to the original theme — have all been busied not merely with pictures presented by words or with music as found in meter and rhyme. They have also had something to say. They use imagery and sound to help them say it because they could not say it in abstract thought alone.

Thus, Milton was concerned in *Paradise Lost* to "justify the ways of God to man." Virgil sang of "arms and the man," Homer of "the wrath of Achilles," Dante of virtually all Catholic theology. The same judgment could be reached by a study of great novels — the novels of Dostoevsky, Tolstoy, Henry James, and Thackeray.

Because he treats truth as embodied in images and as communicable not merely by the thought in words but also by their sound, the poet in one way drives deeper than the scientist into the concrete. But the report on the real by literature, while less abstract than science, is also less certain and less universal and less compelling upon the listening mind.

Where literature becomes abstract as in certain poems of Tennyson and Whitman and in several of the novels of Aldous Huxley, it simply becomes poor literature if literature it remains. The kind of impression aimed at would belong by natural temperament in some more suitable form of discourse. On the other hand, there are compositions sometimes alleged as literary, which have no meaning and would, except for their play of sound, hardly claim serious attention. The most obvious case of this is Carroll's "The Jabberwocky."

Literature and reason. It is unfair to ask that a paraphrase of a poem represent the original; but it is not unfair to ask a poet or other literary artist what he means. It would be defective literature that was written in the austere and abstract language proper to science; but at the same time, a writer, even though using infralogical and infrarational techniques of images and sound, can never claim immunity from the laws of reason.

Other arts like painting and sculpture do not involve discourse, and their constructions, while by and for the mind, are not, like literature, in the mind itself. By contrast to painting and sculpture, literature remains within the liberal arts as one of the four forms of logical discourse.

On the scope of logic. By this time the reader is no doubt aware that logic, as conceived by an Aristotelian and a Thomist, is quite different from an upstairs closet of lifeless rules. It lives in homes as different as mathematics and literature. A good logician should be able to identify any of the four forms of discourse and, according to the different standards required by each case, lend a critical eye or ear to each of them. Only a most summary treatment has been possible here of the kinds of syllogism which a student will make and meet; courses in literary criticism may supplement our chapters on literature and possibly rhetoric. But a more advanced study of how to read and listen to other kinds of argument is often not possible in many college programs. A good logician should possess in a personal and integrated way an ability to interrelate the four forms of discourse we have studied. These have been summed up by Newman in a brilliant passage on liberal education that can bring our four-fold treatment of general logic to a fitting close: "It is the education which gives a man a clear, conscious view of his own opinions and judgments, a truth in developing them, an eloquence in expressing them, and a force in urging them."* As a review of

---

* John Henry Newman, *The Scope and Nature of University Education,* Everyman edition (London and New York: J. M. Dent, Ltd., and E. P. Dutton, 1915), p. 171.

the last four chapters, the reader is invited to compare Newman's words with each of the four forms of syllogism.

Problems

1. Explain why literature is a form of discourse.
2. What is the originality of the literary syllogism?
3. Explain the relation between thought and medium in literature and contrast this with the relation between these two components in science.
4. Explain the relation of literature to its paraphrase.
5. Show why literature is a liberal art pertaining to logic, whereas painting and sculpture are not liberal arts.
6. Analyze the following poem in the light of the principles discussed in this chapter:

"On His Blindness"

25.3.   When I consider how my light is spent,
        Ere half my days, in this dark world and wide,
        And that one talent which is death to hide,
        Lodged with me useless, though my soul more bent,
        To serve therewith my Maker, and present
        My true account, lest He returning chide,
        Doth God exact day-labour, light denied?
        I fondly ask; but Patience, to prevent
        That murmur, soon replies, God does not need
        Either man's work, or his own gifts: who best
        Bear his mild yoke, they serve Him best; His state
        Is kingly. Thousands at His bidding speed
        And post o'er land and ocean without rest:
        They also serve who only stand and wait.

                                        JOHN MILTON

7. Write an evaluation of either of the following short stories to show the elements of discourse which they contain.

> Guy de Maupassant, "The Necklace."
> Edgar Allen Poe, "The Cask of Amontillado."
> Anton Chekov, "The Cherry Tree."
> Katherine Ann Porter, "Flowering Judas."
> Henry James, "The Turn of the Screw."

8. Evaluate as literary discourse either of the following poems:

> Samuel Taylor Coleridge, "Kubla Khan."
> Alfred Lord Tennyson, "In Memoriam."

Chapter 26: THE NATURE OF HISTORY

26.1. Thucydides, an Athenian, wrote the history of the war between the Peloponnesians and the Athenians, beginning at the moment that it broke out, and believing that it would be a great war, and more worthy of relation than any that had preceded it. This belief was not without its grounds. The preparations of both the combatants were in every department in the last state of perfection; and he could see the rest of the Hellenic race taking sides in the quarrel; those who delayed doing so at once having it in contemplation. Indeed this was the greatest movement yet known in history, not only of the Hellenes, but of a large part of the barbarian world — I had almost said of mankind. For though the events of remote antiquity, and even those that more immediately preceded the war, could not from lapse of time be clearly ascertained, yet the evidences which an inquiry carried as far back as was practicable leads me to trust, all point to the conclusion that there was nothing on a great scale, either in war or in other matters.

For instance, it is evident that the country now called Hellas had in ancient times no settled population; on the contrary, migrations were of frequent occurrence, the several tribes readily abandoning their homes under the pressure of superior numbers. Without commerce, without freedom of communication either by land or sea, cultivating no more of their territory than the exigencies of life required, destitute of capital, never planting their land (for they could not tell when an invader might not come and take it all away, and when he did come they had no walls to stop him), thinking that the necessities of daily sustenance could be supplied at one place as well as another, they cared little for shifting their habitation, and consequently neither built large cities nor attained to any other form of greatness.

THUCYDIDES

Thus far a number of different forms of human knowledge have been identified. In the four forms of discourse, the requirements for strict science have been sketched, and a place has been found within the fourfold hierarchy for such widely divergent fields of human knowledge as the modern dialectical approaches to nature on the one hand and literature on the other. But where does history fit within such a framework?

History, science, other fields. The foregoing passage from Thucydides can help us understand what historical knowledge is. Is history science? If so, it would have to demonstrate, and pure history resembles a descriptive catalogue of fact rather than a series of demonstrations. It is, as Thucydides illustrates, a record of what happened in the past.

Moreover, history in the natural order has no first principles, and such principles, we saw, are necessary for a science. Such a judgment might even be turned around. There is no necessity in historical events, and necessity is surely one of the characteristics of a science.

Finally, when examined as to its scientific character, history will be found to own no universality. Every historical event is, in the last analysis, an individual event, and our knowledge of that event is a knowledge of something individual. In short, our study of pure history does not rise above space and time to the universal and necessary connections among things as reasoned out from first and certain principles. Consequently, for a number of reasons, history cannot be put down as a science.

Is history opinion? True enough Thucydides freely introduces opinion into his history, but if history is no more than opinion, it must share the uncertainty of opinion. In such a case, we would know only as probable that Caesar invaded Gaul, that Wellington conquered Napoleon, that Washington spent a winter at Valley Forge, that Clovis, king of the Franks, became a convert. No respectable historian would want to assign all such events to the limbo of probable knowledge. Hence, history would seem to give us more than merely probable knowledge.

Is history perhaps rhetoric? If so, it would be an art of persuasion, even weaker in certitude than dialectic. It is true that an excellent rhetorician like Lincoln or Pericles may use historical events as devices of persuasion, and it is also true that many textbooks in history take a rhetorical position in favor of a viewpoint held beforehand by their authors, such as nationalism or Communism. But history if it is not dialectic, certainly is not mere rhetoric either.

Nor can history be identified with literature. It is true that both the historical and literary writer are concerned somehow with the individual. But literature, we have seen, involves discourse, whereas in history events follow not *from* each other but only *after* each other in temporal sequence. Furthermore, genuine history must always be true, but literature need only be plausible. Alike under certain aspects, the historian and literary man, from other angles, are profoundly different in both interest and technique.

Some distinctions. To get at the more positive meaning of historical knowledge, it is important to make some distinctions. As Hegel remarked, the word *history* applies unfortunately both to what actually happened in the past and to our study of such happenings. History is a stream of events having physical reality outside the mind and at the same time it is a subject studied by the mind and having a place in the curriculum of schools. Chemistry is also a subject; but when we name what the subject is about, we do not call it chemistry. Chemistry is about physical things, not about chemistry. So too with literature, theology, mathematics, and all other subjects. But history, as a study, is not distinguished in name from its subject matter. History designates the study, and it designates what that study is about. In order to avoid ambiguity, the term *history* will be employed throughout this chapter to mean history as a form of knowledge rather than history as a stream of events, though the material studied by the historian will affect our verdict concerning the kind of knowledge he enjoys. Moreover, in the interests of simplification, only human history will be considered throughout this chapter, thus omitting natural history with its descriptions of the cosmos in a pre-scientific way.

A second and even more capital distinction obtains between the facts of history, like the date of Charlemagne's coronation, and the opinion about those facts expressed by this or that historian. Thucydides records a number of facts in the passage quoted, but even more striking are his opinions, even his generalizations, about those facts. In a similar vein, it is true that the Roman Empire collapsed and that by the sixth century it had ceased to exist; but the causes of Rome's decline and fall are a matter of constant controversy among students of the phenomenon. That Thomas Jefferson and Alexander Hamilton were prominent figures in the early American government is beyond dispute, but the relative merits of their different economic views can be argued back and forth among their admirers. The ordinary history book includes the dimension of fact and that of opinion. In order to evaluate history, however, these two aspects of the typical text book must be distinguished. In what follows, the concern will be with history as factual knowledge, the knowledge of dates and places and figures of the past. Such knowledge is the fundamental kind of historical knowledge since upon it all opinions by historians claim their base.

History and faith. What then about our knowledge of the facts of history? These facts are usually made known to us by the testimony of men who witnessed them. Such eyewitnesses either wrote reports of what they observed or by word of mouth informed those who later wrote reports. Sometimes the testimony of witnesses to historical events did not pass into written form for centuries after the event itself. While unwritten, such testimony forms that kind of historical knowledge which is called tradition. Illiterate primitive peoples can often recite their ancestry back through many generations. History for them never assumes a written form at all.

Actually, the recent as well as the more remote past constitutes the field of historical knowledge. News stories tonight of what happened this morning are history when we read about them. But again we are dependent on witnesses and reporters.

But however known and whether of the recent or remote past, what we call historical knowledge usually is known on somebody else's word. That George Washington was the first president of the United States is known to us on the authority of those who witnessed his presidency and handed down their testimony in the form of oral or written records or both. To accept a proposition on the authority of another is knowledge by faith. Our knowledge of history then depends on our faith.*

---

* Faith must be distinguished into natural and supernatural. In either case, a truth is accepted on someone else's word. To accept a truth on the word of another human being is natural or human faith. To accept a truth because God has said it is supernatural faith. Though the Bible and tradition, considered

What has been said about historical knowledge as a form of faith must be qualified in one important respect. All of an individual's past is history and can be known by him as an historian. Events, important or trivial, which we have personally witnessed we do not know only on the authority of a witness. We remember them. However, in discussing history as a subject, we are usually referring to events distant from us in space and time and not coming within our own experience except in some accidental way. Hence, although our own memory can attest to the history of our own past, the kind of knowledge that usually gets into history books is known by the testimony of witnesses and accepted by us on a faith in their words. The historian must test the authenticity and credibility of the witnesses which he uses to reconstruct the past. But such tests involve another problem that we need not consider here.

History and other knowledges.   There is then a crucial distinction between history and any of the forms of natural knowledge, inductive or syllogistic, studied so far. All such knowledge, from the scientific to the literary, depends upon what is called intrinsic evidence. The evidence from which such knowledge begins is open to our own observation and our own personal experience. Anything so observed and experienced contains, in principle, enough intrinsic evidence so that we can know something about it and even conclude to its causes. But the facts of our direct experience do not enable us to deduce that Washington was president or even that he existed at all. Such knowledge depends on evidence outside our experience and indeed, it rests on the word of somebody else. Such evidence may be called extrinsic. History is therefore a record of the past compiled by extrinsic evidence, like the testimony of witnesses. Knowledge here is a form of faith.

It is true of course that the historian sometimes depends upon unwritten and unspoken records to achieve a knowledge of his subject. He uses such devices as monuments or coins or drawings as evidence for facts he establishes concerning man's past. But even here the study of the past proceeds by instrumental signs extrinsic to the men and the events they signify, and requiring, to the extent that they are purely historical phenomena, a faith

---

merely as historical records, make the Catholic Church credible, it is history in general that is the concern of this chapter.

that what they signify is true. A monument or an excavated city, like Pompeii, are signs as artificial in principle as the language of an eyewitness would be.

History is neither science nor art. It rests on natural faith. The opinions by historians about historical events can be formed into dialectical syllogisms and inductions, but history, the record of the past, on which such opinion rests, differs in kind from the arts and sciences so far studied. History rests on extrinsic evidence, while science depends upon evidence intrinsic to experience.

Though neither a science nor an art, history serves a function, as no other subject, in initiating us to the tradition of which we are the heirs and continuators. By extending our individual experience to the dimensions of our whole culture, it enables us to profit from the triumphs and failures of the human spirit. By showing us what others have said and done, it aids us to know what we ourselves should think and do. In this respect, history is a valuable preparation for science, giving us in the intellectual order those opinions where dialectic must begin and in the moral order that experience of others' conduct which aids us to regulate our own.

Problems

1. Compare and contrast history as a subject and history as a reality.

2. Distinguish between the facts of history and the opinions of historians. Which item in the above question is more fundamental?

3. Show how the facts of history are established.

4. What is the difference between intrinsic and extrinsic evidence? How, in terms of this distinction, does history differ from the four forms of discourse so far studied and also from induction?

5. What is the function of history in the education of man?

6. Comment on any or all of the following passages; indicate by analyzing them any insights into the nature of history:

> 26.2 It being my purpose to write the lives of Alexander, the king, and of Caesar, by whom Pompey was destroyed, the multitude of their great actions affords so large a field that I were to blame if I should not, by way of apology, forewarn my reader that I have chosen rather to epitomize the most celebrated parts of their story, than to insist at large on every particular circumstance of it. It must be borne in mind that my design is not to write histories, but

lives. And the most glorious exploits do not always furnish us with the clearest discoveries of virtue or vice in men; sometimes a matter of less moment, an expression or a jest, informs us better of their characters and inclinations, than the most famous sieges whatsover. Therefore, as portrait painters are more exact in the lines and features of the face in which the character is seen, than in the other parts of the body, so I must be allowed to give my more particular attention to the marks and indications of the souls of men, and while I endeavour by these to portray their lives, may be free to leave more weighty matters and great battles to be treated of by others.

PLUTARCH

26.3. Rome at the beginning was ruled by kings. Freedom and the consulship were established by Lucius Brutus. Dictatorships were held for a temporary crisis. The power of the decemvirs did not last beyond two years, nor was the consular jurisdiction of the military tribunes of long duration. The despotisms of Cinna and Sulla were brief; the rule of Pompeius and of Crassus soon yielded before Caesar; the arms of Lepidus and Antonius before Augustus; who when the world was weary of civil strife, subjected it to empire under the title of "Prince." But the successes and reverses of the old Roman people have been recorded by famous historians; and fine intellects were not wanting to describe the times of Augustus, till growing sycophancy scared them away. The histories of Tiberius, Caius, Claudius, and Nero, while they were in power, were falsified through terror, and after their death were written under the irritation of a recent hatred. Hence, my purpose is to relate a few facts about Augustus — more particularly his last acts, then the reign of Tiberius, and all which follows, without either bitterness or partiality, from any motives to which I am far removed.

TACITUS

26.4. Bowing down in blind credulity, as is my custom, before mere authority and the tradition of the elders, superstitiously swallowing a story I could not test at the time by experiment or private judgment, I am firmly of the opinion that I was born on the 29th of May, 1874, on Campden Hill, Kensington; and baptized according to the formularies of the Church of England in the little church of St. George opposite the large Waterworks that dominated that ridge.

G. K. CHESTERTON

26.5. In the first place, the historian describes the activity of individuals who in his opinion have directed humanity (one historian considers only monarchs, generals, and ministers as being such men, while another includes also orators, learned men, reformers, philosophers, and poets). Secondly, it is assumed that the goal toward which humanity is being led is known to the historians; to one of them this goal is the greatness of the Roman, Spanish, or French realm; to another it is liberty, equality, and a certain kind of civilization of a small corner of the world called Europe.

LEO TOLSTOY

26.6.   In the second century of the Christian era, the Empire of Rome comprehended the fairest part of the earth, and the most civilized portion of mankind. The frontiers of that extensive monarchy were guarded by ancient renown and disciplined valour. The gentle but powerful influence of laws and manners had gradually cemented the union of the provinces. Their peaceful inhabitants enjoyed and abused the advantages of wealth and luxury. The image of a free constitution was preserved with decent reverence; the Roman senate appeared to possess the sovereign authority, and devolved on the emperors all the executive powers of government. During a happy period (A.D. 98–180) of more than fourscore years, the public administration was conducted by the virtue and abilities of Nerva, Trajan, Hadrian, and the two Antonines. It is the design of this, and of the succeeding two chapters, to describe the prosperous condition of their empire; and afterwards from the death of Marcus Antoninus, to deduce the most important circumstances of its decline and fall; a revolution which will ever be remembered, and is still felt by the nations of the earth.

EDWARD GIBBON

26.7.   Long before that day a decree had been issued by order of Caesar Augustus that a census of the whole world be taken. This census was the first to take place while Cyrinus was in charge of Syria.

Accordingly, the people went, each to the city of his ancestor, to be registered; and so Joseph, too, being a member of the house and family of David, went up from the town of Nazareth in Galilee to David's town in Judea, called Bethlehem, in order to be registered. He was accompanied by his espoused wife Mary, who was with child. In the course of their stay there, the time came for her delivery; and she gave birth to her first-born son. She wrapped him in swaddling clothes, and laid him in a manger, because there was no accommodation for them in the lodging.

ST. LUKE

Chapter 27: THE DIVISION AND ORDER OF THE SCIENCES

27.1. "Odd" and "even," "straight" and "curved," and likewise "number," "line," and "figure," do not involve motion; not so "flesh," and "bone," and "man" — these are defined like "snub nose," not like "curved."

ARISTOTLE

The speculative and the practical. Science, as a certain knowledge through causes, has been contrasted in the past several chapters with dialectic, rhetoric, literature, and history. The next project is to determine how many sciences there are and how they are related to each other.

The first and most important division of human science is into the speculative and the practical. These two kinds of science differ in their end or purpose. Any speculative or liberal science has for its aim to know truth in an absolute way; the object which it considers, for example God or the human soul, is not within our power to make but only to know. Practical science, on the other hand, seeks truth in order to make or to do something; it deals with a world that is open to human control. An engineer, for instance, studies stresses in metals in order to build bridges or airplanes. In ethics, man studies the acts of his will so as to put order into them with respect to his moral purpose in the universe. Because of its aim, speculative or liberal science is always abstract. Practical science, on the other hand, cannot be completely abstract because it must take into account the contingent and concrete circumstances of human actions.

Practical sciences, like engineering or ethics, are divided from each other by their ends since end or purpose is always the organizing principle at the level of making or doing something. Speculative or liberal sciences differ from each other according to the way in which they abstract. There are three levels of speculative science because there are three kinds of abstraction that human reason can make. Put in another way, there are three orders of knowing within which the mind can meet the different sets of first principles that would be necessary for differences among sciences.

The three orders of abstraction. In the first or physical order of abstraction, the mind considers the natural or physical world which undergoes change and is characterized by its sensible qualities. Thus it considers "flesh," "bone," "man," "rosebush," "copper," etc. Scientific knowledge of such things is made possible by observing their various motions or activities. In reaching the universal necessary for science at the physical level, the abstracting mind retains sensible qualities in the objects of its consideration. It does not study *this* flesh or *that* bone, but in the study of flesh and bone, sensible qualities such as color or hardness must be considered. The point is that in a scientific knowledge of the physical world they are considered in an abstract or general sense where the mind represents color or flesh but not *this* particular color, and hardness for the bone but not *that* individual hardness which is in *this* particular bone. In the physical order of abstraction, the mind represents the sensible world in a universal way in order to construct a science about it by observing its motions.

The subject of science at the physical level is mobile being.

Pre-experimental knowledge occurs to us prior to the knowledge gained through experiment in the more specialized studies of modern physics, chemistry, and biology. Accordingly, what must be known prior to experiment — the nature of motion, the definition of time and place, and other such presuppositions of experiment — should be studied before modern physics, chemistry, and biology. Indeed, by the definition of science in Chapter 22, there is only one science of nature, because in nature itself there is but one set of first principles. What is called the philosophy of nature is the first and pre-experimental part of this single science, and the technical and experimentally based fields of physics, chemistry, and biology form for the most part dialectical extensions of our initial scientific knowledge.

In the second or mathematical order of abstraction, the mind leaves aside motion and the sensible world to consider only quantified being. Triangles or circles do not change; they are not, like copper, affected by the sunshine or rain. They simply have no principle of motion within them. Nor do mathematical objects come within the reach of our senses. A circle or the number five cannot be seen or heard or felt. The mind at this level leaves behind sensible matter. But mathematics still considers a kind of matter which need not be named and discussed here. It is matter if only for the reason that mathematical objects, like numbers or figures, have parts and can be divided.

At the third level of abstraction, the mind leaves aside all matter whatsoever. This is the metaphysical order, and the object which it considers is being in so far as it is being. Thus, God and the angels exist without any matter at all. Causes, the good, the true, substance, etc., happen to exist in matter, but they do not require matter in order to exist. Realities of this sort are studied by metaphysics. Metaphysics is a science reached by reason alone. Because it deals with the highest things, it is called a wisdom. As wisdom, it integrates all of the lower sciences.

Logic, even in its wide sense (Chapter 3), belongs also in the third order of abstraction, since the object of logic exists only in an immaterial way. Logic and metaphysics differ because each has a different set of first principles.

In the third order of abstraction, there is yet another science and indeed another wisdom. It is sacred theology whose subject is God and all things to the extent that they belong to God. The first principles of theology are in a different genus from those of the other sciences. The theologian's first principles are the articles of faith, whereas none of the other sciences uses supernatural revelation as its starting point.

There are thus six fundamental departments of human knowledge which claim first principles and hence constitute separate sciences: ethics, the science of nature, mathematics, metaphysics, logic, and sacred theology. Two of these disciplines, logic and mathematics, are the liberal arts. The science of nature includes modern physics, chemistry, and biology, and in a similar fashion, ethics includes all social studies. History is not included among the fundamental disciplines for the reason that it is not a science. It serves to broaden our experience so that science, especially ethics and its affiliated social studies, may have a firm basis to begin with and may be continually enlarged and enriched. Thus, though not a science, history, as the record of human experience, is a presupposition of truly scientific knowledge.

The order of learning. The order in which the basic sciences have been discussed in the course of the present chapter is not the order of their acquisition. The order of learning is considerably different. The general principle which governs the pedagogical order of the sciences is that subjects requiring little experience be taught first, followed by subjects that demand progressively more and more experience. This is a general rule governing all the sciences in the natural region of human knowledge, but it has one exception. Logic, as a study of the instruments of science, must be taught first if scientific knowledge of the real is to be reached at all. In its fuller sense, logic extends to a wider area than the principles of reasoning discussed in this book. As shown by our consideration of the literary and rhetorical modes of argument, logic reaches out to enlighten the work of grammar. Words and sentences depend upon a correct ordering of logical relations, and in this sense, grammar, like rhetoric, is a part of logic considered in its widest amplitude.

Mathematical science follows logic in the order of learning because it requires scanty experience and can be taught to the young. It enables the mind, acquainted through logic with the nature of a science, to gain actual experience in the construction of a science.

Next comes the science of nature which requires more experience than mathematics. This science has the two phases mentioned earlier, the general phase usually called the philosophy of nature and special phases like biology, physics, and chemistry. The study of the living world involves, of course, a study of man.

Following the science of nature comes ethics which requires more experience than the other disciplines discussed so far. In ethics, man's earthly destiny is considered and defined, and as a result all of the social studies, for example sociology and economics, can be organized in the light of an end.

Metaphysics, the highest reach of native reason, is reserved to the last place in the order of natural learning, because it requires the maximum of experience, in short all the resources that reason musters for its loftiest achievement, to contemplate God as He is knowable from creatures.

Sacred theology, unlike metaphysics, does not depend in any way on previous sciences. Its principles are the articles of faith. Such principles can be possessed without going through any other science. Metaphysics, on the other hand, presupposes in some way the four sciences that precede it in the natural order of learning.

Theology is the integrating wisdom of the Christian school. Only when the learning of the Catholic scholar is seen in the light of theology does such learning become in itself truly Catholic. Hence, all other subjects in a Catholic school are preparatory to a greater knowledge of theology.

Problems

1. Distinguish between speculative and practical knowledge.
2. What is the basis for dividing speculative sciences?
3. Characterize each of the three orders of abstraction.
4. Name the sciences in each order of abstraction.
5. What is the fundamental principle governing the order of acquiring scientific knowledge? Why is logic an exception to this principle?
6. Show how logic in the wide sense includes all of the linguistic arts.
7. Explain the reason and purpose of studying mathematics as the second science in the order of learning.
8. Show how the study of nature is organized and unified.
9. Explain how ethics organizes all social studies.
10. What is the difference between metaphysics and theology?
11. Explain how theology is the aim and purpose of all learning achieved by Catholics.

PART VI: SPECIAL QUESTIONS

Chapter 28: THE EXPERIMENTAL METHOD

28.1. A piece of wooden moulding or scantling, about 12 cubits long, half a cubit wide, and three finger-breadths thick, was taken; on its edge was cut a channel a little more than one finger in breadth; having made this groove very straight, smooth, and polished, and having lined it with parchment, also as smooth and polished as possible, we rolled along it a hard, smooth, and very round bronze ball. Having placed this board in a sloping position, by lifting one end some one or two cubits above the other, we rolled the ball, as I was just saying, along the channel, noting, in a manner presently to be described, the time required to make the descent. We repeated this experiment more than once in order to measure the time with an accuracy such that the deviation between two observations never exceeded one-tenth of a pulse-beat.

GALILEO

The problem of experiment. For those who recognize the solid achievements of great logicians in the past, one of the pressing problems of our day is the correct evaluation of the modern advances in logic and method. To a certain extent, some of these problems have already been approached in our treatment of induction and dialectic. Yet there is reason to group into a separate section of this book a few central considerations of modern problems in method — the nature of experiment, reasoning by hypothesis or theory, the use of models, the canons of induction, statistical reasoning, and mathematical logic. All of these topics involve what is usually termed the scientific method, and all of them are important fields for a logician who wishes to use the undoubted principles of the general logic studied so far to assimilate whatever progress recent studies have made toward the improvement of the instruments to reach truth.

The study of experiment and of the experimental method can hardly be detached from the consideration of hypotheses in the next chapter, but in the interest of simplification, it may be well to emphasize here the empirical side of the scientific method. What then is experiment or the experimental method?

The "inclined plane" experiment, designed to clock the fall of bodies when subjected to no force save that of gravity, enabled Galileo to reach his famous law of falling bodies: that all freely falling bodies traverse a distance proportional to the square of their time of descent. In order to slow down the "fall" of a body so that its rate of descent could be measured by the crude timing device he had to employ, Galileo allowed his ball to roll down an inclined plane on the principle that in his experiment the same downward forces were acting on bodies that would be present in a perfectly vertical fall.

Galileo's work is of interest here as a sample of experiment. It is often said that the chief trait of modern research is its experimental attitude. This is one of those vague generalizations that are at most only partially true and, upon a closer reading of history, require considerable modification. Observation and experiment as a means of gathering knowledge about nature are as old as Thales. Aristotle, for instance, would differ from the modern explorers of nature not because he shunned experiment in principle but because he also accepted other ways of knowing, e.g., through common, general, pre-experimental experience. He would not demand an experimental test for any knowledge to be valid, though he would allow of no knowledge that did not begin in experience.

The traits of experiment. As shown by Galileo's work, an experiment always involves a deliberate interference by man with the natural course of events. It may be defined as a controlled sense perception or as an artificial experience in which man disturbs the object of his consideration to learn something more about it than general experience can reveal. Experience may be compared to experiment as nature to art. Galileo did not reach his law of falling bodies by observing the fall of leaves or of raindrops. He contrived an artificial arrangement in his inclined plane and, under controlled conditions, allowed artificial bodies to roll down it. In experience, we take nature in the raw and as we find it; in experiment, we always do something to nature through our active inter-ference. Only what in some measure yields to human control is capable of being experimentally studied. Experiment then is a controlled experience.

In the second place, experiment isolates the subject under con-sideration. Galileo took steps to eliminate the influence of any forces on his rolling ball except the pull of gravity. He lined the groove of his plane with polished parchment to diminish the effect of friction on the rolling ball, and the ball itself had to be "smooth and very round" so that it would be free, hence unaltered in its speed by its own geometrical configuration. In approaching the results of his experiment, Galileo was interested only in the time required by his ball to roll down the plane. Whereas experience takes things fully, experiment isolates what it studies from the environment.

Third, experiment is normally interested only in those aspects of its subject matter which can be measured. Whereas experience always involves the qualitative, experiment is for the most part quantitative. The experimenter usually records his data by counting the cases he has examined or by reading instruments. Thus Galileo was interested in measuring the time of descent in the case of balls rolling down his inclined plane, and the law which emerged from his experiment is an equation.

Fourth, experiment is inductive in character, and in this sense it is a special kind of induction by incomplete enumeration. As the outcome of his experiment, Galileo made a generalization involving not merely his bronze ball but bronze in general, and indeed not merely bronze but all physical bodies on the earth. From several measurements or observations regarding his ball, Galileo formulated a general proposition applying to all terrestrial bodies.

There is a final characteristic of experiment that makes a transi-tion to our next chapter which deals with hypotheses. Experiment always requires foreknowledge if only because, as a refined and specialized experience, it can occur only after experience of a less technical and more general kind. But much more than this, experi-ment is always the answer to a definite question that we put to nature through a dialectical plan of inquiry. As a general rule, experiment is not the origin of a theory, but a test of whether a preconceived hypothesis is good or bad. Its results, as in most inductions, are often colored by the theory suggesting it, and the degree of coloring increases as the object of study is more and more remote from what we directly sense. To the extent that experimental results are interlarded with interpretation by the theory which prompted the experiment, the inductive generalizations so attained are qualified by the dialectical framework used in reaching them.

Experiment and dialectic. Another series of experiments that, like the work of Galileo, is one of the classic achievements of modern physics may bring out even more boldly how theory, a dialectical device, conditions experiment. In the eighteenth century, heat was thought to be a fluid called caloric, which clustered around the tiny particles of matter. According to this theory, to heat a body was to transfer to its material particles some of the caloric of the heating agent, and by the same token for a body to grow cold meant the surrender of some of its caloric to its surroundings.

In 1798, Count Rumford made some experiments which he describes in the following lines:

28.2.   Being engaged lately in superintending the boring of cannons in workshops of the military arsenal at Munich, I was struck by the considerable degree of heat that a brass gun acquires in a short time in being bored, and with the still higher temperature (much higher than that of boiling water, as I found by experiment) of the metallic chips separated from it by the borer.

Rumford observed that the gain of heat by the metals was not accompanied by any material change of weight. If heat were a substance, he reasoned, then the great amount of heat communicated to the gun and to the chips should result in an appreciable increase of weight. But Rumford detected no such increase and hence drew the conclusion that the caloric theory of heat was untenable.

What is important here is that Rumford was looking at his experimental results in the light of dialectical knowledge, the caloric theory of heat, and his experiments make sense only within this context. Other theories of heat proposed since the demise of the caloric theory suggest different experiments to test them.

There is no such thing as a pure experiment.

Summary. Experiment is one of the essential stages in what is generally called the modern scientific method, at least in those applications which are found in physics, chemistry, and biology. Not all modern fields of the scientific method are experimental. The course of the stars, not being within our control, does not lend itself to actual experiment, and neither does the study of rock formations in geology.

In the last analysis, experiment poses no new logical problems that have not been already met in the preceding sections of this book. It belongs to the operation of induction by incomplete enumeration. It is simply a refined and controlled case of this kind of induction in which the subject of study is isolated and considered only in its measurable characteristics. Finally, as in all induction by incomplete enumeration, there is a dialectical apparatus or preconceived theory conditioning the experiment and qualifying the interpretation of the results.

Problems

1. Define experiment and contrast it with experience.
2. Discuss experiment in its tendency to control and isolate its subject.
3. Why is experimental knowledge inductive?
4. Show how foreknowledge enters into every experiment.
5. What is the relation between experiment and induction by incomplete enumeration? Between experiment and dialectic?
6. Comment on the following passages in light of the observations made in the chapter. Show how each illustrates the traits of experiment.

28.3. I tried to find out whether bees have a color sense.
By the scent of a little honey, it is possible to attract bees to an experimental table. Here we can feed them on a piece of blue cardboard, for example. They suck up the food and, after carrying it back to the hive, give it to the other bees. The bees return again and again to the rich source of food which they have discovered. We let them do so for some time, and then we take away the blue card scented with honey and put out two new clean pieces of cardboard at the site of the former feeding place — on the left a blue card and on the right a red one. If the bees remember that they found food on blue, and if they are able to distinguish between

red and blue, they should now light on the blue card. This is exactly what happens.

KARL VON FRISCH

28.4. The colors of all natural bodies have no other origin than this, that they are variously qualified to reflect one sort of light in greater plenty than another. And this I have experimented in a dark room, by illuminating those bodies with uncompounded light of divers colors. For by that means any body may be able to appear of any color. They have no appropriate color, but ever appear the color of the light cast upon them, but with this difference, that they are most brisk and vivid in the light of their own daylight color.

ISAAC NEWTON

28.5. Wine frequently "went bad." It became sour. What was the cause? Could it be prevented? These were the questions asked him by the wine-makers of France. Fermentation had been known from the earliest times, and chemists thought they understood its cause. Berzelius and Liebig, who dominated the scientific thinking of Europe, had taught that the fermentation of sugar to form alcohol and carbon dioxide was a purely mechanical process. Pasteur determined to go to the bottom of this question. With his ever-present microscope, he studied every step of the process. Gradually he became convinced that fermentation is the result of a vital change associated with the life of the yeast cells, which are always present in the production of alcohol. He proceeded to prove it. In a series of experiments, now classic, Pasteur demonstrated that alcoholic fermentation can never be set up in fermentable juices which have been sterilized by heating and afterward protected from the germ-laden dust of the air. This precipitated a battle royal with Liebig, but the facts were against the German autocrat, and he was compelled to surrender. Pasteur did more than this. He showed that every kind of fermentation, as well as alcoholic, is due to a specific micro-organism. The souring of wine he traced to an organism which develops in the wine upon long standing. To destroy it, he introduced the practice, known everywhere now as pasteurization, by which he heated the wine at a definite temperature for several minutes, out of contact with the air. The wine might then be kept in sterilized casks indefinitely, if contamination from the air were prevented.

FLOYD L. DARROW

28.6. On sliding the two wires of an ordinary electric bell circuit into a tumbler of water, down opposite sides, bubbles of gas will be found to collect on the wires, and chemical examination shows that the two lots of gas have entirely different properties. They cannot, then, be water-vapour, and in point of fact neither of them is; one proves to be hydrogen and the other oxygen. There is found to be twice as much hydrogen as oxygen, whence we conclude that the electric current has broken up each molecule of water into two parts of hydrogen and one of oxygen.

SIR JAMES JEANS

Chapter 29: SCIENTIFIC THEORY

29.1. In the cells of a man's body there are certain genes which determine the color of his hair, still others which determine the shape of his nose or mouth, the texture of his skin, and so on for each individual characteristic. Every cell of his body contains the same pattern of genes, there are thousands of them in each cell, linked together in chains like the beads of a necklace, and so there are plenty of genes to account for, determine, and control every aspect of our body's form and other characteristics.

Having said this, I must tell you that no one has ever isolated and examined a gene. They are too small for our present microscopes. But we judge the nature of the genes by the ways in which they behave and by the effects which they produce, just as chemists earlier learned the structure and properties of the invisible molecules by observing their chemical behavior.

T. S. PAINTER

Hypothesis and explanation. In the discussion of the conditional syllogism, dialectic, and experiment, mention has been made of scientific theory. However, the meaning of theory in the physical, biological, and social areas of investigation is so important that it deserves to be singled out for special emphasis.

In realms too small, too distant, or too complicated to be grasped by direct observation, we are oftentimes unable to make a direct conclusion to the causes of things. Always seeking to enlarge its knowledge, the mind in such cases may *legitimately* suppose causes and deduce the consequences from each supposition until one of them is found to agree with observation while others do not. Such a supposition concerning unobservable causes which enables the mind to deduce or predict observational fact is called a theory.

Not every supposition antecedent to empirical verification is a theory. Prior to his experimental discovery of the chemical law that bears his name, Robert Boyle may well have supposed that there is an approximately constant ratio between the pressure and volume of gases. If this were the case, the experiment would have simply confirmed Boyle's supposition, and the latter could then have been discarded. Coulomb could have had a similar suspicion, which experiment only confirmed, that electrical charges behave in the way in which his law states, and again the supposition would have become a fairly well-established fact. Suppositions of this sort which are directly verifiable create no special problem and will not be considered as theories for purposes of this chapter. A theory is a supposition like that of atoms, of evolution, of the expanding universe, and of the Freudian unconscious — all of which deal with areas not open to direct observation.

Although a distinction may be drawn between a hypothesis and a theory, the two terms can be considered as synonymous in assessing their logical validity. A hypothesis is a supposition not yet subjected to empirical testing, whereas a theory has received some kind of verification. In another usage of terms, a hypothesis concerns some special or particular fact, while a theory extends through a whole realm of facts and, like evolution in biology and gravitation in physics, unifies a whole field of investigation. Both of these distinctions are valuable, but they will not affect the considerations in this chapter, and so hypothesis and theory can here be taken as synonymous terms. They are supposed causes, not directly observable, from which observational fact may be deduced.

What then is a theory or hypothesis? Is it an explanation, and if not, what is its exact status?

Explanation, to begin with, is the assigning of a reason for something. In its most perfect form, it is either a real definition or a demonstration. An *adequate* explanation is one which excludes all others. An *inadequate* explanation is always uncertain and tentative, leaving open the possibility that other ways of explaining the event or thing might be found.

The gene theory in biology is an explanation of how individual characteristics in living organisms are determined. It is an ingenious theory and is the most successful account of how hereditary traits are transmitted from parent to offspring. But since "no one has ever isolated and examined a gene," as Painter remarks, the gene theory cannot be accepted as an adequate and certain account for the facts of heredity. We define genes "by the effects which they produce," and it is possible that such effects may really be the work of other causes.

An adequate explanation has reached a real and necessary connection between a thing and its causes. A theory, even when tested, can be no more than an inadequate explanation setting forth causes that are consistent with the effects in question but not known to have a real and necessary connection with them.

Hypothesis and logic. Like experiment, reasoning by theory or hypothesis involves no new principle of logic. From the logician's viewpoint, a hypothesis is the antecedent in a conditional proposition. In such a proposition, where scientific certainty is to be attained, the antecedent expresses a cause whose effect is represented by the consequent. In a syllogism which proceeds by affirming the antecedent and then affirming the consequent, the mind is moving from cause to effect and hence proceeding in a manner that can generate science. But where there is reasoning by theory or hypothesis, as in the case of the gene theory, there is danger of affirming the consequent of a conditional syllogism and then affirming the antecedent. In this case, the mind is moving from effect to cause without assurance that the effect could be produced only by the particular cause which is supposed in the antecedent. If the gene theory is true, Painter is saying, then we can explain certain effects by using it; by using it, we can explain certain effects; therefore, the gene theory is true.

The lesson in astronomy should never be forgotten. For almost two thousand years, the geocentric theory seemed to most men of learning to be an adequate explanation of heavenly appearances. Then came Copernicus. Today, according to Einstein, either a heliocentric or geocentric hypothesis may be used in order to map out the motions of the world.

History, as well as logic, should put us on guard against ever taking a theory as certain and final. Atoms and their parts, genes, the missing link, and gravitational forces have today become familiar even in the daily press; in conversation and books they are almost taken for granted. But viewed from the logician's standpoint, they are at most hypothetical realities acceptable because of the consequences to which they lead, because of "the effects which they produce." Perhaps other antecedents could account for the consequences and other causes explain the effects.

The value of hypothesis. However, the approach to reasoning by hypothesis should not be merely negative. For probing worlds too small or too large for direct observation and experience, a hypothetical account is all that can be expected. With the reservation that a tested theory should be embraced until a better one is found, a theory should always be accepted when it is compatible with well-established truth. The only alternative to such a theory is ignorance.

A theory is valuable for several reasons. First of all, it enables us to organize our knowledge into a logical or dialectical system; it is a dialectical instrument of essentially the same character as those discussed in Chapter 23. In the second place, a theory promotes questions and research and investigation; conclusions are deduced from it, as in any dialectic, and then compared with experimental results. Many scientists value a theory only because it suggests experiments and predicts their outcome. It may well be disputed whether a theory should be narrowed down to this function, but it is surely true that all experiments are made in the light of a prior theory that they always put to a test. From one angle then, the uncertainty of a theory is one of its virtues. Because it is always open to question, a theory or hypothesis provokes a constant search for new ways of testing it and thus acts as a leaven for the advancement of experimental knowledge.

A good theory must satisfy several criteria:

1. It must be capable of verification, that is; it must lead to consequences that in some manner can be tested.

2. It must be at least consistent with the facts to be explained and with other facts known to be true.

3. It must be free from all logical contradiction.

4. A simpler theory is to be preferred to one that is more complicated, when all other merits of two theories are equal. The Copernican theory of astronomy is mathematically simpler than the Ptolemaic system.

5. In a similar manner, when all other things are equal, a more

universal theory is preferable to one that is less universal. The theory of wave mechanics extends to both optics and mechanics and thus unifies branches of physics formerly kept distinct.

It would be a mistake to think of theory as a simple abstraction from facts or as a mere generalization of experimental results. Though dependent on previous experiences, a theory is conceived in advance of the experimental data that put it to a test. In this respect, theories in physics, chemistry, and biology show again their dialectical color. They are not themselves the products of induction but of preinductive dialectic.

In the last two chapters, the two principal features of the modern scientific method have been sampled. It is sometimes alleged that this method is a recent invention. It is true that modern scholarship has emphasized such a method even to the point of divorcing it from all other ways of knowing and emphasizing only quantitative characteristics. But whatever is new about this scientific method, it contains no principles new to logic. Experiment is a refinement of induction; and theory, of dialectic.

Problems

1. When is an explanation certain or adequate?
2. What is the reason for the uncertainty of hypotheses or theories?
3. What is the relation between a theory and the antecedent of a conditional proposition?
4. Show how a theory risks the fallacy of affirming the consequent.
5. Why are theories necessary?
6. What is the value of a theory?
7. Name some criteria that a theory must fulfill.
8. In the following passages identify any characteristics of scientific theory and evaluate the reasoning involved:

29.2. Bohr's original quantum theory of spectra was one of the most revolutionary, I suppose, that was ever given to science, and I do not know of any theory that has been more successful. He was in Manchester at the time, and being a firm believer in the nuclear structure of atoms as shown by experiments on scattering, he tried to see how he could arrange the electrons to give the known spectra of the atom.

LORD RUTHERFORD

29.3. People who think a little but not much sometimes ask me, "Why do you believe in the ether? What's the good of it?" I ask them, "What becomes of light for the eight minutes after it has left the Sun and before it reaches the Earth?" When they consider that, they observe how necessary the ether is.

G. K. FITZGERALD

29.4. The readiest way, perhaps, of persuading the reader that we may dispense with great and sudden revolutions in the geological order of events is by showing him how a regular and uninterrupted series of changes in the animate and inanimate world may give rise to such breaks in the sequence . . . as are usually thought to imply convulsions and catastrophes.

CHARLES LYELL

29.5. Anthropologists have always presumed that the primitive human stock must have been dark-skinned. Certainly the degree of pigmentation seen amongst the great anthropoids lends support to this theory. The gorilla is black; there are various races and varieties of chimpanzee, and all of them show a degree of black pigmentation.

SIR ARTHUR KEITH

9. Compare the following passage with the nature of dialectic:

29.6. Is it [the tobacco mosaic virus] alive? Stanley reminds you that it can be crystallized, a property that we think of as purely inanimate and wholly chemical. He points to the additional fact that it has not been cultured in a test tube. This would seem to say that it is not a bacterium. A few bacteria placed in a nutrient soup will rapidly multiply into uncounted millions, but the crystalline protein shows no growth behavior in a glass vessel, no metabolism, no reproduction.

And yet, observe what happens when it comes into contact with the inner tissue of a tobacco plant or other vegetable host. Instantly the molecules begin to multiply. An almost imperceptible particle of a crystal will infect a plant, and in a few days the disease will spread through a field, producing an amount of virus millions of times that of the original. It exhibits a fecund ability to propagate itself, to extend its occupancy of space and time at the expense of its environment. Is not this a characteristic of living things?

GEORGE W. GRAY

Chapter 30: REASONING BY ANALOGY

30.1. The number of electrons in an atom depends upon its nature. The atom of hydrogen has one electron and the number of electrons increases with each of the elements up to 92. The easiest way to think of the electrons is as small "planets" circling round a central nucleus which is made up of neutrons and protons. The electron carries a charge of negative electricity and the proton a charge of positive electricity. We can imagine electrons as planets whirling around the central sun in a solar system, although this example is not quite correct according to the latest theories.

A. M. LOW

Analogy and argument. Reasoning of the sort employed in this passage is called argument by analogy. This is one of the most common forms of reasoning. It turns up in many areas from modern physics to poetry, but at the same time, it is a kind of argument that is easily misused.

In the reasoning above, the atom is compared to a miniature solar system in order to explain certain facts of atomic physics. The electrons are like planets revolving in orbits, and there is a central region or nucleus like a sun.

The most striking aspect of analogy is a comparison between two different kinds or orders of reality. Let us symbolize the two wholes that are being compared — in this case the atom and the solar system — by A and B. Within each order there are various points of likeness. The electrons are like planets; the nucleus like the sun; and the motion of electrons like that of the planets in the solar system.

In every analogy, one term of comparison — in this case the solar system — is comparatively better known than the other, like the atom, and the former is used to make the latter more intelligible to us.

But analogy is not merely a listing of likenesses between things. From known or supposed correspondences between two different things or two different orders of things, the mind concludes that there are or will be other likenesses. That is why analogy is a form of argument. In trying to investigate how far the atom is like the solar system, atomic physicists had to correct the analogy, as Low indicates. But even though the analogy in question broke down, it was a useful tool for advancing our knowledge of the atom. Reasoning by analogy may be defined as an argument in which, from known or supposed likenesses between two things, the mind concludes to other likenesses. The conclusions reached by such argument are subjected to inductive test.

Analogy and the study of nature. The waves produced on the surface of a pond obey a certain kind of mathematical equation; light follows similar equations. From the fact that water waves and light resemble each other in their common obedience to similar mathematical formulae we conclude that they are alike in other respects and that therefore light is undulatory. The known likenesses between water and light prompt the mind to conclude to other likenesses, hitherto unknown.

One of the richest analogies in our investigation of nature was the likening of an atom of matter to a pebble or billiard ball. No one has ever seen an atom even with a microscope. Whatever knowledge of the atom we have is reached by comparing it to things we know, like stones or billiard balls.

When pebbles are thrown against a wall, they exert a pressure depending on their number and speed. In a similar way, the physicist treats the problem of pressure in a gas, conceiving the gas itself as an aggregate of tiny particles.

The likening of molecules and atoms to little billiard balls proved extremely fruitful in the history of physics, especially in the way of suggesting experiments and predicting their results. Lord Kelvin expressed the typical sentiments of nineteenth-century physics when he wrote that he was unable to understand a thing unless he could make a mechanical model of it. A mechanical model or a construct is always an analogy.

Analogy is likewise an extremely useful device for reconstructing the past. From a few fossils of extinct animals, say bones or teeth, a paleontologist, by comparing his discoveries to similar parts of present-day animals, will reconstruct the entire head and perhaps even the whole body of the extinct creature. Nearly all specimens of past life constructed out of fossil remains depend upon a comparison of parts of the dead animal with similar parts of a living one and upon the argument that, similar under certain aspects, the two animals would be similar under others as well.

Biology also employs analogy. Painter did it in 29.1, where genes were compared to beads on a necklace. Many biologists look upon the bodies of living things as merely machines. This is an analogy.

The frequency of analogy in rhetoric and literature is too obvious to merit discussion here.

The value of analogy. The value of analogy depends first of all upon the kind of similarity existing between the two things compared. There may be a likeness that is merely extrinsic and often accidental. Such is the case when a living body, like that of man, is compared to a machine. A machine does not repair itself when it breaks or reproduce itself as in the birth of a child. Indeed, the differences between the body and a machine are more striking than their likenesses.

A second kind of likeness between things is one that is intrinsic and essential. Both God and man are alike, for instance, in being causes, and so from a knowledge of human causality at least something can be known analogically about the causality of God. An angel is intelligent, and so is man. Hence, it is possible for us to gain some kind of analogical knowledge of angelic natures. Metaphysics and especially theology employ this second and intrinsic kind of analogy to gain knowledge of a world above us that we do not completely know through concepts.

However, we must have recourse to the first kind of analogy in order to know the finer structure and function of our material world and this is the reasoning by analogy with which we are concerned. What is too small or too distant in space and time to come within our direct experience can be grasped only by comparing it with familiar things. Analogy is thus characteristic of most theories. It suggests ways in which, from what is familiar and known, reasoning can be made concerning what is unknown, and experiment can then be conducted to test our conclusions. Analogy in rhetoric and literature is too complex to be discussed here and must of course be evaluated by standards different from those governing scientific analogy.

Reasoning by analogy, especially analogy of the extrinsic type, is open to serious abuse. Analogies can always be carried too far. It is not necessary that what is similar in one or several respects be alike under all aspects. To conclude that things having something in common must therefore have everything in common is to commit the fallacy of false analogy. The analogy involved in the billiard ball atom and even in the planetary atom model has turned out to be at most only partially correct.

But with all of its temptations, reasoning by extrinsic analogy is one of the only ways open for us in penetrating the dim or distant recesses of our physical world. Like the theory of which it is so often a part, such analogy is a dialectical instrument, extrinsic and hence not proper to the order under investigation. This may be put in another way. Painter's "beads" or the billiard-ball atom or the reconstructed fossil always involve an idealization of some sort that can have at most a logical, though not a strict physical existence. This does not deny that there is a real component in the analogy, some foundation or other in the physical world for analogies that have worked so well, for instance, as the atomic hypothesis. But in extrinsic analogy, the real as in the three cases listed above is regarded through the idealization and hence through a dialectical system. Once more induction, made after reasoning through analogy, remains qualified by the dialectical construct used in making it. Experimental results, made in the light of the atomic theory or gene hypothesis, are inductions within analogy.

Problems

1. Define analogy and show why reasoning by analogy is argument.
2. Give some examples of reasoning by analogy.
3. Why would analogy be useful in rhetoric and literature?
4. What is the value of reasoning by analogy?
5. What is the danger in such reasoning?
6. What is the fallacy of false analogy?

7. What is the relation of analogy to theory? To dialectic?

8. Characterize the experimental results obtained by reasoning through analogy.

9. Identify reasoning by analogy in the following passages, name the things compared and state the conclusion:

30.2. The relation which the several parts or members, of the natural body have to each other and to the whole body, is here compared to the relation which each particular person in society has to the whole society: and the latter is intended to be illustrated by the former. And if there be a likeness between these two relations, the consequence is obvious: that the latter shows us we were intended to do good to others, as the former shows us that the several members of the natural body were intended to be instruments of good to each other and to the whole body.

JOSEPH BUTLER

30.3. And why are we not willing to acknowledge that the appearance of a daily revolution belongs to the heavens, its *actuality* to the earth? The relation is similiar to that of which Virgil's Aeneas says: "We sail out of the harbor and the countries and cities recede." For when a ship is sailing along quietly, everything which is outside of it will appear to those on board to have a motion corresponding to the movement of the ship, and the voyagers are of the erroneous opinion that they with all that they have with them are at rest. This can without doubt apply to the motion of the earth, and it may appear as if the whole universe were revolving. . .

NICHOLAS COPERNICUS

30.4. If we think to regulate printing, thereby to rectify manners, we must regulate all recreations and pastimes, all that is delightful to man. No music must be heard, no song be set or sung, but what is grave and Doric. There must be licensing dancers, that no gesture, motion, or deportment be taught our youth but what by their allowance shall be thought honest. . .

JOHN MILTON

30.5. I should premise that I use this term [struggle for existence] in a large and metaphorical sense, including dependence of one being on another, and including (which is more important) not only the life of the individual, but success in leaving progeny. Two canine animals, in a time of dearth, may be truly said to struggle with each other which shall get food and live. But a plant on the edge of a desert is said to struggle for life against the drought, though more properly it should be said to be dependent on the moisture. A plant which annually produces a thousand seeds, of which only one of an average comes to maturity, may be more truly said to struggle with the plants of the same and other kinds which already clothe the ground. The mistletoe is dependent on the apple and a few other trees, but can only in a far-fetched sense be said to struggle with these trees, for, if too many of these parasites grow on the same tree, it languishes and dies. But several seedling mistletoes, growing close together on the same branch, may more truly be said to struggle with each other. As the mistletoe is disseminated by birds, its existence depends on them; and it may metaphorically be said to struggle with other fruit-bearing plants, in tempting the birds to devour and thus disseminate its seeds. In these several senses, which pass into each other, I use for convenience' sake the general term of struggle for existence.

CHARLES DARWIN

(NOTE: Has Darwin made a valid induction?)

30.6. Light and other forms of radiation are analogous to water-ripples or waves, in that they distribute energy from a central source. The sun's radiation distributes through space the vast amount of energy which is generated inside the sun. We hardly know whether there is any actual wave-motion in light or not, but we know that light, as well as other types of radiation, are propagated in such a form that they have many of the properties of a succession of waves.

SIR JAMES JEANS

30.7. Hitherto I had stuck to my resolution of not eating animal food, and on this occasion, I consider'd, with my master Tryon, the taking every fish as a kind of unprovoked murder, since none of them had, or ever could do us any injury that might justify the slaughter. All this seemed very reasonable. But I had formerly been a great lover of fish, and, when this came hot out of the frying-pan, it smelt admirably well. I balanc'd some time between principle and inclination, till I recollected that, when the fish were opened, I saw smaller fish taken out of their stomachs; then thought I, "If you eat one another, I don't see why we mayn't eat you." So I din'd upon cod very heartily, and continued to eat with other people, returning only now and then occasionally to a vegetable diet.

BENJAMIN FRANKLIN

Chapter 31: THE CANONS OF INDUCTION

First Canon: Method of Agreement

31.1. If two or more instances of the phenomenon under investigation have only one circumstance in common, the circumstance in which alone all the instances agree is the cause (or effect) of the given phenomenon.

Second Canon: Method of Difference

If an instance in which the phenomenon under investigation occurs, and an instance in which it does not occur, have every circumstance in common save one, that one occurring only in the former; the circumstance in which alone the two instances differ is the effect, or the cause, or an indispensable part of the cause, of the phenomenon.

Third Canon: Joint Method of Agreement and Difference

If two or more instances in which the phenomenon occurs have only one circumstance in common, while two or more instances in which it does not occur have nothing in common save the absence of that circumstance, the circumstance in which alone the two sets of instances differ is the effect, or the cause, or an indispensable part of the cause, of the phenomenon.

Fourth Canon: Method of Residues

Subduct from any phenomenon such part as is known by previous inductions to be the effect of certain antecedents, and the residue of the phenomenon is the effect of the remaining antecedents.

Fifth Canon: Method of Concomitant Variations

Whatever phenomenon varies in any manner whenever another phenomenon varies in some particular manner, is either a cause or an effect of that phenomenon, or is connected with it through some fact of causation.

JOHN STUART MILL

The nature of the canons. Mill, a nineteenth-century logician who is most famous for his doctrine of induction, proposes his five canons as "methods of experimental inquiry." In a tradition begun by Francis Bacon and carried forward by David Hume, Mill regards the five canons as means of finding and proving the causal connections which, on the basis of nature's order, can be framed into inductive generalizations. In his own words, Mill's canons are methods of "discovering and proving laws of nature."

Since Mill aimed to provide a logic for experimental inquiry, it will be interesting to compare his proposals with the actual procedures of induction to see in what respect his proposals are relevant to the scientific method as practiced in physics, chemistry, and biology. But first the canons must be explained.

A brief explanation.

1. *The method of agreement:* Suppose that a given phenomenon P occurs when three circumstances, A, B, C, are present, and that P also occurs under three other circumstances, A, D, E. According to Mill we may conclude that there is a causal connection between A, the common circumstance, and P, the phenomenon under investigation.

2. *The method of difference:* Suppose that a given phenomenon P occurs in the presence of circumstances A, B, C, and that the same phenomenon P does not occur when only two of the circumstances, B and C, are present. According to Mill, we may conclude that there is a causal connection between A, the circumstance absent in the second case, and P.

3. *The joint method of agreement and difference:* Here let us consider A, B, C and A, D, E as two sets of circumstances in which P occurs, and B, C, and D, E, as two sets of circumstances in which P does not occur. In Mill's logic a causal connection is thus established between A and P.

4. *The method of residues:* If, in the case of the antecedents A, B, C, which have consequents a, b, c, we know that b is the effect of B and c the effect of C, we may conclude by subduction that a is the effect of A.

5. *The method of concomitant variations:* If a diminishes with a decrease of A and increases with an increase of A, then there is a causal connection between a and A.

There are several general criticisms that should be leveled against

Mill before proceeding to a consideration of his canons. First of all, he did not fully appreciate the role of hypothesis or theory in our investigations of nature, though he did hold that theories were necessary to make inductions when they became complicated; if our previous analysis is sustained, some sort of dialectical device is necessary not merely in complicated cases of induction by incomplete enumeration but in most of them. Second, Mill was a sensist; he accepted no knowledge except sense knowledge; and he leaves no room for the intellectual judgments of what is relevant to a given experiment and what is not.

To evaluate Mill's canons in more detail, it will be convenient to check them in examples of reasoning simpler than the inductions which require a more complicated and technical knowledge. In these layman's examples, the principles underlying the canons can stand out more sharply:

1. The method of agreement requires us to find two like effects which agree in only one causal circumstance. Apart from the difficulties of finding such cases, this method can easily lead us astray. Consider a coroner trying to find out why two people in adjoining hospital rooms actually died. They are, let us presume, not only different people in different rooms, but they also have different nurses and doctors; suppose further that they are different in age, sex, and even language. To make the case as simple as possible, let them each have a different disease. On examining the witnesses of the two deaths, the sole common circumstance is found to be that a sparrow was sitting on the window sill when each person stopped breathing. By Mill's methods, taken literally, this lone agreeing circumstance could be taken as the cause of the two deaths, but such an analysis would surely not be in accord with reality.

2. The method of difference requires us to reach a causal connection by finding sequences of events which differ in a single circumstance. This is likewise an almost impossible task. But, let us suppose for the sake of simplicity that a man walks into a hotel room on two successive nights and that on the second night he drops dead. Every circumstance on the two different nights is the same except one. There is the same person and the same room. The only observable difference in the two cases would appear to be the time which has elapsed between the two entrances. The second night is

different from the first. What would restrain an observer, using Mill's sensism, from attributing the cause of the death to a simple difference in time?

3. Since the methods of agreement and difference are simply combined in the joint method, what has been urged against each taken singly can apply also to their combination.

4. The method of residues requires us to find an event produced in part by one of several combined causes, and we are to conclude that the remaining part of the event is produced by the rest of the several united causes. Let us suppose that a man has an upset stomach and a headache after a summer picnic and that he has traced his stomach trouble to food that had spoiled in the warm weather. Can he conclude that the headache is due to other causes? Not necessarily, for headache is often the result of a stomach condition, hence of bad food. The two effects may have the same causes.

5. Finally, the method of concomitant variations permits two things that vary together to be causally related. And here too, Mill could lead us astray if we take him at his word. Over a period of years, the accident rate in Brooklyn may vary according to the standing of the Dodgers in the National League, but this certainly does not establish, of itself, any causal sequence between the phenomena. In this connection, according to the miscellany department of *Time* magazine:

> In Concord, N. H., the State Planning and Development Commission squelched some ugly rumors with a press release: "There is no connection between New Hampshire's reputation as an outstanding ski state and the fact that we make 75 per cent of all wooden crutches."

The canons and the study of nature. Mill's logic, when taken literally in its context of sensism, cannot work even in simple examples of human reasoning, and certainly there is even less hope that such a logic can supply the rules for the much more complicated structure of scientific method. In presenting his canons of induction, Mill failed to recognize that the mind rising in a preinductive dialectical operation above mere sense observation must make judgments of relevance, assessing certain circumstances as being unimportant to the investigation in question and other circumstances as being more to the point. Thus, for instance, the sparrow in the method of agreement, the time in the method of difference, and the fate of the Dodgers in the method of concomitant variations would be ruled out of the picture by a good dialectician as being irrelevant to the investigations in our foregoing examples. To charge Mill with a neglect of dialectic is another way of saying that he failed to pay enough attention to the place of theory and hypothesis in science.

Mill's canons, therefore, cannot stand alone, as he would want, and thus pretend to be the sole guides of induction by incomplete enumeration. In a larger context where dialectic is permitted to screen facts for their relevance to a given problem and suggest experimental tests for the solution, the canons have undoubted value. This is true more perhaps in the cases of the methods of difference and of concomitant variations than in regard to the other methods. The greatest value of the canons is in the eliminating of false hypotheses, but far from being only negative in reasoning, they also help to make our dialectical inductions more and more provable. When no other instrument is available, the canons furnish us with the only tools we have for inductions to probable knowledge. For instance, when one phenomenon varies with another one, provided we have been able to achieve a satisfactory isolation of the sequence involved, it is at least probable that the two phenomena are connected, and there are grounds for holding that they form a causal sequence, until a better explanation comes along.

Mill's basic principle through the five canons is that no effect can be present when a cause is absent nor the cause absent when the effect is present. This principle did not originate with Mill. But he did formulate the principle in ways that, with proper dialectical support, make it an extremely useful means of establishing causal connections in our study of nature. In this respect, Mill has emphasized ways of obtaining data for inductive generalization.

Problems

1. State Mill's five canons.
2. Give an example of each canon.
3. What are some of the shortcomings of Mill's general view of human knowledge?
4. Why do Mill's canons taken alone fail to provide a logic of science?

5. Show how the canons can be incorporated into the principles of logic.

6. Assuming that the human intellect, rising above sense experience, is able to make judgments of what is relevant to an inductive problem, identify a canon of induction in each of the following passages. Explain in what way the canon is used:

31.2. The generally accepted theory that both the Greeks and the Jews owe their systems of writing to the Phoenicians is strongly supported by the similarity in the names of the symbols: compare the Greek *alpha, beta, gamma*, with the Hebrew *aleph, beth, ghimel*.

TOBIAS DANTZIG

31.3. This tide increases with the declination of the moon till the 7th or 8th day; then for the 7 or 8 days following it decreases at the same rate as it had increased before, and ceases when the moon changes its declination, crossing over the equator to the south.

ISAAC NEWTON

31.4. The ultimate fate of an ounce of uranium may be expressed by the equation:

$$1 \text{ ounce uranium} = \begin{cases} 0.8653 \text{ ounce lead,} \\ 0.1345 \text{ ounce helium,} \\ 0.0002 \text{ ounce radiation.} \end{cases}$$

The lead and helium together contain just as many electrons and just as many protons as did the original ounce of uranium, but their combined weight is short of the weight of the original uranium by about one part in 4000. Where 4000 ounces of matter originally existed, only 3999 now remain; the missing ounce has gone off in the form of radiation.

SIR JAMES JEANS

31.5. Take away oxygen from the blood. The mind loses its reasoning ability.

WALDEMAR KAEMPFFERT

7. What conclusion would you draw from the following table? State the method used in drawing it.

31.6. Average Annual Expenditures for Magazines and Newspapers

Family Income Bracket	Average Annual Expenditures	
	For Magazines	For Newspapers
$5,000 and over	$16.92	$24.16
3,000–4,999	7.25	19.76
2,000–2,999	4.45	16.57
1,500–1,999	2.78	14.19
1,000–1,499	1.54	11.87
Under $1,000	.53	8.07

Chapter 32:   STATISTICAL REASONING

32.1. Let us suppose, for example, that we have three urns, A, B, C, one of which contains only black balls while the two others contain only white balls; a ball is to be drawn from the urn C and the probability is demanded that this ball will be black. If we do not know which of the three urns contains black balls only, so that there is no reason to believe that it is C rather than B or A, these three hypotheses will appear equally possible, and since a black ball can be drawn only in the first hypothesis, the probability of drawing it is equal to one third. If it is known that the urn A contains white balls only, the indecision then extends only to the urns B and C, and the probability that the ball drawn from the urn C will be black is one half. Finally this probability changes to certainty if we are assured that the urns A and B contain white balls only.

PIERRE SIMON, MARQUIS DE LAPLACE

The known and the unknown. This is an example of statistics. Statistics can be considered as pure mathematics or in its applications to practical problems like the study of gases in chemistry or like the prediction of business cycles in economics. Let us first summarize, in Laplace's example, what the statistics can and cannot do:

1. If two of the three urns, A, B, C, contain white balls and the other black and if, moreover, we do not know which of the urns contains which of the colors, our probability of drawing a black ball on a pick from C is ⅓.

2. On the same conditions mentioned above, the probability that the pick from C will be a white ball is ⅔.

3. Where we know that A contains white balls only, the probability that a black ball will be picked from C is ½.

4. Knowing that A and B contain white balls, we now have a certainty that our draw from C will be black.

As shown by the simple example of Laplace, statistics is a way of gaining knowledge involving an aggregate of things when our knowledge of the initial conditions in the problem is incomplete. As Laplace has elsewhere remarked, probability always involves a mixture of knowledge and ignorance. In Case 1, for instance, there is knowledge that two of the three urns contain white balls but there is ignorance as to which two of the three do so. There is an initial order known and used in every statistical problem so that in Case 1, for example, we can say *exactly* what the probability is of drawing a black ball from C. Statistics as such is always exact and scientific.

Let us consider another example:

32.2. The Democrats run just *under* the 50 per cent mark and the Republicans just *over* the 30 per cent mark. The remaining roughly 20 per cent of the electorate — that is, one out of every five people — must be classified by the student as independents or swing or shift voters.

ELMO ROPER

Here is another statistical problem. Again there is a known initial order but again our knowledge is incomplete. However, Roper's example brings out an important principle that, when violated, leads to one of the frequent fallacies in statistical reasoning. Suppose that in a group of five persons we should encounter four who are either Democrats or Republicans. Does this finding authorize us to conclude that the fifth and final member of the group will be an "independent"? Not at all. The chance that the unexamined person will be of the "swing or shift" class is still $\frac{1}{5}$. Consider the simpler case of a dice thrower who, on five throws of a die, turns up in succession a 1, 2, 3, 4, and 5. This does not mean that the sixth throw will produce a 6. The chances of a 6 on the sixth throw are what they were on the first, namely, $\frac{1}{6}$. Across the entire country, a pollster would encounter in his totals about 5 Democrats to 3 Republicans to 2 Independents, provided of course that Roper is correct, just as in a large number of throws of a die the ratio of sixes to all other five cases will be $\frac{1}{6}$.

Thus statistics, although enabling us to treat aggregates or groups of things in exact form, yields conclusions about individuals which always involve a margin of uncertainty.

Statistics and induction. Statistics, as defined through the example of Laplace, moves from knowledge about an aggregate to conclusions about its parts. Another and perhaps more fundamental application of statistics moves from knowledge of parts to conclusions about the whole aggregate. In election forecasts, for instance, pollsters will interview a representative number of voters, called a sample, and knowing the percentage of Democrats to Republicans in such a group, the statistician can then, by induction, predict the percentage of Democrats to Republicans in the whole electorate. The sample in such a case must involve a sufficient number of voters on the one hand, and on the other hand it must be representative; the voters examined must not be taken only from labor or from management or only from among men or from among women, or only from this or that section of the country. The sample taken must be a kind of miniature of the electorate as a whole.

As in reasoning from whole to part, so in the induction from part to whole statistics requires a prior acceptance of an order in its field of application. The pollster, for instance, must assume that the proportion of Democrats to Republicans disclosed by his sample will prevail throughout the whole electorate to which the predictions extend. An order must not only be assumed in the relation of the sample to the whole aggregate, but it must also remain unchanged during the time required for testing a statistical forecast.

As is well known, the public opinion polls in the 1948 presidential election erroneously predicted the victory of Dewey over Truman. As explained by George Gallup of the Institute of Public Opinion, samplings of voter sentiment must necessarily be taken in advance of the election so that results can be tabulated and published. Moreover, such advance sentiment showed Dewey leading Truman by the margin reported in the press. But there was a last-minute switch of votes in favor of Truman, and this was enough to swing the election to his cause. The statistical prediction of the pollsters failed because the order sampled by the pollsters did not hold constant. Without order, statistics, either in moving from whole to part or in proceeding from part to whole, cannot be employed.

Statistics and logic. A statistical whole or aggregate should never be confused with chance. Chance is always a disorder and can never be predicted. It cannot be reduced to ratios like 1 to 3 or 2 to 3 in the case of the balls or 5 to 3 to 2 in the case of the voters mentioned by Roper. An extraordinary siege of bad weather, for example, could upset election forecasts. Such disturbances would be chance events. They are real disorders.

But in a statistical problem there is always a real order, not a disorder; and this order is shown by the ordered ratios in the whole collection. In statistics the disorder is only in our minds where it takes the form of an inexact knowledge of the real order in things studied. Order is in things but is too complicated for us to know.

Statistics, whether it goes from whole to part as in the case of Laplace's urns or from part to whole as in an election forecast, is essentially a specialized kind of induction. Induction, as discussed so far in these pages, is a movement from particular to universal. But in statistics, there is a collection rather than a universal, and from a partial or particular knowledge about the collection involved, a statistician concludes to more common or universal knowledge. He has, in the beginning of his problem, some knowledge about his collection, and he moves toward a knowledge involving the all.

Uses of statistics. Statistics has widespread applications. Life insurance companies employ it to predict death rates and thus to establish their premiums. Sociologists use it to study social groups. Statistics is applied by physics in the study of such phenomena as heat transfer and radioactivity; by chemistry in its considerations of the kinetic molecular theory; by biology in the study of heredity; by cybernetics in analyzing mechanical brains; by the National Safety Council in predicting holiday deaths; by political studies in dealing with population trends; by the Bureau of Labor Statistics in the study of the relation between wages and the cost of living.

As in the case of experiment, theory, and the use of models, statistics creates no problems new in principle for the kind of logic discussed earlier in this book. Statistics belongs essentially to the realm of induction as a movement from knowledge involving some aspects of a given subject to a knowledge of more such aspects. As a problem of induction, statistics must presuppose an order that holds constant in its subject, and it can work only to the extent that such an order exists. Finally, as in the case of induction, what constitutes a fair statistical sample can be determined not by merely logical considerations, but by the subject matter to which the statistics is applied.

Problems

1. Describe statistics.

2. Show, by means of Laplace's example, that statistics involves both what is known and what is unknown.

3. Show why statistics, to be applied, involves reference to a real order in things.

4. Using Roper's analysis, show one of the fallacies which statistics, when misused, will commit.

5. What is a sample and what are its characteristics?

6. Show how reasoning from a sample in a statistical problem involves reference to a real order in things.

7. Explain why statistics is not a study of chance, in the proper sense of the word.

8. Why is statistics always inductive in character?

9. Mention important applications of statistics.

10. In the light of principles discussed in this chapter, discuss the following passages, to detect the mention or use of any characteristic features of statistical reasoning:

> 32.3. We have seen that probability assigned to an event is a property of a class of events. Usually the class is not directly mentioned in our statement; but there must be an implicit understanding, since otherwise the probability would be indeterminate. Thus I would say that the probability that Mussolini was born on a Friday is 1/7; the understanding is that his birth is assigned to the class of all human births, and I believe (though I may be mistaken) that human births are equally frequent on all days of the week. You may have looked up the date and found it to be, say, Tuesday; if so, you will assign it to the more limited class of human births which have occurred on a Tuesday, and say that the probability is 0. We are both right. The probability relative to the information in my possession is 1/7; relative to the greater information in your possession, it is 0.
>
> ARTHUR EDDINGTON

> 32.4. The American Cancer society said the smoker "who for years smokes heavily — two packages or more a day — has about one in 10 chances of eventually developing lung cancer.
>
> "A man who smokes less than a pack a day has about one in 36 chances of developing the disease. The odds of a nonsmoker developing lung cancer are about one in 270."
>
> THE ASSOCIATED PRESS

32.5. Everybody knows that life or fire insurance companies are based on statistics which tell how many men die or how many houses burn, *on an average*, per year. Experience shows that under determined conditions, in a population of several million inhabitants, the number of yearly deaths varies little, provided these conditions are not modified in a radical manner from one year to another. The same is true for fires. Supposing that out of a million policyholders there is an average annual death rate of 3 per thousand, or 3000 per year. The company will calculate its rates so as to be able, not only to meet its obligations, but to pay a dividend to its stockholders. The accuracy of this calculation is demonstrated by the fact that the company makes a profit except in the case of war, epidemic, or some other cataclysm. It can be easily understood that this accuracy and the profits which are derived therefrom depend on the number of people insured. If there were only ten policyholders, all occupying the same house, and if nine were killed by an epidemic or an accident, the company would be bankrupt. When a hundred individuals are distributed in ten different houses, the chances of the company are greater, for it is unlikely that an epidemic or an accident will destroy the whole hundred. If there are ten million policyholders, the chances of the company become almost a certitude.

LECOMTE DU NOÜY

Chapter 33: TRUTH FUNCTIONS: I

Instead of using sentences to express propositions, let us now use symbols such as p, q, and r.

Let p represent any proposition like: *The sky is cloudy*, and let q stand for any other proposition, such as: *It will rain*. The expressions p and q mean that the respective propositions symbolized by each are true. p means, for instance, *The sky is cloudy*; it is true that *The sky is cloudy*;* and q of course has a corresponding meaning.

The truth functions. Moreover, let us agree to represent the negative proposition by the symbol $\sim$, which in certain of its functions resembles the negative sign in arithmetic $-$. Where p and q have the same meanings as above, $\sim p$ means, it is false that *The sky is cloudy* and $\sim q$, it is not the case that *It will rain*. $\sim q$ can also be read, *It will not rain*, and $\sim p$, *The sky is not cloudy*.

In our study of the hypothetical proposition, we found three types: the conjunctive proposition which has the form *both . . . and . . .*; the disjunctive proposition which has the form *either . . . or . . .*; and the conditional proposition which has the form *if . . . then . . . .* It is possible to use an abbreviated expression for the connectives in each of the three kinds of hypothetical proposition.

As $\sim$ was taken as the symbol of negation, a dot ($\bullet$) will be considered from now on to be the symbol for conjunction. Where p and q continue to have the same meanings as above, the expression $p \bullet q$ means: it is true both that *The sky is cloudy* and that *It will rain*; or simply, *The sky is cloudy* and *It will rain*. $\sim p \bullet \sim q$

---

* In more advanced studies, a distinction might be made between these two expressions, in terms of semantic levels. However, this distinction is not important for present purposes.

means: it is false that *The sky is cloudy* and it is false that *It will rain*; or simply, *The sky is not cloudy* and *It will not rain.* $\sim p \cdot q$ means: it is false that *The sky is cloudy* and true that *It will rain*; or simply, *The sky is not cloudy* and *It will rain.*

The character V (from the Latin *vel* for "or") will be taken as the symbol for disjunction. Where *p* and *q* have meanings as above, $p \vee q$ means: Either *the sky is cloudy* or *it will rain*; $\sim p \vee \sim q$ means that either the first proposition is false or the second is false; $\sim p \vee q$ means that either the first is false or the second is true.

Finally, the character $\supset$ will be taken to symbolize the conditional, *if . . . then . . .* ; $p \supset q$, in terms of our example, means: *If the sky is cloudy, then it will rain*; i.e., if *p* is true, then *q* is true. $\sim p \supset q$ reads, *If the sky is not cloudy, then it will rain*; i.e., if *p* is false, then *q* is true. $\supset$ is called the implication sign. $p \supset q$ can be read *p implies q*.

Any expression such as *p, q, r . . .* which, when given a specific meaning, becomes a proposition, is called a propositional variable. The signs $\sim$, $\cdot$, V, $\supset$, symbolize truth functions. We have seen at least four such functions:

1. $\sim p$ is an example of the contradictory truth function.
2. $p \cdot q$ is an example of the conjunctive truth function.
3. $p \vee q$ is an example of the disjunctive truth function.
4. $p \supset q$ is an example of the implicative truth function.

Logical punctuation. In algebra, parentheses are used to indicate the range of application of the various signs. Thus in $a - (b + c)$, the minus sign applies not merely to *b* but to the whole expression $(b + c)$. In $a - b + c$, the minus sign applies to *b* only.

The logician has a similar problem of "punctuation." For instance, $\sim p \cdot \sim q$ is not the same as $\sim (p \cdot q)$. The first states that each of the propositions involved is false. The second says only that $p \cdot q$, taken together, are not true. At least one of them is false, but one may be true.

Let us change the meanings we have been assigning to *p* and *q* in order to simplify the following explanations. Let *p* now stand for *The parent has dark hair*, and let *q* represent *The child has dark hair.*

In terms of these meanings, $\sim p \cdot \sim q$ means it is false that

The parent has dark hair and it is false that The child has dark hair.

$\sim (p \bullet q)$ says that p and q are not true together. In other words, it is false that *both parent and child have dark hair.* Now there are three conditions that would render it false to say that *both parent and child have dark hair.*

One of these conditions we have already seen: both p and q are false, i.e., the parent does not have dark hair and the child does not.

A second condition is: p is true but q is false, i.e., the parent has dark hair but the child does not.

A third condition is: p is false but q is true, i.e., the parent does not have dark hair but the child does.

The expression $\sim (p \bullet q)$ says that p and q, taken together, are not true, but it does not tell us which of the three conditions makes $p \bullet q$ false.

Parentheses will therefore be used to indicate the range of truth functions. Where parentheses do not appear after a truth function like $\sim$, $\bullet$, V, or $\supset$, the various functions apply only to the next expression. In $\sim p \bullet q$, the $\sim$ applies only to p and not to q. When parentheses do appear, the sign before them applies to everything that they contain. Thus in $\sim (p \bullet q)$, the $\sim$ applies not merely to p but to the whole conjunctive expression $(p \bullet q)$.

Many variable functions. There may be more than two variables in a truth function. Let p be *Chicago is a large city*; q, *The United States is industrialized*; and r, *The United States has skyscrapers.* With this understanding, $p \bullet q \bullet r$ means that all of the propositions are true. $\sim p \bullet \sim q \bullet \sim r$ means that all of the propositions are false. $\sim p \bullet (q \bullet r)$ says that the first proposition is false but that the other two are true. $p \bullet \sim (q \bullet r)$ means that the first proposition is true but that one or both of the last propositions is false. $\sim (p \bullet q \bullet r)$ says that one or two or all of the propositions is false.

In a similar way, there may be complications of disjunctive arguments.

There can also be complications of disjunctive and conjunctive propositions and of disjunctive, conjunctive, and implicative propositions. Thus $p \bullet q$ V r says: *It is true that both Chicago is a large city and the United States is industrialized or that the United States has skyscrapers.* $p \bullet \sim (q$ V $r)$ means: *It is true that Chicago is a* large city but false that the United States either is industrialized or has skyscrapers. $p \supset (q \cdot r)$ says: If Chicago is a large city, then the United States both is industrialized and has skyscrapers.

Non-exclusive alternatives. One of the rules laid down in dealing with the disjunctive syllogism required that the alternatives be mutually exclusive. Such a rule enables us to conclude that one of the alternatives is true when the other is known to be false and vice versa. A simple conclusion of this sort cannot be drawn if this rule is to be modified to permit nonexclusive alternatives in a disjunctive proposition.

However, it remains a fact that in ordinary English usage there are times when an either-or proposition does not require alternatives to be mutually exclusive. A student may say, "Either I'll pass the examination or become a nervous wreck." Both alternatives may be verified. Neville Chamberlain no doubt thought to himself at Munich, "Either Hitler must be appeased or there will be a second world war." Both alternatives were fulfilled.

Accordingly, unless otherwise indicated, the disjunctive truth function will be taken, in this and the following chapter, in a non-exclusive meaning. An expression like $p \vee q$ will mean that either p is true or q is true or both p and q are true. In other words, $p \vee q$ is equivalent to $p \vee q; \vee (p \cdot q)$. The only condition that would falsify $p \vee q$ would be if both alternatives were false. Put more positively, a disjunctive proposition is true when at least one of its component propositions is true.

Problems

Put the following expressions into truth-functional form, using as variables, p, q, r, and if necessary s.

1. London has subways.
2. Ostriches do not fly.
3. Either houses are heated by coal, or they are heated by oil.
4. Atoms are not indivisible, and their parts are useful.
5. If Jupiter has moons, the solar system is heliocentric.
6. It is not the case that Bacon wrote the plays of Shakespeare and also not the case that the Earl of Oxford wrote them.
7. At least one of the following statements is false: bananas are healthful; monkeys imitate human beings; mathematicians mature young.

8. If horses have hooves, then they can walk on rough ground, and they will not injure their feet.

9. If either a cold spell occurs in Florida or a heat wave strikes Alaska, the weatherman checks his records.

10. Either Christmas trees are decorated by children or they are decorated by mothers and by fathers.

11. It is not true that both the Redlegs and the Cubs will win the pennant.

12. If both an atmosphere exists on Mars and the climate of Mars is not severe, then life is possible there.

13. If one nation becomes either too powerful or too wealthy, then other nations become jealous and seek its downfall.

14. Tomorrow it will either rain or snow or do both.

15. Either both the short story and the novel are literary forms or neither Poe nor Dickens was a literary writer.

Chapter 34:   TRUTH FUNCTIONS: II

From the discussions in the past chapter, it can already be seen that there is a relationship among the truth functions. It was seen for instance that $\sim (p \cdot q)$ is equivalent to ($\equiv$) $(\sim p \cdot q)$ $V (p \cdot \sim q) V (\sim p \cdot \sim q)$. Here there is a reduction of a conjunction to a disjunction. In fact, all of the four fundamental truth functions can be converted into one another.

Disjunction to conjunction, and vice versa.

34.1. $p V q \equiv \sim (\sim p \cdot \sim q)$

A disjunction is converted into a conjunction by (a) conjoining the parts of the original disjunction; (b) negating the new conjunction; (c) negating each of its parts.

Let p stand for *Joe passed the examination* and let q read *Ann passed the examination*. Our original disjunction reads: *Either Joe passed the examination or Ann passed the examination*. Our equivalent, $\sim (\sim p \cdot \sim q)$, says: *It is false that Joe failed the examination and that Ann failed it*. In other words, if it is true that either one or the other or both passed the examination, it is false that both of them failed.

This is an appropriate place to remark that two negation signs cancel each other and the resulting expression is positive. For instance, $\sim p V \sim q \equiv \sim (p \cdot q)$ and $\sim (p V q) \equiv \sim p \cdot \sim q$.

34.2. $p \cdot q \equiv \sim (\sim p V \sim q)$

A conjunction is converted into a disjunction by (a) disjoining the parts of the original conjunction; (b) negating the new disjunction; and (c) negating each of its parts.

Let p stand for *The Tigers won the pennant*, and q for *The Redlegs won the pennant*. Our original conjunctive proposition

255

states that they both won. And the equivalent disjunction states that it is false that neither of them won. If both of them won, neither of them lost.

Where the original conjunction or any of its parts has a negative sign, the double negative in the resulting disjunction will become positive.

The same rules for equivalences between conjunctions and disjunctions apply where more than two variables are involved. Thus $p \cdot q \cdot r \equiv \sim (\sim p \vee \sim q \vee \sim r)$.

Implication to conjunction and disjunction.

34.3. $p \supset q \equiv \sim (p \cdot \sim q)$

If p implies q, then it is false that p is true and q is false.

An implication is converted into a conjunction by (a) conjoining the parts of the original implication; (b) negating the new conjunction; (c) negating the original consequent.

Let p become: *The businessman is just,* and q: *He pays a fair wage.*

Our original implication reads: *If the businessman is just, he pays a fair wage.* Our equivalent expression says: *It is false that the businessman is just but does not pay a fair wage.*

$\sim (p \supset q) \equiv p \cdot \sim q$. Here we can see once again the effect of double negation. Let p read: *Hogs are animals,* and q: *Hogs have feathers.* Our original proposition now reads: *It is false that if hogs are animals, hogs have feathers,* and the derived proposition says: *It is true that hogs are animals but false that they have feathers.* In other words, they are animals but have no feathers.

34.4. $p \supset q \equiv \sim p \vee q$.

If p implies q, then either p is false or q is true.

An implication is converted into a disjunction by (a) disjoining the parts of the original implication; and (b) negating the original antecedent.

Let p now read: *The Republicans will win,* and q: *The Democrats will lose.* The original implication then says: *If the Republicans will win, the Democrats will lose.* And the equivalent disjunction says: *Either the Republicans will not win or the*

Democrats will lose. In other words, either the Republicans will lose or the Democrats will lose.

Actually, the equivalence in **34.4** could be reached by strictly logical considerations.

By **34.2** $p \cdot q \equiv \, \sim (\sim p \vee \sim q)$.

By **34.3** $p \supset q \equiv \, \sim (p \cdot \sim q)$.

Using the rule from **34.2** on $\sim (p \cdot \sim q)$ just above we find this conjunction to yield $\sim p \vee q$.

Conjunction and disjunction to implication.

34.5. $p \cdot q \equiv \, \sim (p \supset \sim q)$

If p and q are both true, then it is false that p implies that q is false.

A conjunction is converted into an implication by (a) ordering the parts of the original conjunction into an implication; (b) negating the implication; and (c) negating the consequent.

Let p represent *Angels are spirits* and q: *Angels are invisible.* Our original proposition now reads: *Angels are both spirits and invisible.* The derived proposition reads: *It is false that if angels are spirits they are visible.* In other words, what is spiritual cannot be seen.

34.6. $p \vee q \equiv \, \sim p \supset q$.

If either p is true or q is true, then if p is false, q must be true.

A disjunction is converted into an implication by (a) ordering the parts of the original disjunction into implication; and (b) denying the antecedent.

Suppose that a biologist is examining a newly discovered kind of organism to decide whether it is a plant or an animal. Let p be: *The organism is a plant,* and q: *The organism is an animal.* Then our original disjunction reads: *Either the organism is a plant or it is an animal.* And the equivalent proposition reads: *If the organism is not a plant, then it is an animal.* If in our original proposition we say that the living thing is either a plant or animal, then when we know it is not the one we can certainly conclude that it is the other.

Material implication. The relation expressed by $\supset$ is called material implication. The examples we have chosen in order to illustrate it have all been simple and straightforward. Logic is concerned not with the content of thought objects but with form, and in this respect, material implication raises a serious problem. Let us approach it through an example involving **34.6**: $p \lor q \equiv \sim p \supset q$.

Let p be: *Bears have fur,* and q: *Bears are protected from the cold.*

The disjunction in **34.6** says: *Either bears have fur or they are protected from the cold (or both).* The equivalent implication reads: *If bears do not have fur, they are protected from the cold.* Here we began with the alternative that *Bears either have fur or are protected from the cold,* and we "concluded" that *If bears lack fur, they are protected from the cold.* Clearly, in such a framework, p can be false while q is true as **34.6** indicates.

Let us examine some conditions that would make $p \supset q$ to be true or false:

By **34.3**, it is impossible for p to be true while q is false. Therefore, if p is true, q is true. But by **34.4**, p can be false while q is true. Indeed, there is only one condition where $p \supset q$ is false, and that is where p would be true and q false. Hence, $p \supset q$ can be true whether p is true or false, as long as q is true.

In terms of our example, if it is true that *Bears are protected from the cold,* then the following propositions are true:

If bears have fur, they are protected from the cold. (**34.3**)

If bears do not have fur, they are protected from the cold. (**34.4**)

This state of affairs where opposites seem to prevail is called a paradox, and the present problem is called the paradox of material implication. According to our earlier rule governing the conditional syllogism, it is impossible to have a false antecedent and a true consequent; any proposition with a false antecedent and a true consequent would, according to this earlier rule, be false. But here we have seen a conditional proposition that is true so long as the consequent is true, whether the antecedent be true or false.

Evaluation. The past two chapters have briefly examined what is called the propositional calculus. This is a branch of modern symbolic or, as it is usually called, mathematical logic. Such a logic is often presented as a rival to the traditional or Aristotelian logic presented in the earlier part of this book. From the principles of their logic, modern mathematical logicians claim to derive the whole of mathematics. It will be useful to comment on the issues between an Aristotelian logician and the modern logician to the extent that they can be focused from what has been so simply presented.

1. Modern logicians did not invent the presentation of logic through symbols, but to their great credit they have evolved and refined remarkable techniques for expressing complicated thoughts, especially in connection with the three kinds of hypothetical propositions. Where arguments are complicated and expression involved, it is much easier to see logical relations and correctly to manipulate them if we employ such techniques as those outlined in the past two chapters. Formalizing a complex expression by reducing it to symbolic form enables us to make a quick and easy test of consistency that would be difficult to conduct were the composition merely left in its original form.

2. But modern logic takes no account of the logical considerations which go beyond mere symbolisms to discuss arguments in terms of their scientific, dialectical, rhetorical, and literary character. One of the chief concerns of logic is to name the conditions that an argument must fulfill to be, for instance, a demonstration. In analyzing a conditional syllogism that is truly scientific, an Aristotelian would insist that such an argument is no mere algebraic manipulation of linguistic symbols or the propositions which these symbols stand for. On the contrary, where such a syllogism is solved by affirming the antecedent and then affirming the consequent, the antecedent represents the cause of what is expressed by the conclusion. Hence, in a truly scientific sense, $p \supset q$ can only hold where p is related to q not merely as a symbolic antecedent but as representing a genuine cause.

Let us return to 34.6 $(p \lor q \equiv \sim p \supset q)$ to see what happens if the rules for scientific reasoning are applied.

Science is not open like dialectic. Its conclusions express a truth with no fear that the opposite can hold, because the premises themselves also represent truth known to be certain. Demonstration would not tolerate a set of alternatives where either p is true or q is true, or both p and q are true. In accordance with the principles laid down earlier in this book, the alternatives in a scientific disjunction must be mutually exclusive because in science reason is not open to a proposition where opposites are true. Such an openness is characteristic of dialectic but not of demonstration.

If these observations are applied now to the equivalence $p \vee q \equiv\, \sim p \supset q$, it will be seen that the mind in quest of science will accept the proposition: *Either bears lack fur or they are protected from cold.* But it will not accept the simultaneous truth of both parts of the disjunction. Such a disjunction, $p \vee q$ is equivalent to $\sim p \supset q$, *If bears do not lack fur, they are protected from cold.* Hence, though everyday language will tolerate such expressions as, "Either I'll pass the examination or become a nervous wreck," strict demonstration will require a more precise disjunction where the alternatives are mutually exclusive. Such expressions as "Either Hitler must be appeased or there will be a second world war," may well be acceptable in the ordinary conventions of language, but they do not involve the kind of consideration of which science is made. Logic should not imitate the conventions of language. It is concerned primarily with natural signs rather than with those that are arbitrary and conventional.

Reference to the various kinds of arguments, such as the demonstrative and the dialectical, is one way out of the paradox of material implication. The logician, as such, cannot find the reason why bears are protected from cold, but he can name the conditions for a scientific discourse about the subject.

3. What has been said, however, should by no means be construed as a rejection of the new logic. Like other modern developments studied in this Part, mathematical logic, even with its paradox of material implication, has a place within a wider whole. All of it may well be accepted as an intellectual method, but the fact remains that its strictly scientific value is limited by its ignoring of causality in argument. Even in material implication, modern logic is an extension of the Aristotelian principles developed earlier in this book. In the dialectical syllogism, for example in reasoning by hypothesis, the antecedent may be false while the consequent is true, as shown by the history of astronomy. The advances of mathematical logic are especially useful then in those areas where the mind, unable to find true causes and principles, must construct a dialectical system, more or less complicated in character but sub-

ject, when tested, to the fundamental fact that truly scientific reasoning takes place through certain causes and principles.

Problems

Change the following functions as directed:

1. $\sim p \lor q$ to implication.
2. $p \cdot \sim q$ to disjunction.
3. $\sim (\sim p \lor q)$ to conjunction.
4. $\sim p \supset \sim q$ to conjunction.
5. $\sim (p \cdot q)$ to disjunction.
6. $\sim p \supset q$ to disjunction.
7. $\sim (\sim p \cdot \sim q)$ to conjunction.
8. $p \lor \sim q$ to implication.
9. $\sim (\sim p \supset \sim q)$ to disjunction.
10. $(p \cdot q) \lor r$ to conjunction.
11. $(\sim p \lor q) \cdot r$ to disjunction.
12. $(p \lor q) \cdot r$ to implication.

13. Show the paradox involved in material implication and discuss the relevance of material implication to the logic of Aristotle.

PART VII: THE FALLACIES

Chapter 35: FALLACIES

35.1. We repudiate all morality taken apart from human society and classes. We say that it is deception, a fraud, a befogging of the minds of the workers and peasants by the landlords and capitalists.

NICOLAI LENIN

35.2. There is an incredible amount of empty space in the universe. The distance from the sun to the nearest star is about 4.2 light years, or 25 followed by 12 noughts miles. . . And as to mass: the sun weighs about 2 followed by 27 noughts tons, the Milky Way weighs about 160,000 times as much as the sun and is one of a collection of galaxies of which, as I said before, about 30 million are known. It is not very easy to retain a belief in one's own cosmic importance in view of such overwhelming statistics.

BERTRAND RUSSELL

35.3. If it were permitted to reason consistently in religious matters, it is clear that we all ought to become Jews, because Jesus Christ was born a Jew, lived a Jew, and died a Jew, and because he said that he was accomplishing and fulfilling the Jewish religion.

VOLTAIRE

35.4. No, there is only one most sacred human right, and this right is at the same time the most sacred obligation, namely, to see to it that the blood is preserved pure, so that by the preservation of the best human material a possibility is given for a more noble development of these human beings.

ADOLF HITLER

35.5. It did not occur to Macaulay that a closely similar indictment might be drawn against the religion founded by one who said that man does not live by bread alone. But more recent disciples of the Baconian philosophy have not hesitated to accuse Christianity of failing to achieve its one practical aim: to make men love one another. Both failures must be frankly admitted.

F. M. CORNFORD

These are examples of common fallacies in reasoning.

In nearly every chapter of this book it was noted that the laws of logic can be violated. Any violation of logical laws is a fallacy. It is not necessary here to review the fallacies already mentioned, as in the deviation from the rules of syllogism. Nor is it feasible to consider all of the various possible cases of fallacious reasoning. It will be sufficient here to comment briefly on the principal kinds of fallacy which were not treated in earlier sections and which result from bad reasoning and not simply from faulty language.

Begging the question. It is clear in Lenin's argument that he proves nothing. Instead of supporting his charge that morality apart from classes should be repudiated, he proceeds to engage in a name-calling attack which merely restates his original proposition. Such a procedure is called begging the question. It consists in attempting to prove a point while assuming it, and hence involves a vicious circle.

Begging the question is one of the more common of the fallacies. Some philosophers argue that only what is measurable is meaningful, because mathematics, the science of measurement, is the only certain and meaningful science. Such an argument assumes the point rather than proves it. Another example of begging the question is the charge by a powerful educational association in this country that private schools are divisive and hence undemocratic. This argument assumes that private schools are divisive and undemocratic without attention to the very opposite point of view that private education, free from government control, is the best educational weapon of democracy against any future tyrant who would control, like Stalin or Hitler, the spread of truth. It also overlooks the important fact that the moral training in parochial schools makes for good, law-abiding citizens.

Ignoring the question. In 35.2 Russell commits a fallacy called ignoring the question. This fallacy consists in proving something other than the point to be established and hence in evading the original issue. Russell's figures show that our cosmos is immense. But they do not either add or detract from the dignity of man. For the importance of man does not consist in his physical dimensions but rather in his spiritual soul. Russell has therefore proved something other than the conclusion he wishes to draw and hence has ignored the question he would answer.

John Dewey, one of America's most influential philosophers, often declared that his sole aim was to apply to social and cultural problems the kind of method that has worked so well in physics and chemistry. But such an aim ignores the issue of whether human problems can be solved by the same methods that succeed in the study of mere matter. Dewey's whole philosophy is based on ignoring the question in the area that he wished to study.

False cause. In 35.3 Voltaire commits the fallacy of false cause. This fallacy consists in assuming that when one event precedes another it is therefore its cause. It is true, of course, that Christ was a Jew before He founded the Catholic Church, but such a temporal sequence does not require a similar succession in Christ's followers. The fact that Jew preceded Christian in time does not mean that Jew must precede Christian in causality.

The fallacy of false cause is a constant threat to all those studies of the past like paleontology and archaeology. It is tempting to argue, where two forms of life are found after one another in time, that therefore the first was the cause of the second. Early apologists for Christianity had to meet the argument from the pagans that Christianity was the cause of Rome's decline because the rise of Christianity preceded the failure of the empire. It was once thought that yellow fever was spread by bodily contact because victims had been close to previous victims. All such reasoning involved the fallacy of false cause.

Fallacy of accident. In 35.4 Hitler commits a fallacy called the fallacy of accident. This error consists in treating what is accidental to a subject as something essential to that subject. In our present case, Hitler treats blood or race as essentially involved in human superiority when, as history attests, genius is found in many different stocks. In any case, greatness is not a property of any particular race; race or blood is accidental to "noble development."

The fallacy of accident is common in propaganda including campaign oratory. It is certainly involved in the claims of white superiority among anti-segregationists. Materialists commit this fallacy by emphasizing only what man can see and feel about himself without attending to his most essential part, namely, his spiritual soul.

The fallacy of accident makes its appearance when we measure the greatness of a civilization by the number of its bathtubs or powerhouses, the greatness of a man by his income, the quality of a nation by its armies. In all such cases what is accidental is taken for the essential.

Part and whole. A final kind of fallacy that will be considered here is illustrated by **35.5.** Cornford is repeating a familiar argument by blaming Christianity for the conduct of individual Christians. Such a fallacy is called the fallacy of part and whole. It consists in attributing to a whole what belongs only to its parts or of attributing to the part what belongs only to the whole. Cornford violates logic in the first regard; he attributes to Christianity as a whole what is the failure of individual Christians. There is an error of the second kind in arguing, for instance, that because America is such a prosperous nation all of its citizens must be well off. Here what belongs only to a whole is predicated, wrongly, of the parts.

One of the ways of committing this fallacy is to condemn labor unions on the grounds that some of their members and even some of their leaders have been racketeers. Another case of this fallacy occurs in book reviewing where a work as a whole is given a scorching criticism because this or that part is somehow inadequate. In statistics, as was previously observed, there is no warrant to argue, after successive rolls of 1, 2, 3, 4, and 5 that the next throw of the die will be 6. The ratio of 6's as $\frac{1}{6}$ holds only over a large collection of throws (the whole) and does not necessarily hold for any individual throw (the part).

The present chapter has considered some of the more common fallacies. It should be emphasized again that the list is incomplete. To catalogue all of the fallacies would be indeed an impossible task. An argument can be right in only one way, but the number of ways of being wrong are endless. Because truth is one while error is multiple, a bad argument will often involve more than one fallacy and hence will be exposed to criticism on more than one score.

The study of fallacies has, it is true, only a negative value, but the value is nevertheless of considerable proportion. For whenever the mind analyzes error, it can learn something of the truth, and a mind that makes a mistake will, when it is pointed out, be less likely to commit a similar pitfall again.

Man is the only animal that can profit from his enemies no less than from his friends.

Problems

1. Define the five fallacies studied in this chapter.
2. Explain why a list of fallacies would be endless.
3. Name the fallacy involved in each of the following arguments:

    35.6.   Since cancer runs in families, it must be hereditary.

    35.7.   Birth prevention is wrong because it is forbidden.

    35.8.   Since the life span of the American is increasing, children born this year will live longer than those born last year.

    35.9.   The human soul cannot exist because it cannot be measured.

    35.10.   Great men should be respected because they are so rare.

    35.11.   Economists were wrong in forecasting a postwar depression and therefore economics is not a reliable study.

    35.12.   The reason why Wagner was a good composer was because he wrote such wonderful compositions.

    35.13.   As human, the Holy Father can sin and hence is not infallible.

    35.14.   Deficit spending is good because it is approved by the majority of the people.

    35.15.   Since this boy is a juvenile delinquent, he must have come from a poor section of town.

    35.16.   Since Hollywood has widespread divorce, no movie star can long remain married.

4. Criticize the arguments implied in the following paragraphs:

    35.17.   Leopold lives on, a sad, heavy-set man of 51, deeply read in many languages, and fascinated by medical research which he works at, along with his job as technician in the Stateville prison hospital. Leopold declares, with medical pedantry, that no cell in his body is the same as that of the boy who once killed another.

                                                         TIME

    35.18.   Being anti-individualistic, the Fascist system of life stresses the importance of the State and recognizes the individual only in so far as his interests coincide with those of the State, which stands for the consciousness and universality of man as an historic entity.

                                        BENITO MUSSOLINI

    35.19.   Let us go to the animal and try to track the sense of beauty to its source. We are wrong if we suppose that man alone is gifted with esthetic feeling. Many animals are more beautiful than the featherless biped that transiently rules the earth; and for all we know they may realize it more clearly than ourselves, and may look upon us, as sometimes they seem to do, with a calm and leisurely contempt.

WILL DURANT

35.20.   Just as in astronomy the difficulty of admitting the motion of the earth lay in the immediate sensation of the earth's stationariness and of the planets' motion, so in history the difficulty of recognizing the subjection of the personality to the laws of space and time and causation lies in the difficulty of surmounting the direct sensation of the independence of one's personality.

LEO TOLSTOY

35.21.   I smoke and am a better Christian for doing so!

MOREHOUSE, BISHOP OF MANCHESTER

35.22.   Good sense is, of all things among men, the most equally distributed; for everyone thinks himself so abundantly provided with it, that those even who are the most difficult to satisfy in everything else, do not usually desire a larger measure of this quality than they already possess.

RENÉ DESCARTES

35.23.   One day he was at table in the man's home, and many tax collectors and sinners were reclining at table with Jesus and his disciples, for the number of his followers was considerable. When now the Scribes of the Pharisaical party noticed that he was taking a meal with sinners and tax collectors, they said to his disciples: "He takes a meal with tax collectors and sinners! How is that?"

SAINT MARK

35.24.   If we take in our hand any volume; of divinity or school metaphysics, for instance; let us ask, *Does it contain any abstract reasoning concerning quantity or number?* No. *Does it contain any experimental reasoning concerning matter of fact and existence?* No. Commit it then to flames; for it can contain nothing but sophistry and illusion.

DAVID HUME

35.25.   One of the oldest paradoxes is that of the wealthy Arab who at death left his stable of seventeen beautiful horses to his three sons. He specified that the eldest was to have one half the horses, the next one third, and the youngest one ninth. The three young heirs were in despair, for they obviously could not divide seventeen horses this way without calling in the butcher. They finally sought the advice of an old and wise friend, who promised to help them. He arrived at the stable the next day, leading one of his own horses. This he added to the seventeen and directed the brothers to make their choices. The eldest took one half of the eighteen, or nine; the next, one third of the eighteen, or six; and the youngest, one ninth of the eighteen or two. When all seventeen of the original horses had been chosen, the old man took his own horse and departed.

EUGENE P. NORTHROP

35.26. The only freedom which deserves the name, is that of pursuing our own good in our own way, so long as we do not attempt to deprive others of theirs, or impede their efforts to obtain it. Each is the proper guardian of his own health, whether, bodily, or mental and spiritual.

JOHN STUART MILL

35.27. Now the gates of hell ofttimes had the papacy in their power, at times the pope was not a pious man, and the office was occupied by a man without faith, without grace, without good works; which God would never have permitted if the papacy were meant in Christ's word concerning the rock.

MARTIN LUTHER

35.28. THE PURE SCIENCES EXPRESS RESULTS OF COMPARISON exclusively; comparison is not a conceivable effect of the order in which outer impressions are experienced — it is one of the house-born portions of our mental structure; therefore, the pure sciences form a body of propositions with whose genesis experience has nothing to do.

WILLIAM JAMES

35.29. There is no short cut to truth, no way to gain a knowledge of the universe except through the gateway of scientific method. The hard and stony path of classifying facts and reasoning upon them is the only way to ascertain truth.

KARL PEARSON

35.30. Things are interesting because we care about them, and important because we need them.

GEORGE SANTAYANA

35.31. There is evidence in plenty that I exist and there is none that God exists.

For my existence is an object of such a nature that it can be inferred from other objects of belief.

G. E. MOORE

35.32. Man walks because things in nature move. . . Similarly, man digests because nature is chemical. . . Man predicts because nature is mechanical. . . Once more man is free because nature is contingent.

STERLING P. LAMPRECHT

(In the foregoing argument, apart from any other fallacy committed by one or more of the enthymemes, do the arguments violate any of the rules of the syllogism?)

35.33. Common-sense says, we lose our fortune, are sorry and weep; we meet a bear, are frightened and run; we are insulted by a rival, are angry and strike. The hypothesis here to be defended says that this order of sequence is incorrect, that one mental state is not immediately induced by the other, that the more rational statement is that we feel sorry because we cry, angry because we strike, afraid because we tremble, not that we cry, strike, or tremble because we are sorry, angry, or fearful as the case may be.

WILLIAM JAMES

REFERENCES FOR CASE HISTORIES

1.1. Galileo Galilei, *Dialogues Concerning the Two New Sciences*, First Day. Translated by Henry Crew and Alfonso de Salvio (Evanston, Ill.: Northwestern University Press, 1946), p. 72.

1.2. Euclid, *The Thirteen Books of Euclid's Elements*, Bk. I, First Theorem. Translated by Sir Thomas L. Heath, Everyman edition (London and New York: J. M. Dent, Ltd., and E. P. Dutton, Inc., 1933), p. 7.

1.3. St. Thomas Aquinas, *On Kingship*, Bk. I, Ch. 1, par. 5. Translated by G. B. Phelan, revised with Introduction and Notes by I. Th. Eschmann (Toronto: Pontifical Institute of Mediaeval Studies, 1949), p. 3.

1.4. John Dalton, "On the Constitution of Bodies," in *Foundations of the Atomic Theory*. Alembic Club Reprints, No. 2 (Edinburgh: E. & S. Livingstone, Ltd., 1948), p. 1. With permission of the Royal Society of Edinburgh.

1.5. Charles Darwin, *Origin of Species*, Ch. 5, "Laws of Variation" (New York: Hurst and Company, n.d.), pp. 136–137.

1.6. Charles Saunders Peirce, "The Essence of Mathematics," in *Collected Papers of Charles Saunders Peirce*, edited by C. Hartshorne and P. Weiss (Cambridge: Harvard University Press, 1931), Vol. I, ch. iv. Originally an article, "The Architecture of Theories," in *The Monist* (January, 1891).

2.1. Hilaire Belloc, *The Path to Rome* (New York: Doubleday Image, 1956), pp. 114–115. With permission of Henry Regnery Company.

2.2. Alexander Pope, *Essay on Criticism*, lines 182–183.

2.3. Samuel Taylor Coleridge, *Biographia Litteraria*.

2.4. Gilbert Keith Chesterton, *A Handful of Authors*. Edited by Dorothy L. Collins (New York: Sheed and Ward, Inc., 1953), p. 93.

3.1. St. Augustine, *Good and Evil*, ch. 12, I, 1, 3.

3.2. Aristotle, *On the Parts of Animals*, I, 1; 639 a 1–12. Translated by William Ogle. In *The Basic Works of Aristotle*, edited by Richard McKeon (New York: Random House, Inc., 1941), p. 643. With permission of Oxford University Press.

3.4. Bertrand Russell, *Unpopular Essays* (New York: Simon and Schuster, Inc., 1950), p. 31.

4.1. St. Luke 21:25–31. In *The New Testament*, translated by James Kleist, S.J., and Joseph Lilly, C.M. (Milwaukee: The Bruce Publishing Company, 1954), p. 214.

4.2. Suzanne K. Langer, *Philosophy in a New Key* (Cambridge: Harvard University Press, 1951), p. 72.

4.3. Ernst Cassirer, *The Philosophy of Symbolic Forms*. Translated by Ralph Manheim (New Haven: Yale University Press, 1955), Vol. I, p. 85.

4.4. Charles Morris, *Signs, Language, and Behavior* (New York: Prentice-Hall, Inc., 1946), p. 3. Reprinted with permission.

5.1. Alexis Carrel, *Man, the Unknown* (New York: Harper and Brothers, 1935), pp. 236–237.

5.2. Sir Isaac Newton, *Mathematical Principles of Natural Philosophy*, Axioms or Laws of Motion, Law 1. Translated by Andrew Motte, revised by Florian Cajori (Berkeley, Calif.: University of California Press, 1946), p. 13.

5.3. Alexander Hamilton, *The Federalist Papers*, No. 83. In *Great Books of the Western World*, edited by Robert Maynard Hutchins (Chicago: Encyclopaedia Britannica, Inc., 1952), Vol. 43, p. 248. This series will hereinafter be abbreviated *GBWW*.

5.4. Plato, *Theaetetus*, 185. Translated by Benjamin Jowett and found in *The Dialogues of Plato* (New York: Random House, Inc., 1937), Vol. II, p. 187. With permission of Oxford University Press.

5.5. Jean-Jacques Rousseau, *On the Origin of Inequality*. Translated by G. D. H. Cole, in *GBWW*, Vol. 38, pp. 341b–342a. Reprinted by permission of J. M. Dent & Sons, Ltd., London and E. P. Dutton & Co., Inc., New York.

5.6. William James, *Principles of Psychology*, in *GBWW*, Vol. 53, p. 447b. Reprinted by permission of Henry Holt & Co., Inc.

5.7. George Berkeley, *Principles of Human Knowledge*, Introduction, Section 18. In *British Empirical Philosophers*, edited by A. J. Ayer and Raymond Winch (London: Routledge and Kegan Paul, 1952), pp. 173–174.

6.1. Plato, *The Statesman*, 279. Translated by Benjamin Jowett and found in *The Dialogues of Plato* (New York: Random House, Inc., 1937), Vol. II, p. 306. With permission of Oxford University Press.

6.2. John Locke, *An Essay Concerning Human Understanding*, Bk. III, Ch. 3, section 9. Edited and annotated by Alexander Campbell Fraser (Oxford: The Clarendon Press, 1894), Vol. II, p. 19.

6.3. Jacques Maritain, *Man and the State* (Chicago: University of Chicago Press, 1951), p. 2.

6.4. St. Thomas Aquinas, *Commentary on the Ethics*, Bk. VIII, lect. 3. Translation adapted from *St. Thomas Aquinas on Aristotle's Love of Friendship*, by Pierre Conway, O.P. (Providence: Providence College Press, 1951), p. 10.

7.1. Charles Darwin, *The Descent of Man*, in *GBWW*, Vol. 49, p. 332.

7.2. Antoine Lavoisier, *Elements of Chemistry*. Translated by Robert Kerr, in *GBWW*, Vol. 45, p. 4c.

7.3. Homer Smith, *From Fish to Philosopher* (Boston: Little, Brown, and Company, 1953), p. 210.

7.4. Alexis de Tocqueville, *Democracy in America*. Edited by Richard D. Heffner (New York: Mentor Books, 1956), p. 157.

7.5. René Descartes, *Objections against the Meditations and Replies*, Reply to Fourth Set of Objections. Translated by Elizabeth S. Haldane and G. D. T. Ross. In *GBWW*, Vol. 31, p. 154. Reprinted by arrangement with The Open Court Publishing Co.

8.1. Nicomachus of Gerasa, *Introduction to Arithmetic*, Bk. I, Ch. VII. Translated by Martin L. D'Ooge, Frank Egleston Robbins, and Louis Charles Karprinski. In *GBWW*, Vol. 11, p. 814. Reprinted by arrangement with the Regents of the University of Michigan, The University of Michigan Press.

8.2. Edwin Markham, "The Man With the Hoe."

8.3. Aristotle, *On the Parts of Animals*, I, 1; 641 a 5. Translated by William Ogle. In *The Basic Works of Aristotle*, edited by Richard McKeon (New York: Random House, Inc., 1941), p. 647. With permission of the Oxford University Press.

8.4. René Descartes, *Objections against the Meditations and Replies*, Reply to Fourth Set of Objections. Translated by Elizabeth S. Haldane and G. D. T. Ross. In *GBWW*, Vol. 31, p. 154. Reprinted by arrangement with The Open Court Publishing Co.

8.5. Louis Agassiz, *Gists from Agassiz*, selected by John Kasper. Square Dollar Series (New York: Kasper and Horton, 1953), pp. 12–13.

8.6. Herman Melville, *Moby Dick*, ch. xxxii, "Cetology."

8.7. Julian S. Huxley, cited by Paul A. Meglitsch, "On the Nature of Species," *Systematic Zoology*, Vol. III, No. 2 (June, 1954).

8.8. Dmitri I. Mendeleyev, reprinted in John Warren Knedler, Jr., *Masterworks of Science* (New York: Doubleday and Company, 1947), p. 562. Reprinted by permission.

9.1. Aristotle, *Categories*, I, 4; 1b 24–2a. In *Aristoteles Graece*, ed. I. Bekker (Berlin: Georg Reimer, 1831). (Translation, mine; emphasis mine.) I have found it necessary to re-translate this passage because the existing English translation renders the Greek terms for the nine accidents into abstract rather than concrete nouns. We do not predicate quantity, e.g., fourness but *quantum*, e.g., four; we do not predicate quality, e.g., redness, but *quale*, i.e., red.

9.2. Henry David Thoreau, *Walden*, ch. vi (New York: Grosset and Dunlap, 1910), p. 184.

9.3. Homer, *The Iliad*, Bk. III. Translated by A. Lang, W. Leaf, and C. Myers (New York: The Modern Library, n.d.), pp. 54–55.

9.4. Leo Tolstoy, *War and Peace*. Translated by Constance Garnett (New York: The Modern Library, n.d.), p. 140.

9.5. St. Augustine, *Confessions*, Bk. 4, ch. xvi. Translated by F. J. Sheed (New York: Sheed & Ward, Inc., 1945), pp. 78–79.

10.1. Plato, *The Sophist*, 219. Translated by Benjamin Jowett and found in *The Dialogues of Plato* (New York: Random House, Inc., 1937), Vol. II, p. 224. With permission of the Oxford University Press.

10.2. Julius Caesar, *The Gallic Wars*, Bk. I, 1.

10.3. Charles de Secondet, Baron de Montesquieu, *The Spirit of Laws*, Bk. VIII. Translated by Thomas Nugent, revised by J. V. Prichard. In *GBWW*, Vol. 38, p. 51. Reprinted by arrangement with G. Bell & Sons, Ltd., London.

10.4. Marie Curie, *Radioactivity*. Digested in *The Masterworks of Science*, edited by John Warren Knedler, Jr. (New York: Doubleday and Company, Inc., 1947), p. 576. Reprinted by permission.

10.5. St. Thomas Aquinas, *Commentary on the Ethics*, Bk. I, lect. 1.

10.6. Bertrand Russell, *Unpopular Essays* (New York: Simon and Schuster, Inc., 1950), p. 34.

10.7. Michael Faraday, *Experimental Researches in Electricity*, Third Series. In *GBWW*, Vol. 45, p. 267.

10.8. Louis Agassiz, *Gists from Agassiz*, selected by John Kasper. Square Dollar Series (New York: Kasper and Horton, 1953), pp. 7–8.

11.1. John Henry Newman, *The Idea of a University*. Edited by Charles Frederick Harrold (New York: Longmans, Green, and Co., 1947), p. 185.

11.2. C. F. von Weizsaecker, *The World View of Physics*. Translated by M. Grene (Chicago: University of Chicago Press, 1949), p. 42.

11.3. Euclid, *The Thirteen Books of Euclid's Elements*, Bk. I, Definitions, Definition 3. Translated by Sir Thomas L. Heath, Everyman edition (London and New York: J. M. Dent, Ltd., and E. P. Dutton, Inc., 1933), p. 1.

11.4. St. Thomas Aquinas, *Summa Theologiae*, I–II, 110, 1.

11.5. Ralph Barton Perry, *Characteristically American* (New York: A. A. Knopf, 1949), p. 127.

11.6. William James, *Principles of Psychology* in *GBWW*, Vol. 53, p. 8a. Reprinted by permission of Henry Holt & Co., Inc.

11.7. Plato, *The Republic*, Bk. II, 357–358. Translated by Benjamin Jowett and found in *The Dialogues of Plato* (New York: Random House, Inc., 1937), Vol. I, p. 621. With permission of Oxford University Press.

11.8. Ernst Mach, *Principles of Physical Optics* (New York: Dover Publications, 1953), p. 2.

12.1. Thomas Hobbes, *Leviathan*, Part I, ch. 14. Everyman edition (London and New York: J. M. Dent, Ltd., and E. P. Dutton, Inc., 1950), p. 106.

12.2. Herbert Spencer, *Education: Intellectual, Moral, and Physical*, ch. 2 (New York: D. Appleton and Company, 1900), p. 119.

12.3. Ernst Mach, *The Science of Mechanics*. Translated by Thomas J. McCormack (Chicago: The Open Court Publishing Co., 1893), p. 194.

12.4. Bertrand Russell, *Principles of Mathematics* (2nd ed.: New York: W. W. Norton and Company, Inc., 1938), p. 136.

12.5. William James, *Varieties of Religious Experience*, Lect. II, "Circumscription of the Topic" (New York: Modern Library, n.d.), p. 28.

12.6. Ralph Waldo Emerson, *Essays on Friendship*, First Series.

12.7. Herbert Spencer, *Principles of Biology*, ch. 4, sect. 24.

12.8. Plato, *Timaeus*, 48. Translated by Benjamin Jowett and found in *The Dialogues of Plato* (New York: Random House, Inc., 1937), Vol. II, p. 29. With permission of Oxford University Press.

12.9. Gerald Ellard, S.J., *Christian Life and Worship* (2nd ed.: Milwaukee: The Bruce Publishing Company, 1950), p. 116.

12.10. Jeremy Bentham, *Principles of Morals and Legislation*, ch. 1, n. iii.

12.11. Michel Montaigne, *Essays*, Bk. III, ch. 5.

12.12. Sir Isaac Newton, *Mathematical Principles of Natural Philosophy*, translated by Andrew Motte, revised by Florian Cajori (Berkeley, Calif.: University of California Press, 1946), p. 2.

12.13. Parton, *The Life and Times of Aaron Burr*, Vol. I, p. 149.

12.14. Percival M. Symonds, *Dynamic Psychology* (New York: Appleton-Century-Crofts, Inc., 1949), p. 321.

12.15. Vauvenargues, *Reflexions*, no. 251.

12.16. Plato, *The Republic*, V, 460 e. Translated by Benjamin Jowett and found in *The Dialogues of Plato* (New York: Random House, Inc., 1939), Vol. I, p. 723. With permission of Oxford University Press.

12.17. U. S. Atomic Energy Commission, Report of January, 1950.

12.18. St. Thomas Aquinas, *Summa Theologiae*, I–II, 90, 4, 1.

12.19. Euclid, *The Thirteen Books of Euclid's Elements*, Bk. I, Definitions, Definition 14. Translated by Sir Thomas L. Heath, Everyman edition (London and New York: J. M. Dent, Ltd., and E. P. Dutton, Inc., 1933), p. 3.

12.20. Monroe Beardsley, in *Philosophical Writings of Peirce*. Edited by Justus Buchler (New York: Dover Publications, 1955), p. 170.

12.21. Thomas Jefferson, *Writings*, Vol. VI, p. 186.

12.22. Orestes Brownson, *Brownson's Quarterly Review*, April, 1873. In *Orestes Brownson: Selected Essays*, edited by Russell Kirk (Chicago: Henry Regnery, 1955), p. 192.

12.23. Charles Augustin Sainte-Beuve, *Monday-Chats*, translated by William Mathews (Chicago: S. C. Griggs & Co., 1877), p. xlviii.

12.24. Walter M. Mason, *The Wonderful World of Books*. Edited by Alfred Stefferud (New York: Mentor Books, 1952), p. 199. Published by The New American Library of World Literature. Copyright, 1952, by Alfred Stefferud.

12.25. Joseph Conrad, *Nigger of the Narcissus*, Preface.

12.26. Aristotle, *Politics*, III, 3; 1275 b 24–34. Translated by Benjamin Jowett and found in *The Basic Works of Aristotle*, edited by Richard McKeon (New York: Random House, Inc., 1941), p. 1178. With permission of Oxford University Press.

12.27. R. W. Jepson, "When Worlds Fail Us," in *Teach Yourself to Think* (London: English Universities Press, Ltd., 1949).

12.28. Diogenes Laertius, 4.

12.29. Adam Smith, *The Wealth of Nations*, in GBWW, Vol. 39, p. 123bc. Reprinted by arrangement with Methuen & Co., Ltd., London.

12.30. Arnold Toynbee, *An Historian's Approach to the Religions of the World* (London and New York: Oxford University Press, 1956), p. 4.

12.31. George Santayana, *The Sense of Beauty* (New York: Dover Publications, 1955), p. 49.

13.1. Immanuel Kant, *Critique of Pure Reason*, Transcendental dialectic, Bk. II, ch. iii, sect. iv. Translated by J. D. M. Meiklejohn, Everyman Edition(London and New York: J. M. Dent & E. P. Dutton, 1933), p. 350.

13.2. Leslie Stephens, *The Life of Samuel Johnson*, ch. 3.

13.3. Thomas B. Macaulay, *History of England*, ch. 2.

13.4. St. Augustine, *Sermo de Ascensione*.

13.5. William Makepeace Thackeray, *Vanity Fair*, ch. 2.

13.6. Plato, *Apology*, 40. Translated by Benjamin Jowett and found in *The Dialogues of Plato* (New York: Random House, Inc.,

1939), Vol. I, p. 422. With permission of Oxford University Press.

13.7. Edward Fitzgerald, "Rubaiyat of Omar Khayyam."

13.8. Voltaire, *Oeuvres Complètes*, Vol. I, p. 1076.

13.9. Alexander Pope, *Thoughts on Various Subjects*.

13.10. Livy, *History*, V, 4.

13.11. William Shakespeare, *Hamlet*, I, 3.

13.12. Francis Bacon, *Of Studies*.

13.13. Dante, *Divine Comedy*, Inferno, Canto III, line 19.

13.14. Samuel Johnson, *Rasselas*, ch. 44.

13.15. Samuel Clemens, *An American Claimant*, Foreword.

13.16. Blaise Pascal, *Pensées*, no. 93. Translated by H. F. Stewart, (London: Routledge and Kegan Paul, 1950), p. 51.

13.17. Leo Tolstoy, *Anna Karenina*, Bk. I, ch. i.

13.18. John Dryden, "The Hind and the Panther," Pt. II, line 59.

13.19. John Ray, *English Proverbs*.

13.20. George Herbert, *Jacula Prudentium*.

13.21. Thomas Jefferson, *Writings*, Vol. XV, p. 40.

13.22. G. K. Chesterton, *A Handful of Authors*. Edited by Dorothy L. Collins (New York: Sheed and Ward, Inc., 1953), p. 1.

14.1. René Descartes, *Discourse on the Method*. Translated by John Veitch, Everyman edition (London and New York: J. M. Dent, Ltd., and E. P. Dutton, Inc., 1951), pp. 28–29.

14.2. Bertrand Russell, *Unpopular Essays* (New York: Simon and Schuster, 1950), pp. 26–27.

14.3. La Chausée, *La Gouvernante*, Act 1, sc. 3.

14.4. Benjamin Disraeli, *Tancred*.

14.5. Karl Marx and Friedrich Engels, *Communist Manifesto*.

14.6. La Rochefoucauld, *Maximes*, no. 287.

15.1. Herbert Spencer, *Education: Intellectual, Moral, and Physical* (New York: D. Appleton and Co., 1900), p. 119.

15.2. Thomas Carlyle, *Heroes and Hero Worship*, ch. 3.

15.4. Samuel Taylor Coleridge, *Biographia Litteraria*, ch. 10.

15.5. Madame de Cornuel, *Mlle. Aisse, Lettres*, p. 161.

15.6. W. S. Landor, *Imaginary Conversations*, Everyman edition (London and New York: J. M. Dent, Ltd., and E. P. Dutton, Inc., 1933), "Diogenes and Plato," p. 79.

15.7. Alexander Pope, *Essay on Criticism*, Pt. II, line 230.

15.8. Herman J. Muller, "Will Science Continue?" *Bulletin of Atomic Research Scientists*, December, 1952.

15.9. John Stuart Mill, *On Liberty*, ch. III. In *Utilitarianism, Liberty, and Representative Government*, Everyman edition (London and New York: J. M. Dent, Ltd., and E. P. Dutton, Inc., 1950), p. 165.

15.10. Ralph W. Ingersoll, *Liberty of Man, Woman, and Child.*
15.11. Oscar Wilde, *Decay of Lying.*
15.12. Plautus, *Trenummus,* Act II, sc. 2.
15.13. Cicero, *De Officiis,* Bk. I, ch. 27, sect. 94.
15.14. John Keats, "Ode on a Grecian Urn."
15.15. Georg Hegel, *Philosophy of Right,* Preface. Translated by T. M. Knox (Oxford: The Clarendon Press, 1942), p. 10.
15.16. John Stuart Mill, *Utilitarianism,* ch. IV. In *Utilitarianism, Liberty, and Representative Government,* Everyman edition (London and New York: J. M. Dent, Ltd., and E. P. Dutton, Inc., 1950), p. 43.
15.17. William James, *Pragmatism,* Sixth Lecture, "Pragmatism's Conception of Truth" (New York: Meridian, 1956), p. 135.

16.1. Gottfried Leibniz, "Preface to the General Science," in *Leibniz: Selections,* edited by Philip Wiener (New York: Charles Scribner's Sons, 1951), p. 12.
16.2. St. Thomas Aquinas, *Summa Theologiae,* I, 12, 6.
16.3. Thomas Carlyle, *Heroes and Hero Worship,* ch. 3.
16.4. St. Paul, 1 Cor. 15:44–45. In *The New Testament,* translated by James Kleist, S.J., and Joseph Lilly, C.M. (Milwaukee: The Bruce Publishing Company, 1954), p. 443.
16.5. Charles Darwin, *The Origin of Species,* ch. III, "Struggle for Existence" (New York: Hurst and Co., n.d.), pp. 56–57.
16.6. John Dalton, "On the Constitution of Bodies," in *Foundations of the Atomic Theory,* Alembic Club Reprints, No. 2 (Edinburgh, E. & S. Livingstone, 1948), p. 27. With permission of the Royal Society of Edinburgh.
16.7. Walt Whitman, "A Backward Glance O'er Traveled Roads."
16.8. St. Thomas Aquinas, *De Veritate,* 14, 1.
16.9. Eric Gill, *Autobiography* (New York: Sheed and Ward, Inc., 1945), p. 244.
16.10. William Hazlitt, cited by George Russell Harrison, *What Man May Be* (New York: William Morrow and Company, 1956), p. 19.
16.11. Adam Smith, *The Wealth of Nations,* in *GBWW,* Vol. 35, p. 13a. Reprinted by arrangement with Methuen & Co., Ltd., London.
16.12. St. Thomas Aquinas, *Summa Theologiae,* I, 10, 2.
16.13. Hendrick Ibsen, *An Enemy of Society,* Act V. Translated by William Archer (Boston: Walter H. Baker & Co., 1900), pp. 127–128.
16.14. Alfred Lord Tennyson, "The Song of the Brook."
16.15. Sir Isaac Newton, *Mathematical Principles of Natural Philosophy,* Translated by Andrew Motte, revised by Florian Cajori (Berkeley, Calif.: University of California Press, 1934), p. 414.

16.16. E. I. Watkin, *Catholic Art and Culture* (New York: Sheed and Ward, Inc., 1944), p. 75.

16.17. Thucydides, *History of the Peloponnesian War*, Bk. II, ch. vi, "Funeral Oration of Pericles." Translated by Richard Crawley, Everyman edition (London and New York: J. M. Dent, Ltd., and E. P. Dutton, Inc., 1945), p. 95.

16.18. Albert Jay Nock, *Free Speech and Plain Language*, ch. 11, "The Disadvantages of Being Educated" (New York: William Morrow and Company, 1937), pp. 219–220.

16.19. Joseph Fourier, *The Nature of Heat*, in GBWW, Vol. 45, p. 177a.

16.20. C. S. Lewis, *Mere Christianity* (New York: The Macmillan Company, 1952), pp. 3–4.

17.3. David Hume, *Treatise Concerning Human Nature*, Book I, Part I, Sect. VII. In *British Empirical Philosophers*, edited by A. J. Ayer and Raymond Winch (London: Routledge and Kegan Paul, 1952), p. 312.

17.7. Adam Smith, *The Wealth of Nations*, in GBWW, Volume 39, p. 340 bc. Reprinted by arrangement with Methuen & Co., Ltd., London.

17.10. Arthur Eddington, *The Nature of the Physical World*, Everyman edition (London and New York: J. M. Dent, Ltd., and E. P. Dutton, Inc., 1935), p. 273.

17.15. Julian Huxley, "Man as a Relative Being," from *Science in a Changing World*. Edited by Mary Adams (London and New York: Allen and Unwin and D. Appleton-Century, 1933).

17.16. Donald Culross Peattie, *Flowering Earth* (New York: G. P. Putnam, 1939), "The Rise of the Modern Floras."

17.17. Edmund Callis Berkeley, *Giant Brains* (New York: John Wiley and Sons, 1949), "Machines That Think."

17.18. Leo Tolstoy, *War and Peace*. Translated by Constance Garnett (New York: Modern Library, n.d.), Epilogue.

17.19. David Hume, *An Enquiry Concerning Human Understanding*, Section X, Part I. In *Hume's Enquiries Concerning Human Understanding and the Principles of Morals*, edited by L. A. Selby-Biggs (Oxford: The Clarendon Press, 1902), p. 114.

17.20. George Berkeley, *Principles of Human Knowledge*, sect. 118. In *British Empirical Philosophers*, edited by A. J. Ayer and Raymond Winch (London: Routledge and Kegan Paul, 1952), p. 225.

17.21. Bertrand Russell, *Unpopular Essays* (New York: Simon and Schuster, 1950), p. 85.

17.22. Immanuel Kant, *Critique of Pure Reason*, in GBWW, Vol. 42, p. 103d.

17.23. Rudolph Carnap, *Philosophy and Logical Syntax* (London: Routledge, 1935), p. 28.

17.24. Albert Einstein, *Geometry and Experience*, reprinted in *Readings in the Philosophy of Science*. Edited by Herbert Feigl and Mary Brodbeck (New York: Appleton-Century-Crofts, 1953).

17.25. Stuart Chase, *The Tyranny of Words* (New York: Harcourt, Brace, 1938), p. 49.

17.26. William Pepperell Montague, *Belief Unbound* (New Haven: Yale University Press, 1938), "God, Finite and Infinite."

17.27. Jean-Jacques Rousseau, *Social Contract*, in GBWW, Vol. 38, p. 389a.

18.4. Georg Hegel, *The Science of Logic*, translated by W. H. Johnson and L. G. Struthers (London and New York: Allen and Unwin, and The Macmillan Company, 1931), Vol. 1, Bk. 1, "The Doctrine of Being," passim.

18.5. George Santayana, *The Sense of Beauty* (New York: Dover Publications, 1955), p. 26.

18.6. St. Thomas Aquinas, *Summa Theologiae*, I, 3, 1.

18.7. Gilbert Highet, *The Art of Teaching* (New York: Vintage Books, 1954), p. 237.

18.8. Mircea Eliade, in *Selections II*, edited by Cecily Hastings and Donald Nicholl (New York: Sheed & Ward, Inc., 1954), p. 22.

18.9. W. V. Houston et al., *The Scientists Look at Our World* (Philadelphia: University of Pennsylvania Press, 1952), p. 22.

18.10. Blaise Pascal, *Pensées*, no. 43. Translated by H. F. Stewart (London: Routledge and Kegan Paul, 1951), p. 21.

18.11. Joseph Wood Krutch, *The Measure of Man* (Indianapolis: Bobbs-Merrill, 1954), p. 218.

18.12. Ortega y Gasset, *Revolt of the Masses* (New York: Mentor Books, 1950), p. 74.

18.13. Immanuel Kant, *Foundations of the Metaphysics of Morals*, sect. 2.

19.7. Samuel Butler, *Sermons*, Sermon II, "*Upon the Natural Supremacy of Conscience.*"

19.8. St. Augustine, *De immortalitate animae*, ch. iv.

19.9. Blaise Pascal, *Pensées*, no. 223. Translated by H. F. Stewart (London: Routledge and Kegan Paul, 1951), p. 119.

19.10. Benedetto Croce, *History as the Story of Liberty* (London: Allen and Unwin, 1952), p. 32.

19.11. John Dewey, *Reconstruction in Philosophy* (Boston: The Beacon Press, 1948), p. 156.

19.12. W. T. Stace, in *Mind*, Vol. 43 (1934).

19.13. Ptolemy, *The Almagest*, Bk. 1.

19.14. Galileo Galilei, *Dialogues Concerning the Two Chief World*

Systems. Translated by Stillman Drake (Berkeley, Calif.: University of California Press, 1953), pp. 116–117.

19.15. St. Matthew, 5:24. In *The New Testament,* translated by James Kleist, S.J., and Joseph Lilly, C.M. (Milwaukee: The Bruce Publishing Company, 1954), p. 25.

19.16. William James, *Pragmatism,* Lecture Two, "What Pragmatism Means" (New York: Meridian Books, 1955), p. 45.

20.1. Sir Isaac Newton, *The Mathematical Principles of Natural Philosophy,* Part III, Rules of Reasoning, Rule III. Translated by A. Motte, revised by Florian Cajori (Berkeley, Calif.: The University of California Press, 1934), p. 399.

20.14. Aristotle, *Prior Analytics,* Bk. II, ch. 23 (passim); cf. the discussion of this point in H. W. B. Joseph, *An Introduction to Logic* (Oxford: The Clarendon Press, 1916), pp. 378–380.

21.1. Lancelot Hogben, *Mathematics for the Millions* (New York: W. W. Norton, 1947), p. 16.

21.2. Robert M. Hutchins, *Freedom, Education, and the Fund* (New York: Meridian Books, 1956), p. 99.

21.3. Alexis Carrel, *Reflexions on Life* (New York: Hawthorne Books, 1953), p. 63.

21.4. David Hume, *Enquiry Concerning the Principles of Morals,* Section III, Part 2. In *Hume's Enquiries Concerning Human Understanding and the Principles of Morals,* edited by L. A. Selby-Biggs (Oxford: The Clarendon Press, 1902), p. 202.

21.5. Howard Mumford Jones, *The Pursuit of Happiness* (Cambridge: Harvard University Press, 1953), "The Technique of Happiness."

21.6. Amram Scheinfeld, *The New You and Heredity* (Philadelphia: J. B. Lippincott, 1950), p. 16.

21.7. Ralph Barton Perry, *Characteristically American* (New York: A. A. Knopf, 1949), p. 126.

21.8. Euclid, *The Thirteen Books of Euclid's Elements,* Bk. I, Axioms, Axiom 1. Translated by Sir Thomas L. Heath, Everyman edition (London and New York: J. M. Dent, Ltd., and E. P. Dutton, Inc., 1933), p. 6.

21.9. Charles Darwin, *The Origin of Species,* Ch. III, "Struggle for Existence" (New York: Hurst and Company, n.d.), pp. 66–67.

21.10. Joseph Gay-Lussac, in John Dalton, et al., *Foundations of the Molecular Theory.* Alembic Club Reprints, No. 4 (Edinburgh: Oliver and Bayds, 1923), p. 15. With permission of the Royal Society of Edinburgh.

21.11. Thomas R. Malthus, *Essay on the Principle of Population,* Bk. I, Ch. 1, 8th ed. (London: Reeves and Turner, 1878), p. 4.

21.12. Gilbert Keith Chesterton, *A Handful of Authors.* Edited by

Dorothy L. Collins (New York: Sheed and Ward, Inc., 1953), p. 142.

23.1.   Aristotle, *Physics*, I, 2, 184b 15–22. Translated by R. P. Hardie and R. K. Gaye, in *The Basic Works of Aristotle*, edited by Richard McKeon (New York: Random House, 1941), p. 219. With permission of Oxford University Press.

23.3.   Paul B. Sears, *Deserts on the March* (Tulsa: University of Oklahoma Press, 1947), "Man, Maker of Wilderness."

23.4.   Sir James Jeans, "Is There Life on Other Worlds," in *A Treasury of Science*, edited by Harlow Shapeley, Samuel Rapport, and Helen Wright (New York: Harper and Brothers, 1943), pp. 84–85.

23.5.   Friedrich Miescher, in *Annual Review of Physiology*, XVI (1954), p. 10.

23.6.   Charles Darwin, "Instinct in Men and Animals," in *Expressions of the Emotions in Men and Animals* (New York: Philosophical Library, 1955), pp. 110–111.

23.7.   Budd Schulberg, "Movies in America — After Fifty Years," in *The Atlantic Monthly*, Nov., 1947.

23.8.   Sir Isaac Newton, *Optics*, Query 29. Reprinted in *Newton's Philosophy of Nature*, edited by H. S. Thayer (New York: Hafner, 1953), p. 156.

24.1.   Abraham Lincoln, *Gettysburg Address*.

24.2.   George Santayana, *The Sense of Beauty* (New York: Dover Publications, 1955), p. 79.

24.3.   Norbert Wiener, *The Human Use of Human Beings* (New York: Doubleday Anchor Books, 1954), p. 183. Reprinted with permission of the Houghton Mifflin Company.

24.4.   Samuel Johnson, *Lives of the English Poets: Selections* (Chicago: Henry Regnery, 1955), pp. 369–370.

24.5.   J. Arthur Thompson and Patrick Geddes, *Life: Outlines of General Biology* (New York: Harper and Brothers, 1954), "Characteristics of Organisms."

24.6.   Thomas Babington Macaulay, Review of Ranke's *History of the Popes*. Quoted in *The Catholic Bedside Book* by C. C. Martindale, et al. (New York: D. J. McKay, 1953), pp. 229–230.

24.7.   David Ewen, *Music for the Millions* (New York: Mentor Books, 1950), p. 22.

24.8.   William Shakespeare, *Julius Caesar*, Act III, sc. 2.

25.1.   John Keats, "On First Looking into Chapman's Homer."

25.3.   John Milton, "On His Blindness."

26.1. Thucydides, *History of the Peloponnesian War*, Bk. I, Ch. 1. Translated by Richard Crawley, Everyman edition (London and New York: J. M. Dent, Ltd., and E. P. Dutton, Inc., 1945), p. 1.

26.2. Plutarch, *Lives*, "Alexander and Caesar," in *GBWW*, Vol. 14, pp. 540b–541a.

26.3. Tacitus, *Annals*, in *GBWW*, Vol. 15, p. 1 ab.

26.4. Gilbert Keith Chesterton, *Autobiography* (New York: Sheed and Ward, Inc., 1936), p. 1.

26.5. Leo Tolstoy, *War and Peace*, translated by Constance Garnett (New York: Modern Library, n.d.), epilogue.

26.6. Edward Gibbon, *The Decline and Fall of the Roman Empire*, in *GBWW*, Vol. 40, p. 1 ab. Reprinted by permission from J. M. Dent & Son, Ltd., London and E. P. Dutton & Co., Inc., New York.

26.7. St. Luke 2:1–7. In *The New Testament*, translated by James Kleist, S.J., and Joseph Lilly, C.M. (Milwaukee: The Bruce Publishing Company, 1954), pp. 5–6.

27.1. Aristotle, *Physics*, Bk. II, ch. 2, 194a 1–6. Translated by R. P. Hardie and R. K. Gaye, in *The Basic Works of Aristotle* edited by Richard McKeon (New York: Random House, 1941), p. 239. With permission of Oxford University Press.

28.1. Galileo Galilei, *Dialogues Concerning the Two New Sciences*, Third Day. Translated by Henry Crew and Alfonso de Salvio (Evanston, Ill.: Northwestern University Press, 1946), pp. 178–179.

28.2. Count Rumford, cited in G. Holton, *Introduction to Concepts and Theories in Physical Science* (Cambridge, Mass.: Addison-Wesley Press, 1952), p. 381.

28.3. Karl von Frisch, *Bees, Their Vision, Chemical Sources, and Language* (Ithaca: Cornell University Press, 1950), p. 4.

28.4. Sir Isaac Newton, *A New Theory About Light and Colors.*

28.5. Floyd L. Darrow, *Masters of Science and Invention* (New York: Harcourt, Brace, 1923), pp. 189–190.

28.6. Sir James Jeans, *The Universe Around Us* (New York: The Macmillan Company, 1929), p. 97.

29.1. T. S. Painter, in *The Scientists Speak*, edited by Warren Weaver (London: Boni and Gaer, 1947), pp. 214–215.

29.2. Lord Rutherford, in *Background to Modern Science*, edited by Joseph Needham and Walter Pagel (New York: The Macmillan Company, 1938), p. 71.

29.3. G. K. FitzGerald, in *A Century of Science*, edited by Herbert Dingle (New York: Roy Publishers, 1951), p. 25.

29.4. Charles Lyell, *Principles of Geology* (New York: D. Appleton and Company, 1873), Vol. I, ch. viii.

29.5. Sir Arthur Keith, *Man: A History of the Human Body* (New York: Henry Holt and Company, n.d.), p. 175.

29.6. George W. Gray, *The Advancing Front of Science* (New York: McGraw-Hill Book Company, Inc., 1954), "Where Life Begins."

30.1. A. M. Low, *Electronics Everywhere* (New York: John Day Co., 1952), p. 17.

30.2. Joseph Butler, *Sermon I*, "Upon the Social Nature of Man."

30.3. Nicholas Copernicus, *Concerning the Revolution of the Heavenly Spheres*, Bk. I.

30.4. John Milton, *Areopagitica*.

30.5. Charles Darwin, *The Origin of Species*, *Ch. III*, "The Struggle for Existence," (New York: Hurst, n.d.), p. 56.

30.6. Sir James Jeans, *The Universe Around Us* (New York: The Macmillan Company, 1929), pp. 107–108.

30.7. Benjamin Franklin, *Autobiography of Benjamin Franklin* (New York: Pocket Books, 1954), p. 45.

31.1. John Stuart Mill, *System of Logic*, Bk. III, ch. viii (New York: Longmans, Green and Company, 1930), pp. 255, 256, 259, 260, 263.

31.2. Tobias Dantzig, *Number, the Language of Science*, 4th ed. (New York: The Macmillan Company, 1954), p. 294.

31.3. Sir Isaac Newton, *Mathematical Principles of Natural Philosophy*, Bk. 3, Prop. xxiv, theorem xix. Translated by Andrew Motte, revised by Florian Cajori (Berkeley, Calif.: University of California Press, 1934), p. 440.

31.4. Sir James Jeans, *The Universe Around Us* (New York: The Macmillan Company, 1929), pp. 113–114.

31.5. Waldemar Kaempffert, *Science Today and Tomorrow*, Second Series (New York: The Viking Press, 1945).

31.6. *Magazine and Newspaper Penetration by Income Groups*, Report No. 6. Research Department, Crowell-Collier Publishing Company, quoted in *Psychology Applied to Life and Work* by Harry Walker Hepner (New York: Prentice-Hall Inc., 1941).

32.1. Pierre Simon, Marquis de Laplace, *Essay on Probability*.

32.2. Elmo Roper, in *The Saturday Review of Literature*, XXXVIII, May 21, 1955, p. 20.

32.3. Arthur Eddington, *New Pathways in Science* (New York: The Macmillan Company, 1935), p. 117.

32.4. AP, November 29, 1956.

32.5. Lecomte du Noüy, *Human Destiny* (New York: Longmans, Green and Company, 1947), p. 21.

35.1. Nicolai Lenin, *Selected Works* (Moscow: Foreign Language Publishing House, 1951), Vol. II, part 2, p. 482.

35.2. Bertrand Russell, *Unpopular Essays* (New York: Simon and Schuster, 1950), pp. 85–86.

35.3. Voltaire, *Philosophical Dictionary*, "Tolerance."

35.4. Adolf Hitler, *Mein Kampf* (New York: Reynal and Hitchcock, 1940), p. 606.

35.5. F. M. Cornford *et al.*, *Background to Modern Science* (New York: The Macmillan Company, 1938), p. 18.

35.17. *Time*, LXVIII, No. 20, November 12, 1956, p. 130.

35.18. Benito Mussolini, *The Doctrine of Fascism*, translated by E. Cope (3rd ed.; Florence: Vallechi Publishing Company, 1938), p. 30.

35.19. Will Durant, *The Mansions of Philosophy* (New York: Doubleday and Company, 1929), p. 284. With permission of Simon and Schuster.

35.20. Leo Tolstoy, *War and Peace*, translated by Constance Garnett (New York: Modern Library, n.d.), Epilogue.

35.21. Morehouse, Bishop of Manchester, *The Pleasures of Smoking*. Edited by Sylvestre C. Watkins (New York: Henry Schuman, 1948), p. 177.

35.22. René Descartes, *Discourse on the Method*. Translated by John Veitch, Everyman edition (London and New York: J. M. Dent, Ltd., and E. P. Dutton, Inc., 1951), p. 1.

35.23. St. Mark 2:15–16. In *The New Testament*, translated by James Kleist, S.J., and Joseph Lilly, C.M. (Milwaukee: The Bruce Publishing Company, 1954), p. 101.

35.24. David Hume, *Enquiry Concerning Human Understanding*, Sect. XII, Part III, in Hume's *Enquiries Concerning Human Understanding and the Principles of Morals*, edited by L. A. Selby-Biggs (Oxford: The Clarendon Press, 1902), p. 165.

35.25. Eugene P. Northrop, *Riddles in Mathematics: A Book of Paradoxes* (Princeton, N. J.: Van Nostrand, 1944), pp. 8–9.

35.26. John Stuart Mill, *On Liberty*, ch. 1. In *Utilitarianism, Liberty, and Representative Government*, Everyman edition (London and New York: J. M. Dent, Ltd., and E. P. Dutton, 1950), p. 99.

35.27. Martin Luther, *First Principles of the Reformation*. Translated by H. Wace and C. A. Buckheim (Philadelphia: Lutheran Publication Society, 1885), p. 237.

35.28. William James, *Principles of Psychology*, in GBWW, Vol. 53, p. 867c. Reprinted by permission of Henry Holt & Co., Inc.

35.29. Karl Pearson, *The Grammar of Science*, 2nd ed. (London: Adam and Charles Black, 1900), p. 17.

35.30. George Santayana, *The Sense of Beauty*, (New York: Dover Publications, 1955), p. 3.

35.31. G. E. Moore, "The Value of Religion," *The International Journal of Ethics*, XII (1902), p. 89.

35.32. Sterling P. Lamprecht, "Man's Place in Nature," *The American Scholar*, VII (1938) pp. 60–77 (*passim*).

35.33. William James, *Psychology* (Cleveland and New York: The World Publishing Co., 1948), p. 376.

INDEX

Abstraction, 159, 214 ff; degrees or orders of, 215 ff; and theory, 230

Abstractive induction, 158 f; contrasted with induction by incomplete enumeration, 166 ff

Accident, fallacy of, 265 f

Accident, predicable: 42, 46 ff, 52, 56, 61; defined, 47; distinguished from property, 47 f

Accident, predicamental, 57, 61, 86

Act, to, a category, 55, 56, 60 f

Acts of the mind, 18 f

Agassiz, Louis, on division, 73 f; on divisions among animals, 53

Albert the Great, St., and nature of dialectic, 184

Analogy, 247; and argument, 232 f; extrinsic, 234; intrinsic, 234 f; kinds of, 234; reasoning by, 232 ff; and the study of nature, 233; value of, 234 f

Antecedent, in conditional syllogism, 147 f

Anthropology, and evolution, 231

Argument, and analogy, 232 f; division of, 117 ff; elements of, 18 f; finding form of, 124 f; hidden parts of, 195; in implicit forms, 120; kinds of, 19 f, 121, 173, 192, 194, 202, 204, 260; nature of, 1 ff, 117 ff

Aristotle, on accidents, 52; analyzes the categories of being, 55; on categories, 64 f; on the citizen, 91; and dialectic, 182, 186, 187; on general function of logic, 20; on history, viii; on mathematics and physics, 214; on means of knowing nature, 220; on noncomposite charac-

ter of the categories, 57; on persuasion, 193; on principles of nature, 181; on science, 177

Arithmetic, first principle in, 177

Arnauld, M., and the relation of body to mind, 45

Art, according to Conrad, 91; according to Oscar Wilde, 115; distinguished from science, 11; and history, 211; kinds of, 11 ff; Santayana on, 196

Artificial signs, 24

Astronomy, 49, 229, 236, 268; far-reaching effects of, 115; helped by division, 70; possibility of life on other planets, 188 f; in Ptolemy and Galileo, 155; theories in, 185 f; and theory, 228

Atomic theory, 79, 89, 148, 227, 228, 230; and analogy, 233; classic expression of, in Dalton, 118; exposition of, 232; and properties, 53 f

Augustine, St., on categories, 64 f; on the good, 17, 21; on teaching, 154; on vice, 96

Bach, 198

Bacon, Francis, on books, 99; and dialectic methods, 187; and experimental method, 239

Bacteriology, Pasteur's experiments, 224

Beardsley, Monroe, on "hair-splitting," 90

Beauty, 201; according to Santayana, 92; Durant on, 267 f; power of, 99; and truth, in Keats, 115

Bees, color sense, 223 f

Beethoven, 198